The Tanner Lectures on Human Values

THE TANNER LECTURES
ON HUMAN VALUES

21

2000

Scarry, Burkert, Hartman, Pinker,
White, Verba, Sandel

Grethe B. Peterson, *Editor*

THE UNIVERSITY OF UTAH PRESS
Salt Lake City

THE TANNER LECTURES ON HUMAN VALUES
was set in Garamond by The Typeworks, Vancouver, BC, Canada

THE TANNER LECTURES ON HUMAN VALUES

The purpose of the Tanner Lectures is to advance and reflect upon scholarly and scientific learning that relates to human values.

To receive an appointment as a Tanner lecturer is a recognition of uncommon capabilities and outstanding scholarly or leadership achievement in the field of human values. The lecturers may be drawn from philosophy, religion, the humanities and sciences, the creative arts and learned professions, or from leadership in public or private affairs. The lectureships are international and intercultural and transcend ethnic, national, religious, or ideological distinctions.

The Tanner Lectures were formally founded on July 1, 1978, at Clare Hall, Cambridge University. They were established by the American scholar, industrialist, and philanthropist, Obert Clark Tanner. In creating the lectureships, Professor Tanner said, "I hope these lectures will contribute to the intellectual and moral life of mankind. I see them simply as a search for a better understanding of human behavior and human values. This understanding may be pursued for its own intrinsic worth, but it may also eventually have practical consequences for the quality of personal and social life."

Permanent Tanner lectureships, with lectures given annually, are established at nine institutions: Clare Hall, Cambridge University; Harvard University; Brasenose College, Oxford University; Princeton University; Stanford University; the University of California; the University of Michigan; the University of Utah; and Yale University. Other international lectureships occasionally take place. The institutions are selected by the Trustees.

The sponsoring institutions have full autonomy in the appointment of their lecturers. A major part of the lecture program is the publication and distibution of the Lectures in an annual volume.

The Tanner Lectures on Human Values is a nonprofit corporation administered at the University of Utah under the direction of a self-perpetuating, international Board of Trustees. The Trustees meet annually to enact policies that will ensure the quality of the lectureships.

The entire lecture program, including the costs of administration, is fully and generously funded in perpetuity by an endowment to the University of Utah by Professor Tanner and Mrs. Grace Adams Tanner.

Obert C. Tanner was born in Farmington, Utah, in 1904. He was educated at the University of Utah, Harvard University, and Stanford University. He served on the faculty at Stanford University and was a professor of philosophy at the University of Utah for twenty-eight years. Mr. Tanner was also the founder and chairman of the O. C. Tanner Company, the world's largest manufacturer of recognition award products.

Harvard University's former president Derek Bok once spoke of Obert Tanner as a "Renaissance Man," citing his remarkable achievements in three of life's major pursuits: business, education, and public service.

Obert C. Tanner died in Palm Springs, California, on October 14, 1993, at the age of eighty-nine.

GRETHE B. PETERSON
University of Utah

CONTENTS

PREFACE TO VOLUME 21

Volume 21 of the Tanner Lectures on Human Values includes lectures delivered during the academic year 1998–99.

The Tanner Lectures are published in an annual volume.

In addition to the Lectures on Human Values, the Trustees of the Tanner Lectures have funded special international lectureships at selected colleges and universities which are administered independently of the permanent lectures.

On Beauty and Being Just

ELAINE SCARRY

THE TANNER LECTURES ON HUMAN VALUES

Delivered at

Yale University
March 25 and 26, 1998

ELAINE SCARRY is Walter M. Cabot Professor of Aesthetics and the General Theory of Value in the department of English at Harvard University. She was educated at Chatham College and at the University of Connecticut, where she received her Ph.D. She is a member of the American Academy of Arts and Sciences, and has been a fellow of the Center for Advanced Study in the Behavioral Sciences and a senior fellow at the Getty Research Institute. She is also the recipient of a Guggenheim fellowship. Her many published works include *Dreaming By the Book* (1999), *Resisting Representation* (1994), *Literature and the Body: Essays on Populations and Persons* (1988), and *The Body in Pain: The Making and Unmaking of the World* (1985).

I. ON BEAUTY AND BEING WRONG

What is the felt experience of cognition at the moment one stands in the presence of a beautiful boy or flower or bird? It seems to incite, even to require, the act of replication. Wittgenstein says that when the eye sees something beautiful, the hand wants to draw it.

Beauty brings copies of itself into being. It makes us draw it, take photographs of it, or describe it to other people. Sometimes it gives rise to exact replication and other times to resemblances and still other times to things whose connection to the original site of inspiration is unrecognizable. A beautiful face drawn by Verrocchio suddenly glides into the perceptual field of a young boy named Leonardo. The boy copies the face, then copies the face again. Then again and again and again. He does the same thing when a beautiful living plant—a violet, a wild rose—glides into his field of vision, or a living face: he makes a first copy, a second copy, a third, a fourth, a fifth. He draws it over and over, just as Walter Pater (who tells us all this about Leonardo) replicates—now in sentences—Leonardo's acts, so that the essay reenacts its subject, becoming a sequence of faces: an angel, a Medusa, a woman and child, a Madonna, John the Baptist, St. Anne, La Gioconda. Before long the means are found to replicate, thousands of times over, both the sentences and the faces, so that traces of Pater's paragraphs and Leonardo's drawings inhabit all the pockets of the world (as pieces of them float in the paragraph now before you).

A visual event may reproduce itself in the realm of touch (as when the seen face incites an ache of longing in the hand, and the hand then presses pencil to paper), which may in turn then

These lectures are dedicated to Philip Fisher.

reappear in a second visual event, the finished drawing. This criss-crossing of the senses may happen in any direction. Wittgenstein speaks not only about beautiful visual events prompting motions in the hand but, elsewhere, about heard music that later prompts a ghostly subanatomical event in his teeth and gums. So, too, an act of touch may reproduce itself as an acoustical event or even an abstract idea, the way whenever Augustine touches something smooth, he begins to think of music and of God.

BEAUTY PROMPTS A COPY OF ITSELF

The generation is unceasing. Beauty, as both Plato's *Symposium* and everyday life confirm, prompts the begetting of children: when the eye sees someone beautiful, the whole body wants to reproduce the person. But it also—as Diotima tells Socrates—prompts the begetting of poems and laws, the works of Homer, Hesiod, and Lycurgus. The poem and the law may then prompt descriptions of themselves—literary and legal commentaries—that seek to make the beauty of the prior thing more evident, to make, in other words, the poem's or law's "clear discernibility" even more "clearly discernible." Thus the beauty of Beatrice in *La vita nuova* requires of Dante the writing of a sonnet, and the writing of that one sonnet prompts the writing of another: "After completing this last sonnet I was moved by a desire to write more poetry." The sonnets, in turn, place on Dante a new pressure, for as soon as his ear hears what he has made in meter, his hand wants to draw a sketch of it in prose: "This sonnet is divided into two parts . . . "; "This sonnet is divided into four parts. . . . "[1]

The notes that follow specify the English translation and edition used for works originally written in another language. Passages quoted from works originally written in English are not footnoted except where variations occur across different editions (as in the case of Emily Dickinson) or where the work may not be instantly familiar to the reader (as in the book form of Iris Murdoch's 1967 lecture).

[1] The translation used here, and whenever Dante's *Vita nuova* is quoted, is Mark Musa (New York: Oxford University Press, 1992), pp. xv, xvi, 29, 30.

This phenomenon of unceasing begetting sponsors in people like Plato, Aquinas, and Dante the idea of eternity, the perpetual duplicating of a moment that never stops. But it also sponsors the idea of terrestrial plenitude and distribution, the will to make "more and more" so that there will eventually be "enough." Although very great cultural outcomes such as the *Iliad* or the *Mona Lisa* or the idea of distribution arise out of the requirement beauty places on us to replicate, the simplest manifestation of the phenomenon is the everyday fact of staring. The first flash of the bird incites the desire to duplicate not by translating the glimpsed image into a drawing or a poem or a photograph but simply by continuing to see her five seconds, twenty-five seconds, forty-five seconds later—as long as the bird is there to be beheld. People follow the paths of migrating birds, moving strangers, and lost manuscripts, trying to keep the thing sensorily present to them. Pater tells us that Leonardo, as though half-crazed, used to follow people around the streets of Florence once he got "glimpses of it [beauty] in the strange eyes or hair of chance people." Sometimes he persisted until sundown. This replication in the realm of sensation can be carried out by a single perceiver across time (one person staring at a face or listening to the unceasing song of a mockingbird) or can instead entail a brief act of perception distributed across many people. When Leonardo drew a cartoon of St. Anne, for "two days a crowd of people of all qualities passed in naive excitement through the chamber where it hung." This impulse toward a distribution across perceivers is, as both museums and postcards verify, the most common response to beauty: "Addis is full of blossoms. Wish you were here." "The nightingale sang again last night. Come here as soon as you can."

Beauty is sometimes disparaged on the ground that it causes a contagion of imitation, as when a legion of people begin to style themselves after a particular movie starlet, but this is just an imperfect version of a deeply beneficent momentum toward replication. Again beauty is sometimes disparaged because it gives rise to material cupidity and possessiveness; but here, too, we may come to feel we are simply encountering an imperfect instance of an otherwise positive outcome. If someone wishes all the Gallé vases of the world to sit on his own windowsills, it is just a miseducated version of the typically generous-hearted impulse we see when Marcel Proust stares at the face of the girl serving milk at a train stop:

> I could not take my eyes from her face which grew larger as she approached, like a sun which it was somehow possible to stare at and which was coming nearer and nearer, letting itself be seen at close quarters, dazzling you with its blaze of red and gold.[2]

Proust wishes her to remain forever in his perceptual field and will alter his own location to bring that about: "to go with her to the stream, to the cow, to the train, to be always at her side."

This willingness continually to revise one's own location in order to place oneself in the path of beauty is the basic impulse underlying education. One submits oneself to other minds (teachers) in order to increase the chance that one will be looking in the right direction when a comet suddenly cuts through a certain patch of sky. The arts and sciences, like Plato's dialogues, have at their center the drive to confer greater clarity on what already has clear discernibility, as well as to confer initial clarity on what originally has none. They are a key mechanism in what Diotima called begetting and what Alexis Tocqueville called distribution. By perpetuating beauty, institutions of education help incite the will toward continual creation. Sometimes their institutional gravity and awkwardness can seem tonally out of register with beauty, which, like a small bird, has an aura of fragility, as when Simone Weil in *Waiting for God* writes:

---

[2] Marcel Proust, *Remembrance of Things Past,* trans. C. K. Scott Moncrieff and Terence Kilmartin (New York: Vintage–Random House, 1982), 1:706–7.

> The love of the beauty of the world . . . involves . . . the love of
> all the truly precious things that bad fortune can destroy. The
> truly precious things are those forming ladders reaching to-
> ward the beauty of the world, openings onto it.

But Weil's list of precious things, openings into the world, begins
not with a flight of a bird but with education: "Numbered among
them are the pure and authentic achievements of art and sciences."[3] To misstate, or even merely understate, the relation of the
universities to beauty is one kind of error that can be made. A university is among the precious things that can be destroyed.

ERRORS IN BEAUTY: ATTRIBUTES EVENLY AND UNEVENLY PRESENT ACROSS BEAUTIFUL THINGS

The author of the *Greater Hippias,* widely believed to have been
Plato, points out that while we know with relative ease what a
beautiful horse or a beautiful man or possibly even a beautiful pot
is (this last one is a matter of some dispute in the dialogue), it is
much more difficult to say what "Beauty" unattached to any object is. At no point will there be any aspiration to speak in these
pages of unattached Beauty, or of the attributes of unattached
Beauty. But there are attributes that are, without exception, present across different objects (faces, flowers, birdsongs, men, horses,
pots, and poems), one of which is this impulse toward begetting.
It is impossible to conceive of a beautiful thing that does not have
this attribute. The homely word "replication" has been used here
because it reminds us that the benign impulse toward creation
results not just in famous paintings but in everyday acts of staring;
it also reminds us that the generative object continues, in some
sense, to be present in the newly begotten object. It may be

[3] Simone Weil, "Love of the Order of the World," in *Waiting for God,* trans. Emma
Craufurd, introd. Leslie A. Fiedler (New York: Harper & Row, 1951), p. 180.

startling to speak of the *Divine Comedy* or the *Mona Lisa* as "a replication" since they are so unprecedented, but the word recalls the
fact that something, or someone, gave rise to their creation and remains silently present in the newborn object.

In the case just looked at, then, the attribute was one common
across all sites, and the error, when it briefly arose, involved seeing
an imperfect version of the attribute (imitation of starlets or, more
seriously, material greed) and correctly spotting the association
with beauty, but failing to recognize the thousands of good outcomes of which this is a deteriorated version. Rejecting the imperfect version of the phenomenon of begetting makes sense; what
does not make sense is rejecting the general impulse toward begetting, or rejecting the beautiful things for giving rise to false, as
well as true, versions of begetting. To disparage beauty not for the
sake of one of its attributes but simply for a misguided version of
one of its otherwise beneficent attributes is a common error made
about beauty.

But we will also see that many errors made about beauty arise
not in relation to an attribute that is, without exception, common across all sites, but precisely in relation to attributes that
are site-specific—that come up, for example, in relation to a
beautiful garden but not in relation, say, to a beautiful poem; or
come up in relation to beautiful persons but not in relation to
the beauty of gods. The discontinuities across sites are the source
of many confusions, one of which will be looked at in detail in
part two. But the most familiar encounter with error occurs
within any one site.

ERRORS WITHIN ANY ONE SITE

It seems a strange feature of intellectual life that if you question
people—"What is an instance of an intellectual error you have

made in your life?"—no answer seems to come readily to mind. Somewhat better luck is achieved if you ask people (friends, students) to describe an error they have made about beauty. It may be helpful if, before proceeding, the reader stops and recalls—in as much detail as possible—an error he or she has made so that another instance can be placed on the page in conjunction with the few about to be described. It may be useful to record the error, or the revision, in as much detail as is possible because I want to make claims here about the way an error presents itself to the mind, and the accuracy of what I say needs alternative instances to be tested against. The error may be a misunderstanding in the reading of Friedrich Schiller's "Ninth Letter" in his *Aesthetic Education of Man,* or a misreading of page eleven in Immanuel Kant's *Third Critique.* But the question is more directly aimed at errors, and revisions, that have arisen in day-to-day life. In my own case, for example, I had ruled out palm trees as objects of beauty and then one day discovered I had made a mistake.

Those who remember making an error about beauty usually also recall the exact second when they first realized they had made an error. The revisionary moment comes as a perceptual slap or slam that itself has emphatic sensory properties. Emily Dickinson's poem—

> It dropped so low—in my Regard—
> I heard it hit the Ground—

is an instance. A correction in perception takes place as an abrasive crash. Though it has the sound of breaking plates, what is shattering loudly is the perception itself:

> It dropped so low—in my Regard—
> I heard it hit the Ground—

And go to pieces on the Stones
At bottom of my mind—[4]

The concussion is not just acoustic but kinesthetic. Her own brain
is the floor against which the felt impact takes place.

The same is true of Shakespeare's "Lilies that fester smell far
worse than weeds." The correction, the alteration in the perception, is so palpable that it is as though the perception itself (rather
than its object) lies rotting in the brain. In both cases, the perception has undergone a radical alteration—it breaks apart (as in
breaking plates) or disintegrates (as in the festering flower); and in
both cases, the alteration is announced by a striking sensory event,
a loud sound, an awful smell. Even if the alteration in perception
were registered not as the sudden introduction of a negative sensation but as the disappearance of the positive sensory attributes the
thing had when it was beautiful, the moment might be equally
stark and highly etched. Gerard Manley Hopkins confides calmly,
cruelly, to someone he once loved that his love has now almost disappeared. He offers as a final clarifying analogy what happens
when a poem, once held to be beautiful, ceases to be so:

Is this made plain? What have I come across
That here will serve me for comparison?
The sceptic disappointment and the loss
A boy feels when the poet he pores upon
Grows less and less sweet to him, and knows no cause.

No loud sound or bad smell could make this more devastating. But
why? In part, because what is so positive is here being taken away:
sweet is a taste, a smell, a sound—the word, of all words, closest to

---

[4] Emily Dickinson, *The Poems of Emily Dickinson: Variorum Edition,* ed. R. W. Frank-
lin (Cambridge, Mass.: Harvard University Press, Belknap Press, 1998), p. 785. Variants in wording in other editions are given on the same page. My thanks to Helen
Vendler for bringing to my attention this poem as well as "The Beginning of the End,"
the poem by Gerard Manley Hopkins I several times quote.

the fresh and easy call of a bird; and conveying a belovedness, an
acuity of regard, as effortless and unasked-for as honeysuckle or
sweet william. Fading (one might hope) could conceivably take
place as a merciful numbing, a dulling, of perception, or a turning
away to other objects of attention. But the shades of fading here
take place under the scrutiny of bright consciousness, the mind
registering in technicolor each successive nuance of its own be-
reavement. Hopkins's boy, with full acuity, leans into, pores upon,
the lesson and the lessening.

Those who recall making an error in beauty inevitably describe
one of two genres of mistake. The first, as in the lines by Dickinson, Shakespeare, and Hopkins, is the recognition that something
formerly held to be beautiful no longer deserves to be so regarded.
The second is the sudden recognition that something from which
the attribution of beauty had been withheld deserved all along to
be so denominated. Of these two genres of error, the second seems
more grave: in the first (the error of overcrediting), the mistake occurs on the side of perceptual generosity, in the second (the error of
undercrediting) on the side of a failed generosity. Doubting the se-
verity of the first genre of error does not entail calling into question the pain the person feels in discovering her mistake: she has
lost the beautiful object in the same way as if it had remained
beautiful but had suddenly moved out of her reach, leaving her
stranded, betrayed; in actuality, the faithful object has remained
within reach but with the subtraction of all attributes that would
ignite the desire to lay hold of it. By either path the desirable object has vanished, leaving the brain bereft.

The uncompromising way in which errors in beauty make
themselves felt is equally visible in the second, more severe genre
of intellectual error, where something not regarded as beautiful
suddenly alerts you to your error. A better description of the moment of instruction might be to say—"Something you did not
hold to be beautiful suddenly turns up in your arms arrayed in full
beauty"—because the force and pressure of the revision is exactly

as though it is happening one-quarter inch from your eyes. One lets things into one's midst without accurately calculating the degree of consciousness required by them. It is as though, when you were about to walk out onto a ledge, you had contracted to carry something, and only once out on the precipice did you realize that the object weighed one hundred pounds.

How one walks through the world, the endless small adjustments of balance, is affected by the shifting weights of beautiful things. Here the alternatives posed a moment ago about the first genre of error—where the beautiful object vanished, not because the still-beloved object itself disappeared carrying its beauty with it, but because the object stayed behind with its beauty newly gone—are reversed. In the second genre of error a beautiful object is suddenly present, not because a new object has entered the sensory horizon bringing its beauty with it (as when a new poem is written or a new student arrives or a willow tree, unleafed by winter, becomes electric—a maze of yellow wands lifting against lavender clapboards and skies) but because an object, already within the horizon, has its beauty, like late luggage, suddenly placed in your hands. This second genre of error entails neither the arrival of a new beautiful object, nor an object present but previously unnoticed, but an object present and confidently repudiated as an object of beauty.

My palm tree is an example. Suddenly I am on a balcony and its huge swaying leaves are before me at eye level, arcing, arching, waving, cresting and breaking in the soft air, throwing the yellow sunlight up over itself and catching it on the other side, running its fingers down its own piano keys, then running them back up again, shuffling and dealing glittering decks of aqua, green, yellow, and white. It is everything I have always loved, fernlike, featherlike, fanlike, open—lustrously in love with air and light.

The vividness of the palm states the acuity with which I feel the error, a kind of dread conveyed by the words "How many?" How many other errors lie like broken plates or flowers on the floor of my mind? I pore over the floor but cannot see much surface since all the space is taken up by the fallen tree trunk, the big clumsy thing with all its leaves stuffed into one shaft. But there may be other things down under there. When you make an error in beauty, it should set off small alarms and warning lights. Instead it waits until you are standing on a balcony for the flashing sword dance to begin. Night comes and I am still on the balcony. Under the moonlight, my palm tree waves and sprays needles of black, silver, and white; hundreds of shimmering lines circle and play and stay in perfect parallel.

Because the tree about which I made the error was not a sycamore, a birch, a copper beech, a stellata Leonard magnolia but a palm tree, because in other words it was a tree whose most common ground is a hemisphere not my own (southern rather than northern) or a coast not my own (west rather than east), the error may seem to be about the distance between north and south, east and west, about mistakes arising from cultural difference. Sometimes the attribution of a mistake to "cultural difference" is intended to show why caring about beauty is bad, as though if I had attended to sycamores and chestnuts less I might have sooner seen the palminess of the palm, this green pliancy designed to capture and restructure light. Nothing I know about perception tells me how my love of the sycamore caused, or contributed to, my failure to love the palm, since there does not appear to be, inside the brain, a finite amount of space given to beautiful things that can be prematurely filled, and since attention to any one thing normally seems to heighten, rather than diminish, the acuity with which one sees the next. Still, it is the case that if I were surrounded every day by hundreds of palms, one of them would have sooner called upon me to correct my error.

Beauty always takes place in the particular, and if there are no particulars, the chances of seeing it go down. In this sense cultural difference, by diminishing the number of times you are on the same ground with a particular vegetation or animal or artwork, gives rise to problems in perception, but problems in perception that also arrive by many other paths. Proust, for example, says we make a mistake when we talk disparagingly or discouragingly about "life" because by using this general term, "life," we have already excluded before the fact all beauty and happiness, which take place only in the particular: "we believed we were taking happiness and beauty into account, whereas in fact we left them out and replaced them by syntheses in which there is not a single atom of either." Proust gives a second instance of synthetic error:

> So it is that a well-read man will at once begin to yawn with boredom when one speaks to him of a new "good book," because he imagines a sort of composite of all the good books that he has read, whereas a good book is something special, something unforeseeable, and is made up not of the sum of all previous masterpieces but of something which the most thorough assimilation . . . would not enable him to discover.

Here the error arises not from cultural difference—the man is steeped in books (and steeped in life)—but from making a composite of particulars, and so erasing the particulars as successfully as if he lived in a hemisphere or on a coast that grew no books or life.

When I used to say the sentence (softly and to myself) "I hate palms" or "Palms are not beautiful; possibly they are not even trees," it was a composite palm that I had somehow succeeded in making without even ever having seen, close up, many particular instances. Conversely, when I now say, "Palms are beautiful," or "I love palms," it is really individual palms that I have in mind. Once when I was under a high palm looking up at its canopy sixty feet above me, its leaves barely moving, just opening and closing slightly as though breathing, I gradually realized it was looking back down at me. Stationed in the fronds, woven into them, was a large owl whose whole front surface, face and torso, was already angled toward the ground. To stare down at me, all she had to do was slowly open her eyes. There was no sudden readjustment of her body, no alarmed turning of her head—her sleeping posture, assumed when she arrived each dawn in her palm canopy, already positioned her to stare down at anyone below, simply by rolling open her eyes in a gesture as pacific as the breezy breathings of the canopy in which she was nesting. I normally think of birds nesting in cuplike shapes where the cup is upward, open to the sky, but this owl (and I later found other owls entering other palms at dawn) had discovered that the canopy was itself a magnified nest, only it happened to be inverted so that it cupped downward. By interleaving her own plumage with the palm's, latching herself into the leaves, she could hold herself out over the sixty-foot column of air as though she were still flying. It was as though she had stopped to sleep in midair, letting the giant arcing palm leaves take over the work of her wings, so that she could soar there in the shaded sunshine until night came and she was ready to fly on her own again.

Homer sings of the beauty of particular things. Odysseus, washed up on shore, covered with brine, having nearly drowned, comes upon a human community and one person in particular, Nausicaa, whose beauty simply astonishes him. He has never anywhere seen a face so lovely; he has never anywhere seen *any* thing so lovely. "No, wait," he says, oddly interrupting himself. Something has suddenly entered his mind. Here are the lines:

> But if you're one of the mortals living here on earth,
> three times blest are your father, your queenly mother,
> three times over your brothers too. How often their hearts
> must warm with joy to see you striding into the dances—
> such a bloom of beauty. . . .
> I have never laid eyes on anyone like you,
> neither man nor woman . . .
> I look at you and a sense of wonder takes me.
>   Wait,
> once I saw the like—in Delos, beside Apollo's altar—

the young slip of a palm-tree springing into the light.
There I'd sailed, you see, with a great army in my wake,
out on the long campaign that doomed my life to hardship.
That vision! Just as I stood there gazing, rapt, for hours . . .
no shaft like that had ever risen up from the earth—
so now I marvel at *you,* my lady: rapt, enthralled,
too struck with awe to grasp you by the knees
though pain has ground me down.[5]

Odysseus's speech makes visible the structure of perception at the moment one stands in the presence of beauty. The beautiful thing seems—is—incomparable, unprecedented; and that sense of being without precedent conveys a sense of the "newness" or "new-bornness" of the entire world. Nausicaa's childlike form, playing ball on the beach with her playmates, reinforces this sense. But now something odd and delicately funny happens. Usually when the "unprecedented" suddenly comes before one, and when one has made a proclamation about the state of affairs—"There is no one like you, nothing like this, anywhere"—the mind, despite the confidently announced mimesis of carrying out a search, does not actually enter into any such search, for it is too exclusively filled with the beautiful object that stands in its presence. It is the very way the beautiful thing fills the mind and breaks all frames that gives the "never before in the history of the world" feeling.

Odysseus startles us by actually searching for and finding a precedent; then startles us again by managing through that precedent to magnify, rather than diminish, his statement of regard for Nausicaa, letting the "young slip of a palm-tree springing into the light" clarify and verify her beauty. The passage continually restarts and refreshes itself. Three key features of beauty return in the new, but chronologically prior, object of beauty.

[5] I am using Robert Fagles's translation of *The Odyssey,* introd. Bernard Knox (New York: Penguin, 1996), Bk. 6, 168–72, 175–86. Most lines cited are from Book 6; occasionally a phrase from Book 5 or 7 enters.

First, beauty is sacred. Odysseus had begun (in lines earlier than those cited above) with the intuition that in standing before Nausicaa he might be standing in the presence of Artemis, and now he rearrives at that intuition, since the young palm grows beside the altar of Delos, the birthplace of Apollo and Artemis. His speech says this: If you are immortal. I recognize you. You are Artemis. If instead you are mortal, I am puzzled and cannot recognize you, since I can find no precedent. No, wait. I do recognize you. I remember watching a tree coming up out of the ground of Delos.

Second, beauty is unprecedented. Odysseus believes Nausicaa has no precedent; then he recalls the palm and recalls as well that the palm had no precedent: "No shaft like that had ever risen up from the earth." The discovery of a precedent only a moment ago reported not to exist contradicts the initial report, but at the same time it confirms the report's accuracy since the feature of unprecedentedness stays stable across the two objects. Nausicaa and the palm each make the world new. Green, pliant, springing up out of the ground before his eyes, the palm is in motion yet stands firm. So, too, Nausicaa: she plays catch, runs into the surf, dances an imagined dance before her parents and brothers, yet stands firm. When the naked Odysseus suddenly comes lurching out onto the sand, "all those lovely girls . . . scattered in panic down the jutting beaches. / Only Alcinous' daughter held fast . . . and she firmly stood her ground and faced Odysseus."

These first and second attributes of beauty are very close to one another, for to say that something is "sacred" is also to say either "it has no precedent" or "it has as its only precedent that which is itself unprecedented." But there is also a third feature: beauty is lifesaving. Homer is not alone in seeing beauty as lifesaving. Augustine described it as "a plank amid the waves of the sea."[6] Proust makes a version of this claim over and over again. Beauty quickens. It

[6] Augustine, *De Musica,* trans. W. F. Jackson Knight, in *Philosophies of Art and Beauty,* ed. Albert Hofstadter and Richard Kuhns (Chicago: University of Chicago Press, 1976), p. 196.

adrenalizes. It makes the heart beat faster. It makes life more vivid, animated, living, worth living. But what exactly is the claim or— more to the point—exactly how literal is the claim that it saves lives or directly confers the gift of life? Neither Nausicaa nor the palm rescues Odysseus from the sea, but both are objects he sees immediately after having escaped death. Odysseus stands before Nausicaa still clotted with matter from the roling ocean that battered him throughout Book 5, just as Odysseus stood before the young palm having just emerged out of the man-killing sea: "There I'd sailed, you see, with a great army in my wake, / out on the long campaign that doomed my life to hardship." Here again Homer re-creates the structure of a perception that occurs whenever one sees something beautiful; it is as though one has suddenly been washed up onto a merciful beach: all unease, aggression, indifference suddenly drop back behind one, like a surf that has for a moment lost its capacity to harm.

Not Homer alone but Plato, Aquinas, Plotinus, Pseudo-Dionysius, Dante, and many others repeatedly describe beauty as a "greeting." At the moment one comes into the presence of something beautiful, it greets you. It lifts away from the neutral background as though coming forward to welcome you—as though the object were designed to "fit" your perception. In its etymology, "welcome" means that one comes with the well-wishes or consent of the person or thing already standing on that ground. It is as though the welcoming thing has entered into, and consented to, your being in its midst. Your arrival seems contractual, not just something you want, but something the world you are now joining wants. Homer's narrative enacts the "greeting."[7] Odysseus

---

[7] As Nausicaa greets Odysseus on the beach, so a short time later Athena greets him when he arrives at the city: "As he was about to enter the welcome city, the bright-eyed goddess herself came up to greet him there." The idea of beauty as a greeting reappears in many classical, medieval, and Renaissance writings—in the description of beauty's "clear discernibility" in Plato, in the attention to the attribute of *claritas* in Aquinas, in the account of beauty as "a call" in both Albertus Magnus and Marsilio Ficino. In Dante's *Vita nuova* the idea of beauty as a greeting becomes not just a theme or argument but a principle of structure, for the work is organized as a succession of greetings. "It was pre-

hears Nausicaa even before he sees her. Her voice is green: min-gling with the voices of the other children, it sounds like water moving through lush meadow grass. This greenness of sound be-comes the fully articulated subject matter of her speech when she later directs him through her father's groves, meadows, blossom-ing orchards, so he can reach their safe inland hall, where the only traces of the ocean are the lapis blue of the glazed frieze on the wall and the "sea-blue wool" that Nausicaa's mother continually works. Nausicaa's beauty, her welcoming countenance, allows Odysseus to hope that he will be made welcome in "the welcome city," "welcome Scheria"—that "generous King Alcinous" and the Phaeacian assembly will receive him, as in fact they do, with "some mercy and some love."

Odysseus has made a hymn to beauty. One may protest that this description tonally overcredits Odysseus since—something that has so far not been mentioned—Odysseus is here being re-lentlessly strategic. He has a concrete, highly instrumental goal. He must get Nausicaa to lead him to safety. The lines immediately preceding his hymn of praise show him "slyly" calculating how to approach her. How should he walk? Stand? Speak? Should he hold himself upright or kneel on the ground before her? Should he grasp her by the knees or keep his distance, stand reverently back? But just as his hymn to beauty can be seen as an element subordi-nate to the larger frame of his calculation for reentering the human community, so the narrative of calculation can be seen as subordi-nate to the hymn of beauty. The moment of coming upon some-thing or someone beautiful might sound—if lifted away from beauty's own voice and arriving from a voice outside him—like this: "You are about to be in the presence of something life-giving,

---

cisely the ninth hour of that day (three o'clock in the afternoon), when her sweet greet-ing reached me," reports Dante of Beatrice; and his first sonnet begins: "To every loving heart and captive soul . . . greetings I bring." A greeting, either given or withheld, is the central action and issue throughout. The idea continues across the centuries. When James Joyce's Lynch announces that he is devoted to beauty, Stephen Dedalus responds by lifting his cap in greeting.

lifesaving, something that deserves from you a posture of reverence or petition. It is not clear whether you should throw yourself on your knees before it or keep your distance from it, but you had better figure out the right answer because this is not an occasion for carelessness or for leaving your own postures wholly to chance. It is not that beauty is life-threatening (though this attribute has sometimes been assigned it), but instead that it is life-affirming, life-giving; and therefore if, through your careless approach, you become cut off from it, you will feel its removal as a retraction of life. You will fall back into the sea, which even now, as you stand there gazing, is only a few feet behind you." The framework of strategy and deliberation literalizes, rather than undermines, the claim that beauty is lifesaving.

Sacred, lifesaving, having as precedent only those things that are themselves unprecedented, beauty has a fourth feature: it incites deliberation. I have spoken of Odysseus's error toward Nausicaa. But one could just as easily see Odysseus's error as committed against the palm: seeing Nausicaa, he temporarily forgets the palm by the altar, injuring it by his thoughtless disregard and requiring him at once to go on to correct himself. The hymn to Nausicaa's beauty can instead be called a palinode to the beauty of the palm. By either account, Odysseus starts by making an error.

So far error has been talked about as a cognitive event that just happens to have beauty—like anything else—as one of its objects. But that description, which makes error independent of beauty, may itself be wrong. The experience of "being in error" so inevitably accompanies the perception of beauty that it begins to seem one of its abiding structural features. On the one hand, something beautiful—a blossom, a friend, a poem, a sky—makes a clear and self-evident appearance before one: this feature can be called "clear discernibility" for reasons that will soon be elaborated. The beauty of the thing at once fills the perceiver with a sense of conviction about that beauty, a wordless certainty—the this! here! of Rainer Maria Rilke's poetry. On the other hand, the act of perceiving that seemingly self-evident beauty has a built-in liability to self-correction and self-adjustment, so much so that it appears to be a key element in whatever beauty is. This may explain why, as noticed earlier, when the informal experiment is conducted of asking people about intellectual errors, they do not readily remember ever having made one (or, more accurately, they are sure they have made one but do not happen to remember what it is); whereas when you ask them about errors in beauty, they seem not only to remember one but to recall the process of correction in vivid sensory detail. Something beautiful immediately catches attention yet prompts one to judgments that one then continues to scrutinize, and that one not infrequently discovers to be in error.

Something beautiful fills the mind yet invites the search for something beyond itself, something larger or something of the same scale with which it needs to be brought into relation. Beauty, according to its critics, causes us to gape and suspend all thought. This complaint is manifestly true: Odysseus does stand marveling before the palm; Odysseus is similarly incapacitated in front of Nausicaa; and Odysseus will soon, in Book 7, stand "gazing," in much the same way, at the season-immune orchards of King Alcinous, the pears, apples, and figs that bud on one branch while ripening on another, so that never during the cycling year do they cease to be in flower and in fruit. But simultaneously what is beautiful prompts the mind to move chronologically back in the search for precedents and parallels, to move forward into new acts of creation, to move conceptually over, to bring things into relation, and does all this with a kind of urgency as though one's life depended on it. So distinct do the two mental acts appear that one might believe them prompted by two different species of beauty (as Schiller argued for the existence of both a "melting" beauty and an "energetic" beauty)[8] if it weren't for the fact that they turn up

[8]   The English words "energetic" and "melting" occur in various translations of the Sixteenth Letter of Schiller's *On the Aesthetic Education of Man in a Series of Letters,* such as that by Reginald Snell (New York: Frederick Ungar, 1954) and again that by Elizabeth M. Wilkinson and L. A. Willoughby (Oxford: Clarendon, 1967).

folded inside the same lyric event, though often opening out at chronologically distinct moments.

One can see why beauty—by Homer, by Plato, by Aquinas, by Dante (and the list would go on, name upon name, century by century, page upon page, through poets writing today such as Gjertrud Schnackenberg, Allen Grossman, and Seamus Heaney) —has been perceived to be bound up with the immortal, for it prompts a search for a precedent, which in turn prompts a search for a still earlier precedent, and the mind keeps tripping backward until it at last reaches something that has no precedent, which may very well be the immortal. And one can see why beauty—by those same artists, philosophers, theologians of the Old World and the New—has been perceived to be bound up with truth. What is beautiful is in league with what is true because truth abides in the immortal sphere. But if this were the only basis for the association, then many of us living now who feel skeptical about the existence of an immortal realm might be required to conclude that beauty and truth have nothing to do with one another. Luckily, a second basis for the association stands clearly before us: the beautiful person or thing incites in us the longing for truth because it provides by its compelling "clear discernibility" an introduction (perhaps even our first introduction) to the state of certainty yet does not itself satiate our desire for certainty since beauty, sooner or later, brings us into contact with our own capacity for making errors. The beautiful, almost without any effort of our own, acquaints us with the mental event of conviction, and so pleasurable a mental state is this that ever afterward one is willing to labor, struggle, wrestle with the world to locate enduring sources of conviction— to locate what is true. Both in the account that assumes the existence of the immortal realm and in the account that assumes the nonexistence of the immortal realm, beauty is a starting place for education.

Hymn and palinode—conviction and consciousness of error— reside inside most daily acts of encountering something beautiful.

One walks down a street and suddenly sees a redbud tree—its tiny heart-shaped leaves climbing out all along its branches like children who haven't yet learned the spatial rules for which parts of the playground they can run on. (Don't they know they should stay on the tips of the twigs?) It is as though one has just been beached, lifted out of one ontological state into another that is fragile and must be held on to lest one lose hold of the branch and fall back into the ocean. Like Odysseus, one feels inadequate to it, lurches awkwardly around it, saying odd things to the small leaves, wishing to sing to them a hymn or, finding oneself unable, wishing in apology to make a palinode. Perhaps like Dante watching Beatrice, one could make a sonnet and then a prose poem explaining the sonnet; or, like Leonardo looking at a violet, one could make a sketch, then another, then another; or like Lady Autumn, listening with amazement to a stanza Keats has just sung her, one could sit there patiently staring moment after moment, hour by hour. Homer was right: beauty is lifesaving (or life-creating as in Dante's title *La vita nuova,* or life-altering as in Rilke's imperative "You must change your life"). And Homer was right: beauty incites deliberation, the search for precedents. But what about the immortal, about which Homer may or may not have been right? If we look at modern examples of the palinode for a missing precedent, does the plenitude and aspiration for truth stay stable, even if the metaphysical referent is in doubt?

Matisse never hoped to save lives. But he repeatedly said that he wanted to make paintings so serenely beautiful that when one came upon them, suddenly all problems would subside. His paintings of Nice have for me this effect. My house, though austere inside, is full of windows banking onto a garden. The garden throws changing colors into the chaste rooms—lavenders, pinks, blues, and pools of green. One winter when I was bereft because my garden was underground, I put Matisse prints all over the walls—thirteen in a single room. All winter long I applied the paintings to my staring eyes, and now they are, in retrospect, one of the things that make my former disregard of palm trees so startling. The precedent behind each Nice painting is the frond of a palm; or, to be more precise, each Nice painting is a perfect cross between an anemone flower and a palm frond. The presence of the anemone I had always seen—in the mauve and red colors, the abrupt patches of black, in the petal-like tissue of curtains, slips, parasols, and tablecloths, in the small pools of color with sudden drop-offs at their edges. But I completely missed what resided behind these surfaces, what Odysseus would have seen, the young slip of a palm springing into the light.

The signature of a palm is its striped light. Palm leaves stripe the light. The dyadic alternations of leaf and air make the frond shimmer and move, even when it stays still, and if there is an actual breeze, then the stripings whip around without ever losing their perfect alignment across the full sequence. Matisse transcribes this effect to many of the rooms in the Nice paintings. Here is the structure of one entitled *Interior, Nice, Seated Woman with a Book,* where the arcings and archings of the fronds are car-

ried in the rounding curves of the curtain and chair and woman. The striped leaf-light is everywhere in the room, in the louvered slats of the slanted window, in the louvered slats of the straight window, in the louvered slats reflecting in the glass window, in the striped blue-and-white cloth on the lower right and its mirrored echo, in the woman's striped robe, lifting out from its center like an array of fronds from a stalk, and in the large bands of color in the architectural features of the room. On the upper left, lifting high above the woman, a single curved frond cups outward, its red, blue, and green leaf colors setting the palette for the rest of the room: it registers the botanical precedent, in case the small surface of the actual black-green palm (visible in the upper half of the window and indicated in my sketch by dark ink) is missed. Light trips rapidly across the surface of the room: in out in, out in out in, out off on off, on out off in, on off on off. It feathers across the eye, excites it, incites in it saccadic leaps and midair twirls ("retinal arabesques," my friend calls them). It is as though the painting were painted with the frond of a palm, or as though the frond were just

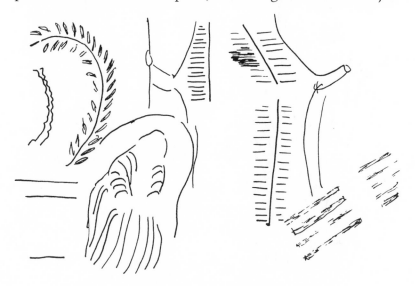

Interior, Nice. Seated Woman with a Book.

laid down on the canvas, as though it swished across the canvas, leaving prints of itself here there here there here there.

In *My Room at the Beau Rivage,* the striping, the stationary equivalent of shimmering, is accomplished through the pink-and-yellow wallpaper stripes and the curved lines of the satin chair, where the leaf-light is so concentrated it simply whites out in one section. The pliant chair, like the woman in *Seated Woman with a*

My Room at the Beau Rivage

Book, is the newborn palm tree, the place where light pools and then spills outward in all directions. Like silver threads appearing and disappearing behind the cross threads of a weaving—not a finished weaving but one whose making is just now under way—the silver jumps of our eyes trip in unison across the stripes, appearing and disappearing beneath the latticing of the guide threads. It is as though white sea-lanes have been drawn on the surface of the ocean and across them Nereids dive in and out.

Missing the print of the palm seems remarkable. The thing so capaciously and luminously dispersed throughout the foreground of the room is concretely specified at the very back of (almost as if behind) the painting. The palm is present in all, or almost all, of the Nice paintings. But the amount of surface that is dedicated to the actual tree, as opposed to the palmy offspring stripings inside the room, is tiny—one-thirtieth of the canvas in *Seated Woman with a Book,* one-fiftieth of the canvas in *My Room at the Beau Rivage,* and similar small fractions in others of the 1920s, such as *The Morning Tea, Woman on a Sofa, Still Life: 'Les Pensées de Pascal,' Vase of Flowers in Front of the Window,* in each of which the tree occupies between one-fiftieth and one sixty-third of the full surface.

Further, the tree's individuated fronds are themselves seldom visible, and the leaves, never. A curtain may be striped; a wall may be striped; a bowl of flowers may be striped; a floor may be striped; a human figure may be striped, a table, bed, or chair may be striped. The fronds are the one thing to which stripes are disallowed, except perhaps in *'Les Pensées de Pascal'* where (on close inspection of the very small tree) the green branchings have a cupped pink underside that sets in motion, inside the room, the soft blocks of gray and pink where the curtain overlaps the windowsill, and the hot pink and gray stripes on the sill below. More typically the tree canopy looks like a knob of broccoli, sometimes lacks a trunk, and may even be positioned in the lower half of the painting. It provides just a fleeting acknowledgment of the fact that it is the precedent that sets in motion all the light-filled

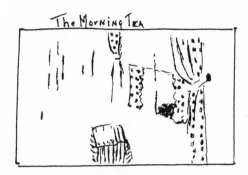

surfaces in the foreground. The tree is the only thing in the paintings to which the palm-style is not applied, just as when Matisse includes a bowl of actual anemones or nasturtiums or fritillarias in his paintings, it is often the one thing to which the anemone-style, nasturtium-style, or fritillaria-style (everywhere else filling the room) will be disallowed.

But at least one painting from the Nice period—*The Painter and His Model, Studio Interior* (1919)—explicitly announces the fact that the palm frond is the model from which, or more accurately the instrument with which, Matisse paints. Perhaps the palm is here openly saluted and seized because the painting is overtly about the act of painting. The room is full of sunlight. Yellow. Cream. Gold. White. These colors cover two-thirds of its surface, which is also awash with lavenders and reds falling in sun-filled stripes from the curtains, the walls, the man, the table,

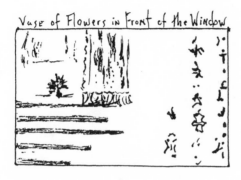

the chair, the dresser. The palm in the window is still only a small fraction of the surface, one thirty-fifth, but unlike many other Nice paintings, it is here stark, self-announcing. The palm now has emphatic fronds. It is brown, like the painter's brush, which has only a shaft and no brush, and so seems supplied by the tree, as though the palm were a continuation of the tool he holds, interrupted by the woman's body (the woman who is technically the model referred to in the title, though the palm seems more model than she). The palm seems not just the model, the thing that inspires him or the thing he aspires to copy, but much more material in its presence. It is what he reaches out for, closes his hand around, and presses down on the surface of the canvas he is lashing with light. It is a graphic literalization of "brush," "to brush," a brush with beauty. Because the palmy stripings incite the silver cross-jumps of light over our face and eyes, it is as though the

The Painter and His Model
1919

painting in turn paints us, plaiting braids of light across the surface of our skin.

Other Nice paintings depicting the act of composition similarly register the palm as instrument. The woman painter in *The
Morning Session* (1924) wears a yellow-and-black striped dress that
covers her torso, lap, and legs—the vertical stripes become hori-
zontal when they reach her lap, raying out like sunlight before becoming vertical again as they turn at her knees and drop to the
floor. She sits in front of a red-and-white striped wall, and long
vertical bands of peach streak down the window, down the walls,
and down the back of her painting. Because of the angle at which
she sits, the brush with which she paints (like the man's in *The
Painter and His Model*) has only a shaft and no brush, but by good
luck there stand directly above her hand the open fronds, the lux-

urious canopy brush, of a distant palm. This vision of creation extends to auditory composition. The musician's bow in *Young Woman Playing the Violin in Front of the Open Window* (1923) is also completed and continued by the fronds of the palm outside her window, turning her bow into a brush. She is safely held in the lap of the striped walls on three sides. Above her head, the huge open window—open sky, open sea, open sail, open palm—seems the picture of the airy music she is playing, a picture painted with the brush of her bow.

Three decades later, Matisse still paints palms in windows, but now as the fulsome, fully saluted precedent. The pictures seem Odyssean palinodes to the once insufficiently acknowledged tree. By 1947 the palm fills not one sixty-third or one-fiftieth or one-thirtieth of the painting but one-quarter. By 1948 it fills one-half. In both pictures it has become the central subject. Formerly deprived of the very style it inspired, it is now the single thing in the picture to which the leaf-light striping is emphatically applied. The palm in *Still Life with Pomegranate* is composed of hundreds of green stripes against light blue. The palm in *Interior with Egyptian Curtain* is composed of hundreds upon hundreds of stripes in black, green, yellow, white. On the wall inside the 1948 canvas *Large Interior in Red* hangs a black-and-white picture with a palm outside the window and another palm inside the room—palm fronds painted with a palm frond on a palm frond—the painter's material, instrument, and subject.

I began here with the way beautiful things have a forward momentum, the way they incite the desire to bring new things into the world: infants, epics, sonnets, drawings, dances, laws, philosophic dialogues, theological tracts. But we soon found ourselves also turning backward, for the beautiful faces and songs that lift us forward onto new ground keep calling out to us as well, inciting us to rediscover and recover them in whatever new thing gets made. The very pliancy or elasticity of beauty—hurtling us forward and

The Morning Session

back, requiring us to break new ground, but obliging us also to bridge back not only to the ground we just left but to still earlier, even ancient, ground—is a model for the pliancy and lability of consciousness in education. Matisse believed he was painting the inner life of the mind; and it is this elasticity that we everywhere see in the leaf-light of his pictures, the pliancy and palmy reach of the capacious mind. Even when the claim on behalf of immortality is gone, many of the same qualities—plenitude, inclusion—are the outcome.

It sometimes seems that a special problem arises for beauty once the realm of the sacred is no longer believed in or aspired to. If a beautiful young girl (like Nausicaa), or a small bird, or a glass vase, or a poem, or a tree has the metaphysical in behind it, that realm verifies the weight and attention we confer on the girl, bird, vase, poem, tree. But if the metaphysical realm has vanished, one may feel bereft not only because of the giant deficit left by that va-

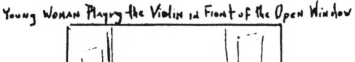

Young Woman Playing the Violin in Front of the Open Window

cant realm but because the girl, the bird, the vase, the book now seem unable in their solitude to justify or account for the weight of their own beauty. If each calls out for attention that has no destination beyond itself, each seems self-centered, too fragile to support the gravity of our immense regard.

But beautiful things, as Matisse shows, always carry greetings from other worlds within them. In surrendering to his leaf-light, one is carried to other shorelines as inevitably as Odysseus is carried back to Delos. What happens when there is no immortal realm behind the beautiful person or thing is just what happens when there *is* an immortal realm behind the beautiful person or thing: the perceiver is led to a more capacious regard for the world. The requirement for plenitude is built-in. The palm will always be found (whether one accidentally walks out onto a balcony, or follows at daybreak the flight path of an owl, or finds oneself washed up in front of Nausicaa or a redbud or *Seated Woman with a*

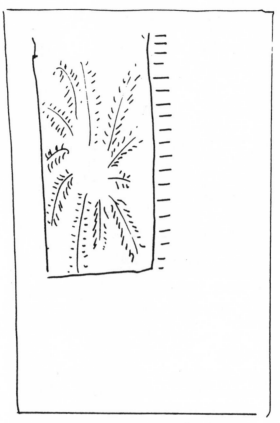

1947 Still Life with Pomegranate

Book) because the palm is itself the method of finding. The material world constrains us, often with great beneficence, to see each person and thing in its time and place, its historical context. But mental life doesn't so constrain us. It is porous, open to the air and light, swings forward while swaying back, scatters its stripes in all directions, and delights to find itself beached beside something invented only that morning or instead standing beside an altar from three millennia ago.

This very plasticity, this elasticity, also makes beauty associate

1948 Interior with Egyptian
Curtain

with error, for it brings one face-to-face with one's own errors: momentarily stunned by beauty, the mind before long begins to create or to recall and, in doing so, soon discovers the limits of its own starting place, if there are limits to be found, or may instead—as is more often the case—uncover the limitlessness of the beautiful thing it beholds. Though I have mainly concentrated here on failures of plenitude and underattribution—mistakes that involve not seeing the beauty of something—the same outcomes can be arrived at by the path of overattribution, as registered in the poems about error by Dickinson, Hopkins, and Shakespeare. This genre of error, however, has the peculiarity that when the beautiful person or thing ceases to appear beautiful, it often incites the perceiver to repudiate, scorn, or even denounce the object as an invalid candidate or carrier of beauty. It is as though the person or thing had not merely been beautiful but had actually made a claim that it was beautiful, and further, a claim that it would be beautiful forever.[9] But of course it is we—not the beautiful persons or things themselves (Maud Gonne, Mona Lisa, "Ode to a Nightingale," Chartres, a columbine, a dove, a bank of sweet pea, a palm tree)—who make announcements and promises to one another about the enduring beauty of these beautiful things. If a beautiful palm tree one day ceases to be so, has it defaulted on a promise? Hopkins defends the tree:

> No, the tropic tree
> Has not a charter that its sap shall last
> Into all seasons, though no Winter cast
> The happy leafing.

The temptation to scorn the innocent object for ceasing to be beautiful might be called the temptation against plenitude; it puts at risk not the repudiated object but the capaciousness of the cognitive act.

Many human desires are coterminous with their object. A person desires a good meal and—as though by magic—the person's desire for a good meal seems to end at just about the time the good meal ends. But our desire for beauty is likely to outlast its object because, as Kant once observed, unlike all other pleasures, the

---

[9] Shakespeare's sonnets (and a small number of other beautiful things) openly promise that they will be forever beautiful; but most beautiful things make no such claim. They only seem to make such a claim because the very moment they enter our minds, there simultaneously enters our minds a wish that this thing should forever be what it is now. So associated are the two events that the object itself seems to have made the announcement that it will always be what it is now.

pleasure we take in beauty is inexhaustible. No matter how long beautiful things endure, they cannot out-endure our longing for them. If the beauty of an object lasts exactly as long as the life of the object—the way the blue chalice of a morning glory blossom spins open at dawn and collapses at noon—it will not be faulted for the disappearance of its beauty. Efforts may even be made to prolong our access to its beauty beyond its death, as when Aristotle, rather than turning away from a dying iris blossom, tracks the changing location of its deep colors, and Rilke, rather than turning away from the rose at the moment it breaks apart, describes the luxurious postures the flower adopts in casting down its petals.

But if the person or thing outlives its own beauty—as when a face believed ravishing for two years no longer seems so in the third, or a favorite vase one day ceases to delight, or a poem beloved in the decade when it is written becomes incomprehensible to those who read it later—then it is sometimes not just turned away from but turned upon, as though it has enacted a betrayal. But the work that beautiful persons and things accomplish is collectively accomplished, and different persons and things contribute to this work for different lengths of time, one enduring for three millennia and one enduring for only three seconds. A vase may catch your attention, you turn your head to look at it, you look at it still more carefully, and suddenly its beauty is gone. Was the beauty of the object false, or was the beauty real but brief? The three-second call to beauty can have produced the small flex of the mind, the constant moistening, that other objects—large, arcing, flexuous—will more enduringly require. We make a mistake, says Seamus Heaney, if, driving down a road between wind and water, overwhelmed by what we see, we assume we will see "it" better if we stop the car. It is there in the passage. When one goes on to find "better," or "higher," or "truer," or "more enduring," or "more widely agreed upon" forms of beauty, what happens to our regard for the less good, less high, less true, less enduring, less universal instances? Simone Weil says, "He who has gone farther, to the very beauty of the world itself, does not love them any less but much more deeply than before."

I have tried to set forth the view here that beauty really is allied with truth. This is not to say that what is beautiful is also true. There certainly are objects in which "the beautiful" and "the true" do converge, such as the statement "1 = 1." This may be why, though the vocabulary of beauty has been banished or driven underground in the humanities for the last two decades, it has been openly in play in those fields that aspire to have "truth" as their object—math, physics, astrophysics, chemistry, biochemistry— where every day in laboratories and seminar rooms participants speak of problems that are "nice," theories that are "pretty," solutions that are "beautiful," approaches that are "elegant," "simple." The participants differ, though, on whether a theory's being "pretty" is predictive of, or instead independent of, its being "true."[10]

But the claim throughout these pages that beauty and truth are allied is not a claim that the two are identical. It is not that a poem or a painting or a palm tree or a person is "true," but rather that it ignites the desire for truth by giving us, with an electric brightness shared by almost no other uninvited, freely arriving perceptual event, the experience of conviction and the experience, as well, of error. This liability to error, contestation, and plurality— for which "beauty" over the centuries has so often been belittled— has sometimes been cited as evidence of its falsehood and distance from "truth," when it is instead the case that our very aspiration for truth is its legacy. It creates, without itself fulfilling, the aspiration for enduring certitude. It comes to us, with no work of our own; then leaves us prepared to undergo a giant labor.

---

[10] Physicist Thomas Appelquist, for example, has told me that in particle physics the beauty of a theory is taken to be predictive of its truth; experimental astrophysicist Paul Horowitz, on the other hand, counsels new physicists not to assume that if they come up with a "pretty" theory, it must be true. Exponents of both positions can no doubt be found within each of the two sciences.

II. ON BEAUTY AND BEING FAIR

The banishing of beauty from the humanities in the last two decades has been carried out by a set of political complaints against it. But, as I will try to suggest, these political complaints against beauty are themselves incoherent. Beauty is, at the very least, innocent of the charges against it, and it may even be the case that far from damaging our capacity to attend to problems of injustice, it instead intensifies the pressure we feel to repair existing injuries. I will try to set forth a sketch of the way aesthetic attributes exert this pressure on us.

When I say that beauty has been banished, I do not mean that beautiful things have themselves been banished, for the humanities are made up of beautiful poems, stories, paintings, sketches, sculpture, film, essays, debates, and it is this that every day draws us to them. I mean something much more modest: that conversation about the beauty of these things has been banished, so that we coinhabit the space of these objects (even putting them inside us, learning them by heart, carrying one wedged at all times between the upper arm and the breast, placing as many as possible into our bookbags) yet speak about their beauty only in whispers.

The Political Arguments against Beauty Are Incoherent

The political critique of beauty is composed of two distinct arguments. The first urges that beauty, by preoccupying our attention, distracts attention from wrong social arrangements. It makes us inattentive, and therefore eventually indifferent, to the project of bringing about arrangements that are just. The second argument holds that when we stare at something beautiful, make it an object of sustained regard, our act is destructive to the object. This argument is most often prompted when the gaze is directed toward a human face or form, but the case presumably applies equally when the beautiful thing is a mourning dove, or a trellis spilling over with sweet pea, or a book whose pages are being folded back for the first time. The complaint has given rise to a generalized discrediting of the act of "looking," which is charged with "reifying" the very object that appears to be the subject of admiration.

Whatever merit either of these arguments has in and of itself, it is clear at the outset that they are unlikely both to be true since they fundamentally contradict one another. The first assumes that if our "gaze" could just be coaxed over in one direction and made to latch onto a specific object (an injustice in need of remedy or repair), that object would benefit from our generous attention. The second assumes that generous attention is inconceivable, and that any object receiving sustained attention will somehow suffer from the act of human regard. Because the two complaints so fundamentally contradict one another, evidence that can be brought forward on behalf of the first tends to call into question the accuracy of the second; and conversely, evidence that can be summoned up on behalf of the second works to undermine the first.

If, for example, an opponent of beauty eventually persuades us that a human face or form or a bird or a trellis of sweet pea normally suffers from being looked at, then when the second opponent of beauty complains that beauty has caused us to turn away from social injustice, we will have to feel relieved that whatever harm the principals are now suffering is at least not being compounded by our scrutiny of them.[1] If instead we are persuaded that beauty has distracted us from suffering, and that our attention to that suffering will help reduce the harm, we will have to assume that human perception, far from poisoning each object it turns toward, is instead fully capable of being benign.

It seems that the two opponents of beauty have a greater quar-

[1] Indeed, at the very moment when beauty was being banished from universities for distracting from social justice, scholars trying to make problems of social justice visible were sometimes accused of "reenacting" the cruelty by making suffering available to the reader's gaze.

rel with each other than with us and should perhaps be encouraged
to press forward their claims, since they will together eliminate
both grounds of opposition and leave us free once more to speak of
beauty. But seasons come and go, decades are passing, and the two
arguments—by never being brought together in a single space—
continue to flourish. So, as bad-tempered as the effort may seem,
some time must be given here to contesting the two views.

The opponents of beauty could conceivably defend the consistency of their two views. They might say the following. It is not
that one of us holds perception to be benign and the other holds
perception to be malicious: we are speaking of two distinguishable
kinds of perception. It is pleasure-filled perception (as when one
listens to the mourning dove terracing its sweet calls or the crow-
ing of the cock on a distant hillside) that is morally bad; and it is
aversive perception (as when one turns on the radio and hears, with
distress, one point of view being systematically suppressed) that is
morally good. But it seems almost inconceivable that anyone with
affection for human beings could wish on them so harsh an edict,
permitting only perceptions that bring discomfort. More important, there is no way to be in a high state of alert toward injus-
tices—to subjects that, because they entail injuries, will bring
distress—without simultaneously demanding of oneself precisely
the level of perceptual acuity that will forever be opening one to
the arrival of beautiful sights and sounds. How will one even notice, let alone become concerned about, the inclusion in a political
assembly of only one economic point of view unless one has also attended, with full acuity, to a debate that is itself a beautiful object,
full of arguments, counterarguments, wit, spirit, ripostes, ironies,
testing, contesting; and how in turn will one hear the nuances of
even this debate unless one also makes oneself available to the
songs of birds or poets?

One other possible way our two opponents might claim they
can reconcile their apparently contradictory complaints about
beauty would be to say that passive perception—looking or

hearing without any wish to change what one has seen or heard (as often happens in the presence of the beautiful)—is unacceptable; whereas instrumental perception—looking or hearing that is prelude to intervening in, changing, what one has seen or heard (as happens in the presence of injustice)—is good. But a moment's reflection will show that this is just a slight rephrasing of the earlier proposal that pleasurable perception is morally bad and aversive perception is morally good. Further, it seeks to make the whole sensorium utilitarian, an outcome laudable only in high emergencies.

It is the argument of this chapter that beauty, far from contributing to social injustice in either of the two ways it stands accused, or even remaining neutral to injustice as an innocent bystander, actually assists us in the work of addressing injustice, not only by requiring of us constant perceptual acuity—high dives of seeing, hearing, touching—but by the more direct forms of instruction sketched in the next part of the chapter. The sketch counters both grounds of attack, but because it more directly addresses the first (the enduring claim that beauty makes us inattentive to justice), it may be helpful to address here very briefly the second (the relatively recent complaint that beauty enlists the perceiver into an act of perception that reifies). It has two major weaknesses.

First, the complaint is often formulated in such a way that, in its force and scope, it seems to be generalized to all objects of beauty—the poems of John Donne or John Keats, mother-of-pearl poppies, gods from both the East and the West, human faces, buildings—even though the particular instances explicitly cited are almost always confined to one particular site of beauty, the beauty of persons. Even if we could be persuaded that looking at beautiful human faces and forms were harmful to the persons we seem to be admiring, it is not clear why the entire world of natural and artifactual, physical and metaphysical beauty should be turned away from. It seems that at most we should be obligated to give up the pleasure of looking at one another.

No detailed argument or description is ever brought forward to justify this generalization, yet the generalization has worked to silence conversations about beauty. If this critique or the other critiques against beauty were crisply formulated as edicts or treatises with sustained arguments and examples, the incoherence would be more starkly visible and the influence correspondingly diminished. They exist instead as semiarticulate but deeply held convictions that—like snow in a winter sky that keeps materializing in the air yet never falls or accumulates on the ground—make their daily way into otherwise lively essays, articles, exams, conversations. Suddenly, out of the blue, someone begins to speak about the way a poet is reifying the hillside or painting or flower she seems to be so carefully regarding.

One way of seeing the weakness of the generalization is to test it across different categories of beautiful objects, categories of objects whose beauty is beloved not just by people in Western countries but by people everywhere. The beauty of persons is honored throughout the world, but so, too, is the beauty of gods, the beauty of gardens, the beauty of poems. So let us take these four—gods, gardens, persons, and poems—and hold one of them, persons, out for the moment, looking only at the other three.

The argument that "noticing beauty brings harm to the thing noticed" makes no sense if the object is not itself susceptible to harm, as seems to be true of something that is all-powerful such as a god or nonsentient such as a poem. Many stories are told about attempts made to put the gods at risk, but the stories are usually about the immunity of the deity, the foolhardiness of the infidel. Those attacking the god do not, in any event, do so by paying attention to the god's beauty. Pentheus expresses sneering contempt for the effeminate beauty of the double-gendered Dionysus; it is instead Dionysus's rhapsodic worshipers who chant encomiums to the beauty of his hair, his body, his voice, his dance, his wine, his theatrical rituals. The face and body of Jesus occasion Aquinas's famous setting forth of the threefold division of beauty into integrity, proportion, and *claritas*—key terms for subsequent aesthetic debate over many centuries up through the conversations of Joyce's Stephen Dedalus and his friend Lynch. Jehovah prohibits anyone from looking at him face-to-face, but only the human perceiver, not Jehovah, is endangered by the act of looking; and though God is not seen, the Hebrew Scriptures revere the beauty of his countenance and his righteousness: "And let the beauty of the Lord our God be upon us."[2] So it is again with Hindu and Buddhist deities. The lotus shapes of the lips, eyes, hands, postures are sculpted into stone and wood by the adoring hands of worshipers, not the hands of detractors.

Noticing beauty, then, does not harm in cases where the object is either perfect (gods) or nonsentient (poem, vase). Further, as the examples suggest, it may even confer a benefit by perpetuating the religion in acts of worship or perpetuating the poem by making certain it does not disappear or get revised by those incapable of seeing its beauty. A vase crafted by Gallé—in whose surface dusky blue plums and purple leaves hang in the soft brown light—can, although nonsentient, be harmed by being mishandled. Noticing its beauty increases the possibility that it will be carefully handled.

Now it may be objected that a less beautiful poem or vase or god may, by receiving less attention, receive less careful protection. This objection inevitably comes up at exactly this moment in conversations about beauty: we saw it earlier in the complaint that what accounted for my disregard of a culturally distant tree was my absorption with sycamores and chestnuts. The complaint can, as a shorthand, be called the problem of lateral disregard, the problem that whatever benefits accrue to an object through its being the focus of our attention are not being equally enjoyed by nearby objects in the same class. The phenomenon of lateral disregard will be returned to in more detail later; but for now it is important to see the following. First, whatever the truth of this

[2] Ps. 90:17 (King James Version).

complaint, it does nothing to confirm the particular complaint that is before us at the present moment—namely, the complaint that our gaze brings harm to gods, poems, gardens, persons, and vases. The problem of lateral disregard assumes our gaze is good, and worries about our failure to distribute it out to objects that are similar to the one we are staring at, but that lack the perfect features that obligate us to stare. Like the political complaint about inattention to problems of social injustice to which it is related, it explicitly confirms the value of human attention. Second, it may well be the case that a less perfectly crafted poem or political debate is less likely to be preserved for posterity; but it is not at all self-evident that this lack of protection is the necessary counterpart of our focus upon the more highly crafted poem or political debate, or that it was in any way prompted by them. If I was about to place a vase on a wide safe ledge and then, finding one more beautiful, I consigned the first vase to a careless spot, we might have a case. But it seems more likely that the concern demanded by the perfect vase or god or poem introduced me to a standard of care that I then began to extend to more ordinary objects (perhaps I began to notice and worry, for the first time, about my neglect of the ordinary object and, inspecting it more closely, may now even discover that it is not ordinary). Far from subtracting or robbing fragility from the ordinary vase, the extraordinary vase *involuntarily* introduced me to the recognition that vases are fragile, and I then *voluntarily* extended the consequences of that recognition to other objects in the same category. I may see that reverence is due not only to a beautiful god but to the god's mother or to nearby angels; that it is not just the poet's best poem that should be published but even the penultimate, nearly-as-beautiful draft, that the flawed political debate should be perpetuated for posterity as part of the large public record of great and lapsed moments of assembly. The benefit of the extraordinary is twofold: first, in the demands it (without our invitation) places on us on its own behalf; second, in the pressure it exerts toward extending the same standard laterally. This pressure toward the distributional is an unusual feature of beautiful persons or things. The fact that it may be one beholder who is singing a hymn of praise to the first object, while it is a second beholder who, as though in harmony, is now demanding that love be equally accorded to a lateral object, should not discourage us from seeing the two as a composite event sponsored by the beautiful object itself.

But for now we need to return to the frame of our concern, whether the charge that staring harms the person being stared at can fairly be generalized to other categories of beautiful things. We have so far spoken about beautiful things to which the argument about perceptual damage seems inapplicable because they are beyond harm (either because perfect and omnipotent or because nonsentient like an artwork). But of course some things are neither omnipotent nor nonsentient but highly vulnerable and simultaneously highly sentient—or more accurately, since there are no degrees of sentience, unnegotiably alive. Persons are the most pressing example, and it may be for this very reason that the argument about the hazards of gazing originates right here, at the site of persons.

Is, then, the aliveness of something a ground on which we might wish to banish it as a candidate for beauty? One can, even in the sites looked at a moment ago, see why this avenue might be in error; for it cannot have escaped our attention that even when the objects we were speaking about were omnipotent or nonsentient, their being perceived as beautiful seemed to bring them to life or to make them life like. In some cases, maybe in all, this can be called a mimesis of life: for each morning when the sun rises and reaches the windowsill where the Gallé vase sits, the amber glass swells with light; the blue-and-brown plums drift in and out of the purple leaves, their veins and stems now flecked with life. The almost-aliveness of a beautiful object makes its abrasive handling seem unthinkable. The mind recoils—as from a wound cut into living flesh—from the possibility that the surface of Jan Brueghel the Elder's painting *Flower Stems in a Clay Vase* should be cut, torn, or roughly touched. Its surface has been accorded the gift of life: this can have nothing to do with the subject, the live flowers, for—look at them, jonquils, roses, fritillaria, tulips, irises, peonies, hyacinths, lily—they were already cut even as the painter painted them into their place inside the vase; and the same mental recoil would be felt if the surface that were roughly touched depicted only a pair of discarded shoes or one of J. M. W. Turner's groundless mists or Paul Klee's colors. The surface of the canvas has become, in the standard of protection we accord it, semisentient. Stone statues of gods, too, in the moment of being revered, come to life, as in Rilke's poems where the mouth of Apollo trembles and the eyebrows of Buddha lift.

We saw in Part One that the moment of perceiving something beautiful confers on the perceiver the gift of life; and now we begin to see that the moment of perceiving beauty also confers on the object the gift of life. The pacific quality of beauty comes in part from the reciprocal, life-granting pact. But we were about to look at sites of beauty—persons and gardens—that do not just, under special circumstances, acquire the gift of lifelikeness but are themselves unequivocally alive; and the question is, are these actually alive things inappropriate subjects for our admiring gaze?

We must still leave to the side the highly puzzling site of persons, because the present question is this: even if it is the case that we can be persuaded to stop looking at persons, ought the negative account of harmful looking be extended to other sites such as gods, poems, and—the site now before us—gardens? Because flowers are alive, they are (unlike omnipotent or nonsentient things) susceptible to damage; but a moment's reflection shows the impossibility of concluding that this damage is brought about by our perception of them, and the deep oddity of banishing them from our regard. Gardens exist for the sake of being beautiful and for the sake of having that beauty looked at, walked through, lingered in. In this one respect the sentient site of gardens and the nonsentient (or only sentient-like) site of poems are alike; for poems too—as well as other art objects such as glass vases and paintings—are brought into being in order to place their beauty in the field of human regard. Prohibiting attention to the beauty of gardens or poems therefore seems even more peculiar than prohibiting attention to the beauty of gods and person.[3] Gods of many traditions are held to be beautiful, but gods do not come into existence to be beautiful: their beauty simply follows from, or is part of, their perfection and cannot be decoupled or held independent from it. If we ceased praising their beauty,[4] the love of them might become less fervent and widespread; but it does not seem our silence would be fatal. Persons, too, though often beautiful, cannot be said to exist for the sake of being beautiful, even if we must grant that at the moment the parents conceive a child, each wishes the beauty of the beloved, already in the world, to enter the world a second time. Of course it is imaginable that someone perceiving a beautiful garden might then trample on it,[5] just as someone perceiving beautiful persons or paintings might then attempt to destroy them; but so many laws and rules are already being broken by these acts that it is hard to comprehend why, rather than bringing these rules and laws to bear on the problem, the rules of perceiving need to be altered to accommodate the violator. Excluding the beauty of gardens and poems from perception would more swiftly destroy them than any occasional act of trampling. Only if

[3] So odd does such a prohibition sound that it may appear I am inventing the idea for the sake of the argument; yet over the last fifteen years, many students, even the brightest and most good-hearted among them, have (as a result of the general prohibition on beauty) spoken in their papers about the way a poet or novelist reifies a garden or a flower or a beautiful bird by his or her lavish regard.

[4] I do not know whether it is possible for a worshiper to have mental pictures of Jesus or Artemis or Krishna or Buddha or Sarasvati, while withholding from mental view their beauty, but for the duration of the one sentence above, I will assume for the sake of argument that this is possible.

[5] It might be objected that even the gardener, in trying to heighten the beauty of a particular bed, might tear out a plant, therefore harming its life; for the gardener, like Keats's poet, carries out "innumerable compositions and decompositions" to arrive at "the snail-horn perception of Beauty." But at most this means that gardeners should be prohibited from tearing out any already existing plant, which should stay where it is or be transplanted to a safe location (a rule some gardeners follow).

the sestinas and the perennials could outlive the edict could there even continue to be gardens or poems.

By now we should be willing to agree that the general form of the complaint—"the perceiver reifies the object of perception"— makes little sense. It does not apply to gods, poems, and gardens. Nor has any evidence been brought forward to suggest its applicability to other sites. The habit of broadening this complaint from the site of persons to the world at large appears to be baseless. Let us agree that we will give it up. Attention to the beauty of all things (gods, gardens, poems—and also the moon, the Milky Way, individual stars, the daylit sky, birds, birdsongs, musical instruments, meadows, dances, woven cloth, stones, staircases, good prose certainly, airplanes of course, mathematical proofs, the sea, its surf, its spray) will be permitted, and only attention to the site of persons will be prohibited. But what about this site of persons?

I suggested at the outset that the complaint had two weaknesses. The first weakness was its generalization from the site of persons to all other things. The second weakness is the claim it makes about the site of persons itself.

People spend so much time noticing one another that the practice will no doubt continue regardless of the conclusions we arrive at about beauty. But many arguments can be made to credit the pleasure people take in one another's countenance. Staring, as we earlier saw, is a version of the wish to create; it is directly connected to acts of drawing, describing, composing, lovemaking. It

---

But what about the case where the gardener, seeking to make the garden more beautiful, *does* roughly dispose of the plant? Should we conclude that beauty imperils, rather than intensifies, the life contract? One way of answering the question is to ask whether the human protection accorded plants is higher or lower in the garden than in the world outside the garden. When we make this comparison we see that although the gardener has only imperfectly protected the plants, he or she has given them far more protection than they ordinarily receive. Another approach is to compare the flower garden, where the plants are grown for their beauty, with a vegetable garden, where the plants are grown for the gardener's table. The gardener in the flower garden places himself or herself in voluntary servitude to the flowers; the gardener in the vegetable garden has subordinated the life of the plant to the dinner table. I am not here objecting to the human need to eat; I am simply making the obvious point that in general "beauty" is associated with a life compact or contract, where the perceiver abstains from harming, or even actively enters into the protection of, this fragment of the world.

is odd that contemporary accounts of "staring" or "gazing" place exclusive emphasis on the risks suffered by the person being looked at, for the vulnerability of the perceiver seems equal to, or greater than, the vulnerability of the person being perceived. In accounts of beauty from earlier centuries, it is precisely the perceiver who is imperiled, overpowered, by crossing paths with someone beautiful. Plato gives the most detailed account of this destabilization in the *Phaedrus.* A man beholds a beautiful boy: suddenly he is spinning around in all directions. Publicly unacceptable things happen to his body. First he shudders and shivers. Then sweat pours from him. He is up, down, up, down, adopting postures of worship, even beginning to make sacrifices to the boy, restrained only by his embarrassment at carrying out so foolish an activity in front of us. Now he feels an unaccountable pain. Feathers are beginning to emerge out of his back, appearing all along the edges of his shoulder blades. Because this plumage begins to lift him off the ground a few inches, he catches glimpses of the immortal realm. Nonetheless, it cannot be denied that the discomfort he feels on the inside is matched by how ridiculous he looks on the outside. The beholder in Dante's *Vita nuova* is equally at risk. Coming face-to-face with Beatrice, Dante undergoes a violent trembling. All his senses go into a huddle, alarmed at the peril to which he has just exposed them. Soon he is so immobilized he might be mistaken for "a heavy inanimate object."

It is hard—no matter how dedicated one is to the principle of "historical difference"—to account for the discrepancy between the aura of radical vulnerability beholders were assigned in the past and the aura of complete immunity they are assigned today. Someone committed to historicism might shrug and say, "We just no longer see beauty in the same way." But how can that be an acceptable answer if—as an outcome of this newly acquired, wretched immunity—people are asking us to give up beauty altogether? A better answer might be to say not that we see the beauty of persons differently but that we do not see it at all. Perhaps only if one spins momentarily out of control, or grows feathers, or begins to write a sonnet can one be said to have seen the beauty of another person. The essentialist who believes beauty remains constant over the centuries and the historicist or social constructionist who believes that even the deepest structures of the soul are susceptible to cultural shaping have no need, when confronting the present puzzle, to quarrel with one another. For either our responses to beauty endure unaltered over centuries, or our responses to beauty are alterable, culturally shaped. And if they are subject to our willful alteration, then we are at liberty to make of beauty what we wish. And surely what we should wish is a world where the vulnerability of a beholder is equal to or greater than the vulnerability of the person beheld, a world where the pleasure-filled tumult of staring is a prelude to acts that will add to the beauty already in the world— acts like making a poem, or a philosophic dialogue, or a divine comedy; or acts like repairing an injury or a social injustice. Either beauty already requires that we do these things (the essentialist view) or we are at liberty to make of beauty the best that can be made—a beauty that will require that we do these things.

I suggested above that in those cases where a perceiver "gazes" with immunity at a person (and convincing instances have been documented by literary critics and art historians), two descriptions are possible: one claims, "In our era we see the beauty of persons in a way different from the way Plato and Dante did"; the other claims, "In our era we no longer see the beauty of persons." If the second is true, then what should be blamed for those occasions on which the person looked at is put at risk is not "seeing beauty" but "failing to see beauty"; and what should be urged is not the banishing of beauty but beauty's immediate return. A third description would say that the documented occasions, though real enough, are aberrations, and that "in our era we still see the beauty of persons the way Plato and Dante did." There is much to support this view: not just the number of new inventions and the number of people who, like Rilke (scratched, then killed, by the thorn of a rose), have died for beauty; but also the evidence of everyday experience. For it simply is the case—isn't it?—that each of us has, upon suddenly seeing someone beautiful, tripped on the sidewalk, broken out in a sweat of new plumage, dropped packages (as though offering a gift or sacrifice)—all while the bus we were waiting for pulls up and pulls away.

If today's beholder were suddenly offered the chance, while keeping his own features, to have a beauty as great as that of the person looked at, would the beholder decline that invitation? If we really believe that "beholders are all-powerful" and "persons beheld are powerless," then wouldn't we decline the offer? Why place oneself at risk by becoming beautiful, and why convert the already beautiful person into a coldly immune surveillant? But might one not instead happily accept? Proust watches the glowing red-haired woman serving milk at the train stop and wishes to accompany her in her daily labor in order to keep her in his field of vision; but he has the equally ardent wish to be included in *her* field of vision, "to feel that I was known to her, had my place in her thoughts." This, too, is why our "appalling" Odysseus washes: he scrubs the cakes of "brackish scurf" from his head and body, rubs himself with oil, and permits Athena's hand to wash over him like the hand of a smith who "washes gold over beaten silver." Athena's washing magnifies his size and stature, and "down from his brow / she ran his curls like thick hyacinth clusters / full of blooms." At last, Odysseus is ready to reenter Nausicaa's field of vision:

> And down to the beach he walked and sat apart,
> glistening in his glory, breathtaking, yes,
> and the princess gazed in wonder . . .

It may be that one reason beautiful persons and things incite the desire to create is so that one can place something of reciprocally great beauty in the shared field of attention. No hyacinth clusters can give homely Socrates the beauty of Phaedrus, but the speeches

Socrates composes for Phaedrus have the same outcome. When Dante composes poems in response to Beatrice's beauty, it is as though he has bathed on the Phaeacian shore.

But we are pursuing a misleading track here, for these are pairs of lovers; and it is important to contemplate the way beauty works not only with respect to someone one loves, but also with respect to the large array of beautiful persons walking through the public sphere. As we will eventually see, the fact that we look at beautiful persons and things without wishing to be ourselves beautiful is one of the key ways in which—according to philosophers like Simone Weil and Iris Murdoch—beauty prepares us for justice. It is then more useful simply to ask the nature of the relation between the person who pursues beauty and the beauty that is pursued. But as this question involves not just persons but many other sites of beauty, it must be postponed a short time.

Before leaving the site of persons, we must recall that we were here looking at only one complaint, the complaint that we might, by looking at such persons, bring them harm. But there are, of course, other arguments less political but equally antagonistic to the site of persons, such as the notion that beautiful persons do not deserve to be attended to for their beauty. Sometimes this idea of undeservingness is urged on the grounds that their beauty is natural: such persons were born with it, lazily inheriting it through no labor or merit of their own. (This argument is not very strong since so many things we unembarrassedly admire—great math skill, a capacity for musical composition, the physical agility of a dancer or speed of an athlete—entail luck at birth.) With equal energy the idea of undeservingness is urged on the grounds that such beauty is artifactual: such persons spend hours running along the beach, plaiting their hair into tiny braids, adorning themselves with beads, bracelets, oil, arrays of color. (This argument is also not very strong since we normally admire feats of artifactual labor, the formation of good government, a well-run newspaper, a twelve-year labor of self-education.) The two complaints contradict one another—one proposing that it is not the natural but the artifactual that should be honored, and the other proposing that it is not the artifactual but the natural that should be honored. More important, they together contradict the complaint we were considering: they say beautiful persons do not deserve to be looked at, whereas the complaint we were wrestling with says beautiful persons deserve not to be looked at (for their own safety). Although, therefore, we have limited ourselves to political arguments, we find—when we step off the straight and narrow path of our present inquiry—an incoherence equal to the one that lies straight ahead.

That straight path—to recover our bearings—has had two parts. First, we saw that the argument that perceiving beauty brings harm is, at most, applicable to the site of persons and cannot be generalized to gods, gardens, poems. Second, we saw that the argument does not stand up even with respect to persons since, if anything, the perceiver is as vulnerable as, or more vulnerable than, the person looked at. The objection is, therefore, neither site-specific nor legitimately diffused out to other sites.

Two other revelations have come forward, almost on their own, that will help us, as we begin to turn now from the negative arguments on behalf of beauty (showing the incoherence of the political complaints against it) to the positive arguments (showing how beautiful things assist us in remedying injustice). We saw that the fact that something is perceived as beautiful is bound up with an urge to protect it, or act on its behalf, in a way that appears to be tied up with the perception of its lifelikeness. This observation first emerged in connection with objects that themselves have no bodily sentience, such as a painted canvas, but that seem to acquire it, or a mimetic form of it, at the very moment of our regarding them as beautiful. Left unanswered was the question of exactly how this lifelikeness bears on persons, flowers, and birds, which can have unevenness of beauty but cannot have an unevenness of aliveness.

The second attribute that emerged was the pressure beauty exerts toward the distributional. This pressure manifests itself in what has been called the problem of lateral disregard, the worry that inevitably follows in the wake of observing the beautiful: "something's receiving attention" seems to involve "something else's not receiving attention." The structure of perceiving beauty appears to have a two-part scaffolding: first, one's attention is involuntarily given to the beautiful person or thing; then, this quality of heightened attention is voluntarily extended out to other persons or things. It is as though beautiful things have been placed here and there throughout the world to serve as small wake-up calls to perception, spurring lapsed alertness back to its most acute level. Through its beauty, the world continually recommits us to a rigorous standard of perceptual care: if we do not search it out, it comes and finds us. The problem of lateral disregard is not, then, evidence of a weakness but of a strength: the moment we are enlisted into the first event, we have already become eligible to carry out the second. It may seem that in crediting the enduring phenomenon of beauty with this pressure toward distribution, we are relying on a modern notion of "distribution." But only the word is new. Plato's requirement that we move from "eros," in which we are seized by the beauty of one person, to "caritas," in which our care is extended to all people, has parallels in many early aesthetic treatises, as when Boethius is counseled by Lady Philosophy, and later, Dante is counseled by Virgil to listen only to a song whose sensory surface will let one move beyond its own compelling features to a more capacious sphere of objects. The metaphysical plane behind the face or song provided the moral urgency for insisting upon this movement away from the particular to the distributional (or as it was called then, in a word that is often now berated, the universal). The vocabulary, but not the ethical direction, differs from the distributional mandate.

One final matter will enable us to move forward to the positive claims that can be spoken on behalf of beauty. We saw that the two political arguments are starkly incompatible with one another; and we also saw along the way that if we move into the intricacy of any one argument and one site—such as the site of persons—the objections on this more minute level are also wildly contradictory. If we were to move not into the intricate interior but outside to the overarching framework—if we were, in other words, to move outside the political arguments and contemplate their relation to the nonpolitical arguments used to assault beauty—we would come face-to-face with the same incoherence.

A case in point is the demotion of beauty that has come about as a result of its juxtaposition with the sublime. It is not the sublime that is incoherent, nor even the way in which the sublime systematically demotes beauty that is incoherent. What is incoherent is the relation between the kinds of claims that are made by this demotion and the political arguments looked at earlier.

The sublime has been a fertile aesthetic category in the last twenty years and has been written about with such intricacy that I will sketch its claims only in the briefest form, so that those unfamiliar with it will know what the aesthetic is. At the end of the eighteenth century, writers such as Kant and Edmund Burke subdivided the aesthetic realm (which had previously been inclusively called beauty) into two realms, the sublime and the beautiful. Kant's early work, the *Observations on the Feeling of the Beautiful and Sublime,* gives so straightforward a list that it can be recited, nearly verbatim, as a shorthand, even though it does not convey the many complications of Kant's own later writing on the subject, nor of the important writings following it. In the newly subdivided aesthetic realm, the sublime is male and the beautiful is female. The sublime is English, Spanish, and German; the beautiful is French and Italian. The sublime resides in mountains, Milton's Hell, and tall oaks in a sacred grove; the beautiful resides in flowers and Elysian meadows. The sublime is night, the beautiful day. "The sublime *moves*" (one becomes "earnest . . . rigid . . . astonished"). "Beauty *charms*." The sublime is dusk, "disdain for the world . . . eternity"; the beautiful is lively gaiety and cheer. The sublime is great; the beautiful "can also be small." The sublime is simple; the beautiful is multiple. The sublime is principled, noble, righteous; the beautiful is compassionate and good-hearted.[6]

Why should this bifurcation have dealt such a blow to beauty (a blow not intended by the original writers of the treatises or by later writers on the sublime)? The sublime occasioned the demotion of the beautiful because it ensured that the meadow flowers, rather than being perceived in their *continuity* with the august silence of ancient groves (as they had when the two coinhabited the inclusive realm of beauty),[7] were now seen instead as a *counterpoint* to that grove. Formerly capable of charming or astonishing, now beauty was the not-astonishing; as it was also the not-male, the not-mountainous, the not-righteous, the not-night. Each attribute or illustration of the beautiful became one member of an oppositional pair, and because it was almost always the diminutive member, it was also the dismissible member.

Furthermore, the path to something beyond both meadow flower and mighty tree, something detachable from their concrete surfaces—one might call it, as Kant did, eternity; or one might instead describe it as the mental realm where, with or without a god's help, the principles of justice and goodness hold sway— suddenly ceased to be a path of free movement and became instead a path lined with obstructions. In its earlier continuity with the meadow flower, the magnificent tree had itself assisted, or at least not interrupted, the passage from blossom to the sphere of just

[6] Immanuel Kant, *Observations on the Feeling of the Beautiful and Sublime*, trans. John T. Goldthwait (Berkeley and Los Angeles: University of California Press, 1960). The terms listed here occur on pp. 46–49 (passim), 60, 78, 93, 97.

[7] The sublime is sometimes credited with having multiplied the kinds of objects that could thereafter be perceived as "aesthetic." But most of the objects in both categories had formerly occupied a territory held under the inclusive rubric of beauty. Plato's or Aquinas's or Dante's conception of beauty had not been limited to the "good-hearted and cheerful." More important, the slightly scornful ring of "the good-hearted and cheerful" in that previous sentence only becomes possible once those adjectives have been severed from their aesthetic siblings, as the laughing angels on the edifice of Rheims Cathedral make clear.

principles; now the magnificent tree served as a giant boulder, a locked gate, a border guard, jealously barring access to the realm that had been reconceived as adjacent to itself and thus as only its own to own. The sublime now prohibited, or at least interrupted, the easy converse between the diminutive and the distributive.

One can see how oddly, yet effectively, the demotion from the sublime and the political demotion work together, even while deeply inconsistent with one another. The sublime (an aesthetic of power) rejects beauty on the grounds that it is diminutive, dismissible, not powerful enough. The political rejects beauty on the grounds that it is too powerful, a power expressed both in its ability to visit harm on objects looked at and also in its capacity to so overwhelm our attention that we cannot free our eyes from it long enough to look at injustice. Berated for its power, beauty is simultaneously belittled for its powerlessness.

The multiple, opposing assaults on beauty have worked in a second way. The sublime—by which I mean the outcomes that followed from dividing a formerly unitary realm into the sublime and the beautiful—cut beauty off from the metaphysical, permitting it to inhabit only the ground of the real. Then the political critique—along with a closely related moral critique and a critique from realism—come forward to assert that beauty (forever discomforting mortals with its idealized conceptions) has no place on the ground of the real. Permitted to inhabit neither the realm of the ideal nor the realm of the real, to be neither aspiration nor companion, beauty comes to us like a fugitive bird unable to fly, unable to land.

BEAUTY ASSISTS US IN OUR ATTENTION TO JUSTICE

The positive case that can be made on behalf of beauty has already begun to emerge into view and will stand forth more clearly if we place before ourselves the question of the relation between the beholder and the object beheld. The question can best be posed if we, for a moment, imagine that we are speaking not about the person who comes upon beauty accidentally, or the person who—after valiantly resisting beauty for all the reasons one should be warned against it—at last succumbs, but instead about a person who actively seeks it out.

What is it that such a person seeks? What precisely does one hope to bring about in oneself when one opens oneself to, or even actively pursues, beauty? When the same question is asked about other enduring objects of aspiration—goodness, truth, justice—the answer seems straightforward. If one pursues goodness, one hopes in doing so to make oneself good. If one pursues justice, one surely hopes to be able one day to count oneself among the just. If one pursues truth, one wishes to make oneself knowledgeable. There is, in other words, a continuity between the thing pursued and the pursuer's own attributes. Although in each case there has been an enhancement of the self, the undertaking and the outcome are in a very deep sense unself-interested since in each case the benefits to others are folded into the nature of my being good, bearing knowledge, or acting fairly. In this sense it may have been misleading to phrase the question in terms of a person's hopes for herself. It would be more accurate to say that one cannot further the aims of justice without (whether one means to or not) placing oneself in the company of the just. What this phrasing and the earlier phrasing have in common, the key matter, is the continuity between the external object and the person who is dedicated to it.

But this continuity does not seem to hold in the case of beauty. It does not appear to be the case that one who pursues beauty becomes beautiful. It may even be accurate to suppose that most people who pursue beauty have no interest in becoming themselves beautiful. It would be hard to make the same description of someone pursuing the other objects of aspiration: could one pursue truth if one had no interest in becoming knowledgeable? This would seem like quite a feat. How exactly would one go about that? Would there be a way to approach goodness while keeping oneself free of becoming good? Again, a path for doing so does not immediately suggest itself. And the same difficulties await us if we try to come up with a way of furthering the goals of justice while remaining ourselves outside its reach.

Now there are at least three ways in which one might wish to say that the same kind of continuity between beauty and its beholder exists. The beholder, in response to seeing beauty, often seeks to bring new beauty into the world and may be successful in this endeavor. But those dedicated to goodness or truth or justice were also seeking to carry out acts that further the position of these things in the world; the particular alteration of self they underwent (the thing for which we are seeking a parallel) is something additional to the fact that they supplemented the world. A second answer is to say that beholders of beautiful things themselves become beautiful in their interior lives: if the contents of consciousness are full of the calls of birds, mental pictures of the way dancers move, fragments of jazz pieces for piano and flute, remembered glimpses of ravishing faces, a sentence of incredible tact and delicacy spoken by a friend, then we have been made intensely beautiful. Still, this cannot be a wholly satisfying reply since though the beautiful object may, like the beholder, have internal beauty, it also has external features; this externality has long been held to be crucial to what beauty is, and even to its particular way of turning us toward justice. But there is a third answer that seems more convincing.

One key source of continuity between beholder and beheld became strikingly evident when we earlier saw the way each affirms the aliveness of the other. First we saw in the opening part that beauty is for the beholder lifesaving or life-restoring—a visionary fragment of sturdy ground: the palm tree on the sand of Delos, the floating plank that Augustine holds on to, the branch Noah sees flying through the sky. Then, when we moved from the first to the second part, it became clear that this act of conferring life had a reciprocal counterpart. The thing perceived, the beautiful object, has conferred on it by the beholder a surfeit of aliveness: even if it is inanimate, it comes to be accorded a fragility and consequent level of protection normally reserved for the animate; if inanimate, like a poem, it may, by being memorized or read aloud to others, thereby be lent the aliveness of the person's own consciousness. If what is beheld is instead a person, he or she may sponsor—literally—the coming into the world of a newborn, so that the person now stands companioned by additional life; the more general manifestation of this same phenomenon is visible in the way one's daily unmindfulness of the aliveness of others is temporarily interrupted in the presence of a beautiful person, alerting us to the requirements placed on us by the aliveness of all persons, and the same may take place in the presence of a beautiful bird, mammal, fish, plant. What has been raised is not the level of aliveness, which is already absolute, but one's own access to the already existing level of aliveness, bringing about, if not a perfect match, at least a less inadequate match between the actual aliveness of others and the level with which we daily credit them. Beauty seems to place requirements on us for attending to the aliveness or (in the case of objects) quasi-aliveness of our world, and for entering into its protection.

Beauty is, then, a compact, or contract between the beautiful being (a person or thing) and the perceiver. As the beautiful being confers on the perceiver the gift of life, so the perceiver confers on the beautiful being the gift of life. Each "welcomes" the other: each—to return to the word's original meaning—"comes in accordance with [the] other's will."[8] Why this reciprocal pact should assist us in turning toward problems of justice will be looked at in conjunction with the second positive attribute of beauty, the pressure toward distribution that we came upon in attending to the problem of lateral disregard, the way in which the requirements

[8] Ernest Klein, *A Comprehensive Etymological Dictionary of the English Language* (Amsterdam: Elsevier Publishing, 1971), s.v. "welcome."

involuntarily placed on us by something extraordinary have as a counterpart the shift toward the voluntary extension of these same perceptions. The compatibility between this distributive feature and a turn toward justice will not be hard to discover, since the language of "distribution" (unlike the language of "aliveness") is already an abiding part of the way we every day think and speak about justice.

The notion of a pact here again comes into play. A single word, "fairness," is used both in referring to loveliness of countenance and in referring to the ethical requirement for "being fair," "play-ing fair," and "fair distribution." One might suppose that "fair-ness" as an ethical principle had come not from the adjective for comely beauty but instead from the wholly distinct noun for the yearly agricultural fair, the "periodical gathering of buyers and sellers." But it instead—as scholars of etymology have shown—travels from a cluster of roots in European languages (Old English, Old Norse, Gothic), as well as cognates in both Eastern European and Sanskrit, that all originally express the aesthetic use of "fair" to mean "beautiful" or "fit"—fit both in the sense of "pleasing to the eye" and in the sense of "firmly placed," as when something matches or exists in accord with another thing's shape or size. "Fair" is connected to the verbs *vegen* (Dutch) and *fegen* (German) meaning "to adorn," "to decorate," and "to sweep." (One recalls Leo Tolstoy, during his decade of deepest commitment to social justice, beginning each day by sweeping his room; as one may think, as well, of the small brooms in Japanese gardens, whose use is sacred, reserved to the priests.) But *fegen* is in turn connected to the verb "fay," the transitive and intransitive verb meaning "to join," "to fit," "to unite," "to pact."[9] "Pact" in turn—the making

---

[9] The conclusions reached about the etymology of "fair" in C. T. Onions's *Oxford Dictionary of English Etymology* (Oxford: Oxford Clarendon, 1966), Klein's *Comprehensive Etymological Dictionary,* and Eric Partridge's *Origins: A Short Etymological Dictionary of Modern English* (New York: Macmillan, 1966) are all in accord with one another, though it is only Klein who directly links the word "fair" to the word for "pact" by focusing on the verb "fay."

of a covenant or treaty or agreement—is from the same root as *pax, pacis,* the word for peace.

Although the two attributes of beauty can each be described in isolation from the other, they together constitute a two-part cognitive event that affirms the equality of aliveness. This begins within the confined circumference of beholder and beheld who exchange a reciprocal salute to the continuation of one another's existence; this two-member salute becomes, by the pressures against lateral disregard, dispersed out so that what is achieved is an inclusive affirmation of the ongoingness of existence, and of one's own responsibility for the continuity of existence. Our status as the bearer of rights, our equality of aliveness, does not rely on the existence of beautiful meadows or skies or persons or poems to bring it about; nor, once there are laws and codified rights in place, should beautiful meadows and skies be needed to keep it in view, but—as will be unfolded below—matters that are with difficulty kept legible in one sphere can be assisted by their counterpart in the other.

How this takes place will be clarified if we look first at the connection between beauty as "fairness" and justice as "fairness," using the widely accepted definition by John Rawls of fairness as a "symmetry of everyone's relations to each other." The discussion will then turn to the idea of "aliveness," a word that, though it enters our discussions of justice less openly and less often than words such as "fairness" and "equality," is what is centrally at stake in, and served by, both spheres.

FAIRNESS AS "A SYMMETRY OF EVERYONE'S RELATIONS TO EACH OTHER"

One day I ran into a friend, and when he asked me what I was doing, I said I was trying to explain how beauty leads us to justice. (It happens that this friend is a philosopher and an economist who has spent many years inquiring into the relation between famine and forms of procedural justice such as freedom of the press. He also tracked demographic figures in Asia and North Africa that revealed more than one hundred million missing women and showed a long-standing practice of neglecting the health of girls.) Without pausing, he responded that he remembered being a child in India and coming upon Aristotle's statement that justice was a perfect cube:[10] he had been completely baffled by the statement, except he knew it had something to do with equality in all directions.

Happening to find myself sometime later walking beside another friend, and again pressed to describe what I was up to, I said I was showing that beauty assists us in getting to justice, and—perhaps because the subject seemed out of keeping with the morning's seaside glee—I for some reason added, "But *you* surely don't believe this." (He is a political philosopher who inquires into the nature of deliberative processes, and has established a series of alternative models for ethics; he served in British intelligence during the Second World War and in the Foreign Office during the period of the Marshall Plan.) "No," he agreed, still laughing, and high above the cresting waves, for we were walking on a steep dune, he cited with delight a proclamation about beauty's inevitable descent into bohemia. "Except, of course," he added, turning suddenly serious, and holding out his two large hands, "analogically, by what they share: balance and the weighing of both sides."

The speed and immediacy with which Amartya Sen and Stuart Hampshire spoke is indicative of the almost self-evident character

---

[10] Because this event happened in childhood, the exact book Amartya Sen was reading has receded from view. Aristotelian philosopher Alan Code suggests several possibilities. In the discussion of distributive justice in *Nicomachean Ethics,* Book 5, chapter 3, Aristotle writes that equality has two terms but justice has four terms; a particular translation of, or commentary upon, this passage may have introduced the figure of the cube, especially since Aristotle observes, "This kind of proportion is termed by mathematicians geometrical proportion" (trans. H. Rackham, in Loeb edition, *Aristotle,* vol. 19 [Cambridge, Mass.: Harvard University Press, 1934]).

of the argument that will be made here: that beautiful things give rise to the notion of distribution, to a lifesaving reciprocity, to fairness not just in the sense of loveliness of aspect but in the sense of "a symmetry of everyone's relations to each other."

When we speak about beauty, attention sometimes falls on the beautiful object, at other times on the perceiver's cognitive act of beholding the beautiful thing, and at still other times on the creative act that is prompted by one's being in the presence of what is beautiful. The invitation to ethical fairness can be found at each of these three sites, and so each will be looked at in turn: the first in statements made by classical philosophers, Plato and Augustine; the second, in observations by mid-twentieth-century philosophers Simone Weil and Iris Murdoch; and the third in an account given by turn-of-the-millennium philosopher Andreas Eshete, whose work is divided between the practical task of establishing constitutional rights in Ethiopia and theoretical writings about fraternity: he argues that of the revolutionary triad—liberty, equality, fraternity—it is fraternity (often omitted from our descriptions) that underwrites liberty and equality, and hence also fraternity that underwrites liberal theories of justice. As this list suggests, I have in this one section of the discussion placed the burden of illustration on those who—by their writings, their practice, or both—have dedicated themselves first and foremost to questions of justice, rather than on those who have dedicated themselves first and foremost to beauty; for the reader may feel that anyone who sets out in the morning to defend beauty will surely by nightfall have arrived at the strategy of claiming that beauty assists justice, whereas political philosophers are unlikely to put justice at risk by placing it in beauty's hands unless they deem it prudent to do so.

When we begin at the first of the three sites—the site of the beautiful object itself—it is clear that the attribute most steadily singled out over the centuries has been "symmetry." Some eras single it out almost to the exclusion of all else (remarkably, one such period is the decade of the 1990s),[11] whereas others insist that it is not symmetry alone but symmetry companioned by departures and exceptions from itself that makes a piece of music, a face, or a landscape beautiful (as in the nineteenth-century romantic modification of the principles of eighteenth-century neoclassicism). The feature, despite these variations in emphasis, never ceases to be, even in eras that strive to depart from it, the single most enduringly recognized attribute. But what happens when we move from the sphere of aesthetics to the sphere of justice? Here symmetry remains key, particularly in accounts of distributive justice and fairness "as a symmetry of everyone's relations to each other." It was this shared feature of beauty and justice that Amartya Sen saluted in the figure of the cube, equidistant in all directions, and that Stuart Hampshire again saluted in the figure of scales, equally weighted in both directions.

But why should we not just accept Hampshire's formulation that this is an "analogy," a feature they share, rather than the much stronger formulation that it is the very symmetry of beauty that leads us to, or somehow assists us in discovering, the symmetry that eventually comes into place in the realm of justice? One answer is this: in periods when a human community is too young to have yet had time to create justice, as well as in periods when justice has been taken away, beautiful things (which do not rely on us to create them but come on their own and have never been absent from a human community) hold steadily visible the manifest good of equality and balance.

[11] Throughout the 1990s, articles appeared in key science journals such as *Nature* claiming (1) that "symmetry" is by birds, butterflies, and other creatures chosen in mating over every other feature (such as size, color), possibly because it is taken as a visible manifestation of overall sturdiness of the genetic material; (2) that infants in different cultures stare longer at faces that are highly symmetrical, and also prefer classical music whose passages are symmetrically arranged over the same classical pieces whose musical phrases have been randomly reordered; and (3) that adults choose faces with symmetrical features (nose and mouth precisely equidistant between eyes), and seem to make identical choices across such distant cultures as Scotland and Japan. The research in all three areas is controversial and may well be overturned or qualified over the next decade. But even if the extreme claims of this research are retracted, symmetry will without doubt remain an important element in assessments of beauty.

Which of the many early writers—such as Parmenides, Plato, and Boethius, each of whom saw the sphere, because equidistant in all directions, as the most perfect of shapes—shall we call on for illustration? Here is Augustine thinking about musical rhythm in the sixth book of *De Musica.* He is not setting forth an attribute of distributive justice; he is not recommending that medieval hierarchies be overthrown and replaced by democracies; yet present to his mind—as present to the mind of the writers of scores of other ancient treatises on cubes, spheres—is a conviction that equality is the heart of beauty, that equality is pleasure-bearing, and that (most important in the shift we are seeking to undertake from beauty to justice) equality is the morally highest and best feature of the world. In other words, equality is set forth as the thing of all things to be aspired to:

> The higher things are those in which equality resides, supreme, unshaken, unchangeable, eternal.

> This rhythm [that, like certain principles of arithmetic, can be elicited from a person who has never before been tutored in it] is immutable and eternal, with no inequality possible in it. Therefore it must come from God.

> Beautiful things please by proportion, *numero,* . . . equality is not found only in sounds for the ear and in bodily movements, but also in visible forms, in which hitherto equality has been identified with beauty even more customarily than in sounds.

> It is easy to love colours, musical sounds, *voces,* cakes, roses and the body's soft, smooth surface, *corpora leniter mollia.* In all of them the soul is in quest of nothing except equality and similitude.

> Water is a unity, all the more beautiful and transparent on account of a yet greater similitude of its parts . . . on guard over its order and its security. Air has still greater unity and internal

regularity than water. Finally the sky . . . has the greatest well-being.[12]

Can we, could Augustine, did any reader, ever emerge from this cascade of paragraphs—of which only a small filigree is given here—without having their yearning for, their commitment to, equality intensified? No claim is being made here about the length of time—a year, a century, a millennium—it might take for the same equality to inhere in social relations. All that is claimed is that the aspiration to political, social, and economic equality has already entered the world in the beauty-loving treatises of the classical and Christian periods, as has the readiness to recognize it as beautiful if and when it should arrive in the world.

To return, then, to the question of whether the symmetry in beauty and that in justice are analogous, or whether instead the first leads to the second, the answer already proposed can be restated and expanded through Augustine's idiom. Imagine, then, a world that has blue sky, musical sounds, cakes, roses, and the body's soft, smooth surface; and now imagine further that this world also has a set of just social arrangements and laws that (like Augustine's water) by their very consistency stand guard over and secure themselves. The equality residing in the song-filled sky light and the equality residing in the legal arrangements need not be spoken about as anything other than analogous, especially since the laws (both written and applied with a consistency across all persons) are now themselves beautiful. But remembering there was a time antecedent to the institution of these laws, and recognizing also that this community will be very lucky if, in its ongoing existence through future history, there never comes an era when its le-

---

[12] This is again the W. F. Jackson Knight translation of *De Musica,* pp. 186, 190, 191, 194, 201. Augustine perceives "equality" not just in a formal feature such as symmetry but in color: a patch of blue (or green or red or yellow) continually iterates itself across the surface it occupies.

gal system for a brief period deteriorates, we can perceive that ongoing work is actively carried out by the continued existence of a
locus of aspiration: the evening skies, the dawn chorus of roosters
and mourning doves, the wild rose that, with the sweet pea, uses
even prison walls to climb on. In the absence of its counterpart, one
term of an analogy actively calls out for its missing fellow; it
presses on us to bring its counterpart into existence, acts as a lever
in the direction of justice. An analogy is inert and at rest only if
both terms are present in the world; when one term is absent, the
other becomes an active conspirator for the exile's return.

But there is also a second way in which even in a community
that has both fair skies and fair legal arrangements, the sky still
assists us. For the symmetry, equality, and self-sameness of the sky
are present to the senses, whereas the symmetry, equality, and self-
sameness of the just social arrangements are not. In the young
worlds and in the lapsed worlds, justice was not available to the
senses for the simple reason that justice was not in the world. But
even when justice comes into the world, it is not ordinarily sensorially available. Even once it has been instantiated, it is seldom
available to sensory apprehension, because it is dispersed out over
too large a field (an entire town or entire country), and because it
consists of innumerable actions, almost none of which are occur-
ring simultaneously. If I step out my front door, I can see the four
petals of each mother-of-pearl poppy, like small signal flags: two
up, two down; three up, one down; all four up; all four down. I
cannot see that around the corner a traffic rule is being followed; I
cannot see that over on the other side of town, the same traffic rule
is being followed. It is not that the following of the traffic rule is
not material: it is that its justice, which is not in a solitary location but in a consistency across all locations and in the resulting
absence of injury, is not sensorially visible, as are the blades of the
poppy, even though each of its component members (each car,
each driver, each road surface with its white dividing line, each

blinking light) is surely as material as the fragile poppy. It is the very exigencies of materiality, the susceptibility of the world to injury, that require justice, yet justice itself is outside the compass of our sensory powers.

Now it is true that once a law or constitutional principle is formulated that protects the arrangement, the sentence can be taken in in a single visual or acoustical glance; and this is one of the great powers of bestowing on a diffuse principle a doctrinal location.[13] Having a phrase at hand—"the First Amendment," "the Fourth Amendment"—gathers into itself what is, though material, outside the bounds of sensory perception. Sometimes it may even happen that a just legal principle has the good fortune to be formulated in a sentence whose sensory features reinforce the availability of the principle to perception: "We hold these truths to be self-evident, that all men are created equal. . . . " The sentence scans. The cadence of its opening sequence of monosyllables shifts suddenly forward to the polysyllabic "self-evident," the rapidity of completion adrenalizing the line, as though performing its own claim (it sounds self-verifying). The table has been cleared for the principle about to be announced. Now the sentence starts over with the stark sequence of monosyllables ("that all men are") and the faster-paced, polysyllabic, self-verifying "created equal." The repeated cadence enables each half of the sentence to authorize the other. Who is the "we" empowered to declare certain sentences true and self-evident? The "we" who count themselves as one another's equals. We more often speak of beautiful laws than of beautiful social arrangements because the laws, even when only pieces of language, have a sensory compression that the diffusely scattered social arrangements do not have, and it is this availability to the senses that is also one of the key features of beauty.

But it may happen on occasion that the fair political arrange-

---

[13] The importance of a doctrinal location is visible in the debates about conscientious objection. See, for example, the special issue of *Rutgers Law Review* 21, no. 7 (Fall 1966) on "Civil Disobedience and the Law."

ment itself (not just the laws prescribing it or guaranteeing it) *will* be condensed into a time and space where it becomes available to the senses, and then—like Augustine's water, sky, cakes, and roses—its beauty is visible. This may be true in a great assembly hall, where the representatives deliberate in a bowl of space available to perception. Now the claim has been made that the principle of rhythmic equality (which we were a moment ago enjoying in Augustine) did in the ancient Greek world also take place in the sphere of social arrangements and—this next step is crucial—in social arrangements contracted down into a small enough physical space that it was available to sensory perception: namely, the trireme ships, the ships whose 170 oars and 170 oarsmen could, like a legislative assembly, be held within the small bowl of visual space of which a human perceiver is capable, and whose rhythmic striking of the water, in time with the pipeman's flute, could also be held within the finite auditory compass of a perceiver. But we have not yet arrived at the claim, and it is this: out of the spectacle of the trireme ship, Athenian democracy was born:

> Democracy was instituted or strengthened in substantial degree by the need for a large navy of relatively poor but free citizens, who were paid for their ship duty by the state. The democratic reforms of Periclean Athens . . . shifted the domestic political and military balance of power toward the poor and the navy. . . . [At] the height of democratic government, trireme rowers were full citizens. With 170 rowers in each of at least 200 ships, no fewer than 30,000 supporters of democracy [were present], generally from the lower classes.[14]

Drawing on the Athenian constitution (which designates the oarsmen as "the men who gave the city its power"), on writings by Thucydides, Xenophon, Euripides, on the almost complete correspondence between those Greek city-states that had democracies and those Greek city-states that had navies, both historians of the

[14] Bruce Russett, *Grasping the Democratic Peace: Principles for a Post–Cold War World* (Princeton: Princeton University Press, 1993), p. 59.

ancient world[15] and democratic theorists have affirmed the association. Here again the meanings of "fair" in the sense of loveliness
of countenance and "fair" in the sense of distribution converge: for
the root *fegen* means not just "to sweep" but also "to strike" or "to
beat," actions that appear to be connected to the sweeping or striking motion of the oars.

Euripides gives a visionary account of oarsmen striking and
sweeping the silver surface of the sea, according to the pace of the
aulete's piped song, the dolphins cresting and diving to the same
flashing meter, as though in fraternal salute. The piper is named
by Euripides as the musician of all musicians, Orpheus; and this
alliance between poetic meter and rowing has endured over many
centuries. Rilke reports that he came to understand "the position
of the poet, his place and effect within time" only when he sailed
in a ship whose powerful rowers counted aloud, and whose singer
would send a "series of long floating sounds" out over the water.[16]
Seamus Heaney, reading aloud from his new translation of *Beo-
wulf*, interrupted himself at the moment when the ships enter the
water, saying, it is here that the poem becomes most beautiful and
alive, because of the deep connection (observed by Robert Graves)
between the rhythm of poetry and the rhythm of rowing—the
motion of the oars, "the dip and drag."

We can be forgiven, in a discussion of beauty, for not wishing
to speak about war ships, whether the Greek triremes or the shells
of the Danes and Geats; but since our subject is also justice, the issue of force must of necessity come forward. Even beauty alone
would eventually have required us to speak of it. The particular

---

[15] J. S. Morrison and J. F. Coates, *The Athenian Trireme: The History and Reconstruction
of an Ancient Greek Warship* (Cambridge: Cambridge University Press, 1986). See also Li-
onel Casson, *Ships and Seamanship in the Ancient World* (Princeton: Princeton University
Press, 1971).

[16] "Concerning the Poet," in *Where Silence Reigns: Selected Prose by Rainer Maria
Rilke*, trans. G. Craig Houston, foreword by Denise Levertov (New York: New Directions, 1978), pp. 65–66.

topic at hand is the way that symmetry across social relations is usually invisibly dispersed out over a large expanse but in rare and exceptional moments comes to be compressed down into a small enough space to be directly available to sensory perception. We can find peaceful illustrations. Historians of the nineteenth-century United States have shown that the parade is a peculiarly American invention, designed to display within the contracted space of the city street the plurality of citizenry moving together on an equal footing.[17] Rowing races, too, take place on level waters: they have been called the "ideal egalitarian" or democratic sport, not only because of the pluralistic crowds that gathered on the riverbanks, but because of the plurality of class and gender among the rowers. Champions included customhouse workers and mechanics like the Biglin brothers, whose famous faces now stare out at us from Thomas Eakins's paintings, and whose races first attracted widespread attention when the brothers issued an open challenge to the "gentlemen-only" rowing clubs of Britain.[18] As poets have felt in their own meter the beat of the rower's heart and the pull of the rower's arms, so Eakins described the painter moving through the world on the surface of his canvas like a rower gliding over water in his weightless scull.[19]

But what makes street parades, river races, and playing fields fair is precisely a dividing up, an equal parsing out, of the unsightly means of force. Beauty is pacific: its reciprocal salute to continued existence, its pact, is indistinguishable from the word for peace. And justice stands opposed to injury: "injustice" and "injury" are the same word. The best guarantee of peace would

[17] Mary Ryan, "The American Parade: Representations of the Nineteenth-Century Social Order," in *The New Cultural History,* ed. Lynn Hunt (Berkeley and Los Angeles: University of California Press, 1989), pp. 131–53.

[18] Rowing as a vehicle of democracy in the United States is argued by Helen A. Cooper in *Thomas Eakins: The Rowing Pictures* (New Haven: Yale University Press and Yale Art Gallery, 1996), pp. 24–25, 36, 44.

[19] Eakins expresses his vision of the painter as rower in a March 6, 1868, letter to his father cited in Cooper, *Thomas Eakins,* p. 32.

seem to be the absence of injuring power from the world (including the absence of discrepancies in bodily size that would enable one person to bring physical force to bear on another). The second-best form (and the first-best form that has ever been available to us) is that whatever means of force exist be equally divided among us all, a distribution of force that has often been called the "palladium of civil rights," for it enables each person to stand guard over and secure the nature of the whole. What, during the first two centuries of the United States, was said to distinguish the distributed militia of democracy from the executive "standing" army of tyranny was that it was, in both the ethical and the aesthetic sense, "fair": a "fine, plain, level state of equality, over which the beholder passed with pleasure"; a bright cloth or fabric spanning the entire country, a canopy of shelter and shared regard.[20]

We have so far shown how features that have been located at the site of the beautiful object (features such as the object's symmetry, equality, and pressure against lateral disregard) assist us in getting to justice. There remain two other sites—the "live" mental action of perceiving and the "live" action of creation—where the complicity between beauty and justice can again be seen.

But it will be helpful to locate ourselves and see what has so far been said. The equality of beauty enters the world before justice and stays longer because it does not depend on human beings to bring it about: though human beings have created much of the beauty of the world, they are only collaborators in a much vaster

---

[20] Cassius, *Considerations on the Society or Order of Cincinnati, Lately Instituted by the Major-Generals, Brigadiers, and Other Officers of the American Army, Proving that It Creates, A Race of Hereditary Patricians, or Nobility, and Interspersed with Remarks on Its Consequences to the Freedom and Happiness in the Republick,* reprinted in *Anglo-American Antimilitary Tracts 1697–1830,* ed. R. Kohn (New York: Arno Press, 1979). The beautiful fabric or canopy of military equality is spoken of by secretary of war General Knox in his 1786 proposal to Congress for a militia, quoted in the 1863 tract by J. Willard, *Plan for the General Arrangement of the Militia of the United States* (Boston: J. Wilson & Sons), p. 29; and again by William Sumner in 1826, *A Paper on the Militia Presented to the Hon. James Barbour, Secretary of War* (Washington, D.C.: B. Homans, 1833), p. 9. See also Ransom Gillet's address to the House of Representatives, *Congressional Globe,* 24th Cong., 1st sess., 1836, pp. 235, 237.

project. The world accepts our contributions but in no way depends on us. Even when beauty and justice are both in the world, beauty performs a special service because it is available to sensory perception in a way that justice (except in rare places like an assembly) normally is not, even though it is equally material and comes into being because of the fragility of the material world. By now we can begin to see that the equality of beauty, its pressure toward distribution, resides not just in its interior feature of symmetry but in its generously being present, widely present, to almost all people at almost all times—as in the mates that they choose to love, their children, the birds that fly through their garden, the songs they sing—a distributional availability that comes from its being external, present ("prae-sens"), standing before the senses.

When aesthetic fairness and ethical fairness are both present to perception, their shared commitment to equality can be seen as merely an analogy, for it may truly be said that when both terms of an analogy are present, the analogy is inert. It asks nothing more of us than that we occasionally notice it. But when one term ceases to be visible (either because it is not present, or because it is present but dispersed beyond our sensory field), then the analogy ceases to be inert: the term that is present becomes pressing, active, insistent, calling out for, directing our attention toward, what is absent. I describe this, focusing on touch, as a weight or lever, but ancient and medieval philosophers always referred to it acoustically: beauty is a call.

RADICAL DECENTERING

We have seen how the beautiful object—in its symmetry and generous sensory availability—assists in turning us to justice. The two other sites, that of the perceiver and that of the act of creation, also reveal the pressure beauty exerts toward ethical equality. Once we move to these two sites, we enter into the live actions of perceiving and creating, and are therefore carried to the subject of aliveness, our final goal.

The surfaces of the world are aesthetically uneven. You come around a bend in the road, and the world suddenly falls open; you continue on around another bend, and go back to your conversation, until you are once more interrupted by the high bank of radiant meadow grass rising steeply beside the road. The same happens when you move through a sea of faces at the railroad station or rush down the aisle of a crowded lecture hall. Or you may be sweeping the garden bricks at home, attending with full scrutiny to each square inch of their mauve-orange-blue surfaces (for how else can you sweep them clean?); then suddenly a tiny mauve-orange-blue triangle, with a silver sheen, lifts off from the sand between the bricks where it had been sleepily camouflaged until the air currents disturbed it. It flutters in the air, then settles back down on the brick, demure, closed-winged, a triangle this big: △. Why should this tiny fragment of flying brick-color stop your heart?

Folded into the uneven aesthetic surfaces of the world is a pressure toward social equality. It comes from the object's symmetry, from the corrective pressure it exerts against lateral disregard, and from its own generous availability to sensory perception. But a reader may object that even if the idea of ethical fairness does come before one's mind at the moment one beholds something beautiful, the idea remains abstract. Nothing requires us to give up the ground that would begin to enact such symmetries. It is here that great assistance is provided by Simone Weil, whose mystical writings and life practices—working side by side with laborers in the Spanish Civil War; carrying out a hunger strike, from which she died, in camaraderie with those who were starving in German concentration camps—were inspired by her commitment to justice. (We are trying to hold steady to the agreement we made that we would, in this section, draw primarily from defenders of justice, not defenders of beauty, even though the two so often converge.)

At the moment we see something beautiful, we undergo a radical decentering. Beauty, according to Weil, requires us "to give up our imaginary position as the center. . . . A transformation then takes place at the very roots of our sensibility, in our immediate reception of sense impressions and psychological impressions."[21] Weil speaks matter-of-factly, often without illustration, implicitly requiring readers to test the truth of her assertion against their own experience. Her account is always deeply somatic: what happens, happens to our bodies. When we come upon beautiful things—the tiny mauve-orange-blue moth on the brick, Augustine's cake, a sentence about innocence in Hampshire—they act like small tears in the surface of the world that pull us through to some vaster space;[22] or they form "ladders reaching toward the beauty of the world,"[23] or they lift us (as though by the air currents of someone else's sweeping), letting the ground rotate beneath us several inches, so that when we land, we find we are standing in a different relation to the world than we were a moment before. It is not that we cease to stand at the center of the world, for we never stood there. It is that we cease to stand even at the center of our own world. We willingly cede our ground to the thing that stands before us.

The radical decentering we undergo in the presence of the beautiful is also described by Iris Murdoch in a 1967 lecture called "The Sovereignty of Good over Other Concepts." As this title indicates, her subject is goodness, not beauty. "Ethics," Murdoch writes, "should not be merely an analysis of ordinary mediocre conduct, it should be a hypothesis about good conduct and about how this can be achieved."[24] How we make choices, how we act, is

---

[21] Weil, "Love of the Order of the World," p. 159.

[22] Ibid., p. 163.

[23] Ibid., p. 180.

[24] Iris Murdoch, *The Sovereignty of Good over Other Concepts: The Leslie Stephen Lecture* (Cambridge: Cambridge University Press, 1967), p. 2

deeply connected to states of consciousness, and so "anything which alters consciousness in the direction of unselfishness, objectivity and realism is to be connected with virtue." Murdoch then specifies the single best or most "obvious thing in our surroundings which is an occasion for 'unselfing' and that is what is popularly called beauty."[25]

She describes suddenly seeing a kestrel hovering: it brings about an "unselfing." It causes a cluster of feelings that normally promote the self (for she had been "anxious . . . resentful . . . brooding perhaps on some damage done to [her] prestige") now to fall away. It is not just that she becomes "self-forgetful" but that some more capacious mental act is possible: all the space formerly in the service of protecting, guarding, advancing the self (or its "prestige") is now free to be in the service of something else.

It is as though one has ceased to be the hero or heroine in one's own story and has become what in a folktale is called the "lateral figure" or "donor figure." It may sound not as though one's participation in a state of overall equality has been brought about, but as though one has just suffered a demotion. But at moments when we believe we are conducting ourselves with equality, we are usually instead conducting ourselves as the central figure in our own private story; and when we feel ourselves to be merely adjacent, or lateral (or even subordinate), we are probably more closely approaching a state of equality. In any event, it is precisely the ethical alchemy of beauty that what might in another context seem like a demotion is no longer recognizable as such: this is one of the cluster of feelings that have disappeared.

Radical decentering might also be called an opiated adjacency. A beautiful thing is not the only thing in the world that can make us feel adjacent; nor is it the only thing in the world that brings a state of acute pleasure. But it appears to be one of the few phenom-

---

[25] Ibid., p. 10.

ena in the world that brings about both simultaneously: it permits us to be adjacent while also permitting us to experience extreme pleasure, thereby creating the sense that it is our own adjacency that is pleasure-bearing. This seems a gift in its own right, and a gift as a prelude to or precondition of enjoying fair relations with others. It is clear that an *ethical fairness* that requires "a symmetry of everyone's relations" will be greatly assisted by an *aesthetic fairness* that creates in all participants a state of delight in their own lateralness.

This lateral position continues in the third site of beauty, not now the suspended state of beholding but the active state of creating—the site of stewardship in which one acts to protect or perpetuate a fragment of beauty already in the world or instead to supplement it by bringing into being a new object. (The latter is more usually described as an act of creation than the former, but we have seen from the opening pages of this book forward that the two are prompted by the same impulse and should be perceived under a single rubric.) The way beauty at this third site presses us toward justice might seem hard to uncover since we know so little about "creation"; but it is not difficult to make a start since justice itself is dependent on human hands to bring it into being and has no existence independent of acts of creation. Beauty may be either natural or artifactual; justice is always artifactual and is therefore assisted by any perceptual event that so effortlessly incites in us the wish to create. Because beauty repeatedly brings us face-to-face with our own powers to create, we know where and how to locate those powers when a situation of injustice calls on us to create without itself guiding us, through pleasure, to our destination. The two distinguishable forms of creating beauty—perpetuating beauty that already exists; originating beauty that does not yet exist—have equivalents within the realm of justice, as one can hear in John Rawls's formulation of what, since the time of Socrates, has been known as the "duty to justice" argument: we have a duty, says Rawls, "to support" just arrangements where they already exist and to help bring them into being where they are "not yet established."

Another feature shared by the kind of creation we undertake on behalf of beauty and the kind of creation we undertake on behalf of justice has been suggested by political philosopher Andreas Eshete.[26] In both realms, the object that one aspires to create may be completely known, partially known, or completely unknown to the creator. It is precisely on this basis that John Rawls differentiates three forms of justice: in "perfect justice" we know the outcome we aspire to achieve as well as the procedure by which that outcome can be brought about (food should be shared equally, and we can ensure this outcome by arranging that the person who slices the cake is also the last to select his own slice); in "imperfect justice" we know the outcome we aspire to achieve, and we know the procedure that gives us the best chance of approximating this outcome (persons guilty of a crime should be convicted and innocent persons should go free; a jury trial gives us the best hope of achieving this outcome, though it by no means guarantees it); in "pure procedural justice," finally, we have no picture of the best outcome, and we must trust wholly in the fairness of the procedures to ensure that the outcome itself is fair (here equality of opportunity is Rawls's illustration).[27] Aesthetic creation, too, has this same variation: one may have a vision of the object to be created and the path by which to bring it into being; one may instead have a vision of the object to be created and a technique that brings only its approximation into being; or one may have no prior vision and may simply entrust oneself to the action of creating (as in Richard Wollheim's account of the way one learns what one has been drawing only when the drawing is done).[28]

[26] Andreas Ashete, conversation with author, January 1998.

[27] John Rawls, *A Theory of Justice* (Cambridge, Mass.: Harvard University Press, 1971), pp. 83–87. Other references throughout part two to John Rawls's ideas about fairness can be found on pp. 12, 115.

[28] Richard Wollheim, "On Drawing an Object," in *On Art and Mind* (Cambridge, Mass.: Harvard University Press, 1974), pp. 3–30.

The nonself-interestedness of the beholder has—to return to the subject of adjacency—been seen in a number of ways: first, in the absence of continuity between the beholder and the beheld (since the beholder does not become beautiful in the way that the pursuer of truth becomes knowledgeable); second, in the radical decenteredness the beholder undergoes in the presence of something or someone beautiful; third, in the willingness of the beholder to place himself or herself in the service of bringing new beauty into the world, creating a site of beauty separate from the self.

The unself-interestedness becomes visible in a fourth odd feature. Since beauty is pleasure-producing, one might assume that one would be avid to have it in one's own life and less avid, or noncommittal, about the part it should play in other people's lives. But is this the case? As was noticed at the opening, over the last several decades many people have either actively advocated a taboo on beauty or passively omitted it from their vocabulary, even when thinking and writing about beautiful objects such as paintings and poems. But if one asks them the following question—"Thinking not of ourselves but of people who will be alive at the end of the twenty-first century: is it your wish for them that they be beauty-loving?"—the answer seems to be "Yes"; and "Yes," delivered with speed and without hesitation. My own sample is informal and small, but does it not seem likely that a larger group would answer in similar fashion? If they would, the response suggests that whatever hardships we are willing to impose on ourselves we are not willing to impose on other people. Or perhaps phrased another way: however uncertain we are about whether the absence of beauty from our own lives is a benefit or a deficit, once we see the subject from a distant perspective, it instantly becomes clear that the absence of beauty is a profound form of deprivation.

A related outcome seems to occur if one asks people who are individually opposed to beauty to think in terms of our whole era or even century: "Do you hope that when people in the twenty-first and twenty-second centuries speak of us (the way we so effortlessly make descriptive statements about people living in the nineteenth or eighteenth or seventeenth centuries), do you hope these future people will describe us as beauty-loving? or instead as neutral with respect to beauty? or instead as beauty-disregarding?" Those I have questioned state their hope that we will be spoken about by future peoples as beauty-loving. Does it not seem reasonable to suppose that many people might give this same answer? Let us suppose this and then see what it would mean: it would mean, oddly, that although beauty is highly particular and plural, one can suffer its loss to oneself, or even to those within the daily circle of one's activities, but cannot wish so grave a loss to the larger world of which one is a part, to the era in which one has lived. Neither from one's own century nor from any future century can one imagine its disappearance as anything but a deprivation.

There is one additional thought experiment that, like those above, seems to reinforce the recognition that beauty (though experienced intimately and acutely on each person's individual pulse) is unself-interested. Picture a population empowered to make decisions about the forms of beauty that will be present in our world and picture also that, in making decisions about this, none among them knew any of his or her own features: not gender, not geography, not talents or powers (level of sensory acuity, compositional abilities, physical agility, intellectual reach), not level of wealth, not intimacy or friendships. The population would make their judgments from behind "the veil of ignorance" that we now (at the invitation of John Rawls) often enlist in picturing decisions about social and economic arrangements but that may also assist us in clarifying our relation to the aesthetic surfaces of the world.

Suppose this population were presented with this question: "In the near future, human beings can arrange things so that there either will or will not be beautiful sky. Do you wish there to be beautiful sky?" (The issue before them is not the presence or absence of life-supporting oxygen for which wholly separate arrangements, due to technological advances, can swiftly be made; the question is about the way the sky's beauty itself is perceived to be part of a life-support system.) Because the sky is equally distributed throughout the world—because its beautiful events are equally distributed—it will not be surprising if the population in large numbers, or even unanimously, agree that the beautiful sky should continue. Because most of its manifestations—its habit of alternating between blue and black, the phases of the moon, the sunrise and sunset—are present everywhere, those voting do not need to know where they are living to know that they will be beneficiaries.

It is true that in addition to the constant sky events there are nonconstant ones, but these varied events are unvarying in the intensity of their beauty. The sky where I now am is subject to motions I have never known before, rivulets of air moving vertically up in streams that wash sideways, so that the black ravens and red-tailed hawks tumble in it all day, somersaulting and ferris-wheeling through the air, placing themselves in invisible fountains that lift them up until suddenly, tucking in their wings, they plunge rapidly down, spinning head over tail until out come their wings and the slow float upward starts over again. But each piece of sky is like every other in being in some feature incomparable: one moves each day across five hundred shades of azure and aquamarine; another is so moist in its lavenders, silvers, and grays that the green ground beneath it glows and becomes a second sky; another on long winter nights becomes black with wide pulsing streams of pink, green, blue. The members of our population need not know the specific ground on which fate has placed them (Antigua, Ireland, Siberia) to know that they will be the beneficiaries of both shared and exceptional beauties of the sky. There is therefore no reason to construe their positive vote as anything other than self-interest.

The same outcome seems likely to occur if we ask this population their decision about blossoms. Although they are not so evenly distributed as the sky—in some latitudes covering the meadows for only six weeks and in other latitudes covering the hillsides almost year round—they are so generously distributed across the earth that it would not be surprising if people, without knowing anything about their own attributes, would affirm the continuous existence of plants and blossoms. The population might reason that whichever geography they find themselves living in (once they step out from behind the "veil of ignorance" and recover knowledge of their own features), their local ground will be better with, than without, flowers. So here again we have no reason to search for descriptions other than vibrant self-interest and self-survival, which are compatible with the intense somatic pleasure, the sentient immediacy of the experience of beauty.

But what if now the deliberation turned to objects and events that instead of being evenly distributed across the world were emphatically nondistributional. "Shall there be here and there an astonishingly beautiful underground cave whose passageways extend several miles, opening into crystal-lined grottos and large galleries of mineral latticework, in other galleries their mute walls painted by people who visited thousands of years earlier?" Those from whom we are seeking counsel cannot assume that they are likely to live near it, for they have been openly informed that the caves about which they are being asked to vote exist in only two places on earth. Nor can they even assume that if fate places them near one of the caves, they will be able to enter its deep interior, for climbing down into the galleries requires levels of physical agility and confidence beyond those that are widely distributed among any population. But here is the question: isn't there every reason to suppose that the population will—even in the face of full knowledge that the cave is likely to be forever unavailable to them—request that such a cave be kept in existence, that it be protected and spared harm? Isn't it possible, even likely, that the population will respond in exactly the same way toward objects that are nondistributional as to those that are shared across the surface of the earth, that they will—as though they were thinking of skies and flowers—affirm the existence of remote caves and esoteric pieces of music (harder to enter even than the cave) and paintings that for many generations are held by private collectors and seen by almost no one's eyes?

People seem to wish there to be beauty even when their own self-interest is not served by it; or perhaps more accurately, people seem to intuit that their own self-interest is served by distant peoples' having the benefit of beauty. For although this was written as though it were a thought experiment, there is nothing speculative about it: the vote on blossoms has already been taken (people over many centuries have nurtured and carried the flowers from place to place, supplementing what was there); the vote on the sky has been taken (the recent environmental movement); and the vote on the caves has innumerable times been taken—otherwise it is inexplicable why people get so upset when they learn that a Vermeer painting has been stolen from the Gardner Museum without any assurance that its surface is being protected; why people get upset about the disappearance of kelp forests they had never even heard of until the moment they were informed of the loss; why museums, schools, universities take such care that beautiful artifacts from people long in the past be safely carried forward to people in the future. We are not guessing: the evidence is in.

What Money Can't Buy:
The Moral Limits of Markets

MICHAEL J. SANDEL

THE TANNER LECTURES ON HUMAN VALUES

Delivered at

Brasenose College, Oxford
May 11 and 12, 1998

MICHAEL J. SANDEL is professor of government at Harvard University, where he has taught political philosophy in the Faculty of Arts and Sciences since 1980. He was educated at Brandeis University and received his Ph.D. from Balliol College, Oxford University, where he was a Rhodes Scholar. He is a member of the National Constitution Center Advisory Panel, the Rhodes Scholarship Committee of Selection, the Shalom Hartman Institute of Jewish Philosophy, and the Council on Foreign Relations. He has received fellowships from the Ford Foundation, the American Council of Learned Societies, and the National Endowment for the Humanities. He is the author, most recently, of *Democracy's Discontent: America in Search of a Public Philosophy* (1996), as well as *Liberalism and Its Critics* (1984) and *Liberalism and the Limits of Justice* (1982).

LECTURE I.
COMMODIFICATION, COMMERCIALIZATION, AND PRIVATIZATION

1. Tipping the Tutor

It is a great honor and pleasure to be back at Oxford to give these lectures. It takes me back to the time when I first arrived here as a graduate student twenty-two years ago. There was a welcoming dinner for new students at Balliol. The Master at the time was Christopher Hill, the renowned Marxist historian. In his welcoming remarks he recalled his early days at Oxford as a young tutor, and he told us of his dutiful, but somewhat patronizing, upper-class students, one of whom left him a five-pound tip at the end of term.

Hill's point, I think, was that times had changed. *We* were not supposed to tip our tutors. Not that the thought had ever occurred to me before he mentioned it. But it does raise an interesting question: Why not? What is wrong with tipping the tutor? Nothing perhaps, if the tutor is an economist. After all, according to many economists, and also non-economists in the grip of economic ways of thinking, money is always a good way of allocating goods, or, I suppose, of expressing thanks.

I assume that Christopher Hill disapproved of the tip because he viewed the monetary payment as an indignity, as a failure to regard teaching with the proper respect. But not everybody views money and teaching in this way. Adam Smith, for one, did not. He saw nothing wrong with compensating university teachers according to market principles. Smith thought that teachers should be paid according to the number of students their classes attracted. For colleges and universities to pay teachers a fixed salary, Smith wrote, is a recipe for laziness, especially where colleges and universities are self-governing. Under such conditions the members of the college are likely "to be all very indulgent to one another, and every man to consent that his neighbor may neglect his duty, provided he himself is allowed to neglect his own."[1]

Where do you suppose Smith found the clearest example of the sloth induced by fixed salaries? "In the University of Oxford, the greater part of the . . . professors have, for these many years, given up altogether even the pretence of teaching."[2]

These two different views of money and teaching, Christopher Hill's and Adam Smith's, bring me to the question these lectures seek to address: Are there some things that money can't buy? My answer: sadly, fewer and fewer. Today, markets and market-like practices are extending their reach in almost every sphere of life.

Consider books. It used to be that the books in the window of the bookshop, or on the display table at the front of the store, were there because someone in the store—the manager or buyer or proprietor—considered these books to be of special interest or importance to prospective readers. Today, that is less and less the case. Publishers now pay bookstores, especially the big chain bookstores, tens of thousands of dollars for placement of their books in windows or other prominent places. I don't know whether this is yet the case with Blackwell's. I pray not.

But in many U.S. bookstores, the books you see up front, even the books that are turned face out on the shelves, are titles that the publisher has paid the store to display. It has long been the case that makers of pretzels, potato chips, and breakfast cereals have paid grocery store chains for favorable shelf space. Now, thanks

---

[1] Adam Smith, *An Inquiry into the Nature and Causes of the Wealth of Nations* (1776), book 5, ch. 1, pt. 3 (New York: Modern Library, 1994), p. 821.

[2] Ibid.

partly to the rise of powerful superstores like Barnes and Noble, books are sold like breakfast cereal.[3]

Is there anything wrong with this? Suppose, under the traditional system, you go into a bookstore and look around for a book you have written, something that authors have been known to do. And you find your cherished work on some obscure lower shelf at the back of the store. Imagine that you bribe the owner of the store to put it in the window. If it is a bribe when you make this arrangement, is it any less a bribe when Random House does it to boost sales of really important authors, like O. J. Simpson or Newt Gingrich?

Consider a second example—prisons. Once the province of government, the incarceration of criminals is now a profitable and rapidly growing business. Since the mid-1980s, more and more governments have entrusted their inmates to the care of for-profit companies. In the United States, the private prison business is now a billion-dollar industry. Twenty-seven states and the federal government have contracted with private companies like the Corrections Corporation of America to house their prisoners. In the mid-eighties when the trend began, scarcely a thousand prisoners occupied private prisons. Today, more than 85,000 U.S. inmates are serving time in for-profit prisons. And the trend has spread to Britain, Australia, New Zealand, Canada, France, the Netherlands, and South Africa.[4]

Or consider a third example, the growing trend toward branding, marketing, and commercial advertising in spheres that once stood aloof from market practices. Once, "rebranding" was a device employed by companies that needed to change the image of a tired product line. Today, we hear of efforts by the Blair government to

[3] Mary B. W. Tabor, "In Bookstore Chains, Display Space Is for Sale," *New York Times,* January 15, 1996, p. A1.

[4] Nzong Xiong, "Private Prisons: A Question of Savings," *New York Times,* July 13, 1997.

"rebrand" Britain as "one of the world's pioneers rather than one of its museums." As the American media has reported, "Rule Britannia" is giving way to "Cool Britannia," the new slogan of the British Travel Authority.[5]

The rebranding of Britain is not an isolated episode, but a sign of the times.[6] Last year the U.S. Postal Service issued a stamp of Bugs Bunny, a cartoon character. Critics complained that stamps should honor historic figures, not commercial products. But the post office is facing stiff competition from e-mail, fax machines, and Federal Express. So it now sees licensing rights as key to its future.

Every Bugs Bunny stamp that is bought for the love of it, rather than used to mail an envelope, earns thirty-two cents profit for the post office. And stamp collecting is the least of it. The licensing deal with Warner Brothers enables the Postal Service to market Looney Tunes ties, hats, videos, and other products at its five hundred postal stores across the country.[7]

Canada has also encountered the licensing craze. In 1995, the Royal Canadian Mounted Police sold to Disney the right to market the Mountie image worldwide. Disney paid Canada's federal police $2.5 million per year in marketing rights, plus a share of the licensing fees for Mountie T-shirts, coffee mugs, teddy bears, maple syrup, diaper bags, and other merchandise. Many Canadians objected. They claimed the Mounties were selling out a sacred national symbol to a U.S. corporate giant. "It's not the price that rankles. It's the sale," complained an editorial in Toronto's *Globe and Mail*. "The Mounted Police have miscalculated on a crucial point. Pride."[8]

---

[5] Warren Hoge, "London Journal; Blair's 'Rebranded' Britain Is No Museum," *New York Times,* November 12, 1997.

[6] In this and the following three paragraphs, I draw upon Sandel, "Branded," *New Republic,* January 19, 1998, pp. 10–11.

[7] Nathan Cobb, "Trading Post," *Boston Globe,* December 20, 1997, pp. D1, D3.

[8] Colin Nickerson, "Canadian Mounties Sign with Disney," *Boston Globe,* July 15, 1995, p. 2.

The effect of the increasing commingling of government and commerce is more far reaching than one might imagine, in part because it works so well. Government, widely disliked, seeks to bolster its popularity, even its legitimacy, by leaning on popular images or icons of the commercial culture. Amidst widespread mistrust of government and dissatisfaction with politics, pollsters have found that the two most popular agencies of the U.S. federal government are the post office and the military. Not coincidentally, perhaps, both advertise heavily on television.

Not only governments, but also universities have gone into the business of licensing their brand names. In the late 1980s, Harvard University established a trademark and licensing office to monitor the commercial use of Harvard's name. One of its jobs is to crack down on unauthorized users, such as the poultry company in Korea that sold "Harvard" eggs in a carton that displayed a mortarboard and the promise that eating the eggs will make you as smart as somebody who goes to Harvard.[9]

Harvard's excuse for being in the licensing business is that a trademark must be used to be protected. So Harvard has been using it. In Japan, it licensed a line of clothing and accessories with the Harvard name, including horn-rimmed eyeglasses, khaki pants, and preppie blazers. So popular were these items that Japanese royalties brought Harvard as much as $550,000 in one year. The competition is not far behind. Princeton has also opened up a product line in Japan.[10]

These three cases—the commodification of books, the privatization of prisons, the commercialization of governments and universities—illustrate one of the most powerful social and political tendencies of our time, namely the extension of markets and of market-oriented thinking to spheres of life once thought to lie beyond their reach.

[9] "Harvard Eggs? Protecting the Name," *Harvard Magazine* (January–February 1998): 72.

[10] Ibid., p. 73.

I'd like to argue in these lectures that this tendency is by and large a bad thing, a development that should be resisted. In explaining why this is so I would like to distinguish two objections to extending the reach of market valuation and exchange. Both figure prominently in arguments about the moral limits of markets. But they are often run together, and it is important to disentangle them.

2. Two Objections: Coercion and Corruption

The first objection is an argument from coercion. It points to the injustice that can arise when people buy and sell things under conditions of severe inequality or dire economic necessity. According to this objection, market exchanges are not necessarily as voluntary as market enthusiasts suggest. A peasant may agree to sell his kidney or cornea in order to feed his starving family, but his agreement is not truly voluntary. He is coerced, in effect, by the necessities of his situation.

The second objection is an argument from corruption. It points to the degrading effect of market valuation and exchange on certain goods and practices. According to this objection, certain moral and civic goods are diminished or corrupted if bought and sold for money. The argument from corruption cannot be met by establishing fair bargaining conditions. If the sale of human body parts is intrinsically degrading, a violation of the sanctity of the human body, then kidney sales would be wrong for rich and poor alike. The objection would hold even without the coercive effect of crushing poverty.

Each objection draws on a different moral ideal. The argument from coercion draws on the ideal of consent, or more precisely, the ideal of consent carried out under fair background conditions. It is not, strictly speaking, an objection to markets, only to markets that operate against a background of inequality severe enough to create coercive bargaining conditions. The argument from coercion offers no grounds for objecting to the commodification of goods in a society whose background conditions are fair.

The argument from corruption is different. It appeals not to consent but to the moral importance of the goods at stake, the ones said to be degraded by market valuation and exchange. The argument from corruption is intrinsic in the sense that it cannot be met by fixing the background conditions within which market exchanges take place. It applies under conditions of equality and inequality alike.

Consider two familiar objections to prostitution. Some object to prostitution on the grounds that it is rarely, if ever, truly voluntary. According to this argument, those who sell their bodies for sex are typically coerced, whether by poverty, drug addiction, or other unfortunate life circumstances. Others object that prostitution is intrinsically degrading, a corruption of the moral worth of human sexuality. The degradation objection does not depend on tainted consent. It would condemn prostitution even in a society without poverty and despair, even in cases of wealthy prostitutes who like the work and freely choose it.

My point is not to argue for or against prostitution, but simply to illustrate the difference between the two objections and also to illustrate the further part of my claim, which is that the second objection is not reducible to the first. The worry about corruption cannot be laid to rest simply by establishing fair background conditions. Even in a society without unjust differences of power and wealth, there would still be things that money should not buy.

I shall try to argue, in the remainder of these lectures, for the independence of the second objection. I hope also to show that it is more fundamental than the first. I shall proceed by considering a range of cases. Before turning to the cases, however, I want to emphasize an important qualification. Even if it can be shown that a particular good should not be bought or sold, it is a further question whether the sale of that good should be legally prohibited.

There may well be cases in which commodification is morally objectionable and yet, all things considered, the practice should not be banned. Prohibition may carry moral and practical costs that outweigh the good of preventing the practice. And there may be other, better ways of discouraging it. My question is not what forms of commodification should be legally restricted but what forms of commodification are morally objectionable. The moral status of a contested commodity should figure as one consideration among others in determining its legal permissibility.

3. THE CASE OF SURROGATE MOTHERHOOD

Having distinguished two different arguments against commodification, I now turn to one hotly contested case, that of commercial surrogacy. Contracts for "surrogate motherhood," as the practice is commonly known, typically involve a couple unable to conceive or bear a child, and a woman who agrees, in exchange for a fee, to be inseminated with the sperm of the father, to carry the child to term, and to give it up at birth.

Some argue that commercial surrogacy represents an objectionable kind of commodification. How can such claims be assessed? Many arguments about commodification proceed by way of analogy. Those who oppose contracts for surrogate motherhood argue that they are morally tantamount to baby-selling. With commercial surrogacy as with baby-selling, a woman is paid a fee (typically $10,000 in the surrogacy market), in exchange for relinquishing a child.

Defenders of commercial surrogacy must either resist the analogy or defend both practices. Those who dispute the analogy argue that commercial surrogacy is more like selling sperm than selling a baby; when a woman agrees to undergo a pregnancy for pay, she does not sell a preexisting child but simply allows another couple to make use of her reproductive capacity. And if it is morally permissible for men to sell their reproductive capacity, this argument goes, why is it not morally permissible for women to sell theirs?

I would like to consider both of those analogies. Each can help clarify the moral status of commercial surrogacy. As is often the case with reasoning by analogy, however, we may find that the intuitions that constitute our moral starting point do not emerge unscathed. Reflecting on the rights and wrongs of surrogacy may lead us to revise our initial views about the moral status of baby-selling and of sperm-selling.

In some cases, baby-selling may actually be better than contract pregnancy. Consider the following case, a true story, reported last year in the *New York Times:* Dr. Thomas J. Hicks was a country doctor in a small Georgia town. He had a secret business selling babies on the side. Jane Blasio, now a thirty-two-year-old Ohio resident, was one of those babies. In 1965, her adoptive parents, a tire maker and his wife, drove eight hours from Akron, Ohio, paid the doctor $1,000, and drove home with a new baby daughter. Included in the purchase price was a fake birth certificate listing the buyers as the birth parents.[11]

Mrs. Blasio discovered Dr. Hicks's sideline business while combing through country birth records many years later, searching for the identity of her birth mother. It turns out that the doctor, who died in 1972, sold some 200 babies between 1951 and 1965.

Baby-selling is not normally a respectable business, but Dr. Hicks's version did have a morally redeeming aspect. Childless couples were not his only clientele. Unmarried pregnant girls from Chattanooga to Atlanta also made their way to his clinic in the north Georgia mountains. Abortions were illegal at the time, but Dr. Hicks was known to perform them. Sometimes he persuaded

---

[11] The remarkable story of Dr. Hicks was reported by Rick Bragg, "Town Secret Is Uncovered in Birth Quest," *New York Times,* August 23, 1997, pp. A1, A7. I draw, in the discussion that follows, on Sandel, "Baby Bazaar," *New Republic,* October 20, 1997, p. 25.

the young women to carry their babies to term, which created the supply that met the demand of his childless customers.

It is difficult to condemn the doctor's morally complicated practice. It can be argued that the moral wrong of selling a child was outweighed in his case by the moral good of avoiding an abortion and placing an unwanted child with loving parents. In any case, compare Dr. Hicks's black market in babies with contemporary commercial surrogate motherhood.

Compared to Dr. Hicks's homespun enterprise, commercial surrogacy, a $40 million industry in the United States, is big business. Professional baby brokers advertise for couples who want a child and also for women willing to give birth through artificial insemination for pay. The broker draws up a contract specifying the payment to the birth mother, typically $10,000 plus medical expenses. She agrees to be impregnated with the father's sperm, to carry the pregnancy to term, and to relinquish the child and all parental rights. For his efforts, the broker collects a $15,000 fee, bringing the cost per child to more than $25,000.

Like all commercial contracts, surrogacy promises benefits to both parties. Infertile couples can acquire a baby who bears the genetic imprint of the father and raise it as their own. Surrogate mothers, meanwhile, can earn $10,000 for nine months' work and give the gift of life to a grateful couple.

But contract pregnancy does not always work out so happily. Sometimes the surrogate mother changes her mind and wants to keep the baby. That is what happened in the celebrated "Baby M case," a surrogacy case that went to court in New Jersey.[12]

The surrogate mother, Mary Beth Whitehead, fled to Florida with her baby rather than surrender it to William and Elizabeth Stern. They were the couple who had paid her to conceive it. A lower court in New Jersey ruled that the contract was valid. A deal was a deal, and the birth mother had no right to break the agree-

[12] In re Baby M., 217 New Jersey Superior Court, 313, 1987.

ment simply because she changed her mind. The New Jersey Supreme Court disagreed, however, and invalidated the contract. It granted custody to the father, Mr. Stern, but voided the adoption by his wife and declared Mrs. Whitehead the legal mother, entitled to visiting rights.[13]

On what grounds did the respective courts justify their rulings? The lower court argued, implausibly in my view, that in contracting with Mrs. Whitehead, Mr. Stern did not really buy a baby—he had, after all, contributed the sperm—but simply hired a woman to perform a service for a wage. But this strained distinction overlooks the fact that the contract not only required Mrs. Whitehead to bear the child: it also required that she renounce her parental rights. In fact, the contract even included a product guarantee: If the baby were born abnormal, the Sterns would not have to take it, though they would be obliged to provide financial support.

The New Jersey Supreme Court invalidated the contract and compared commercial surrogacy to baby-selling: "This is the sale of a child, or at the very least, the sale of a mother's right to her child, the only mitigating factor being that one of the purchasers is the father."[14] But if contract pregnancy is morally equivalent to baby-selling, the question remains whether our repugnance to baby-selling is well founded. What is wrong with letting people buy and sell babies if they choose?

There are two possible answers to this question, answers that take us back to the two objections to commodification in general. One answer worries about coercion or other flaws in the act of consent, while the other worries about corruption of the moral goods and social norms associated with pregnancy, childbearing, and parenthood.

Those who oppose surrogacy and baby-selling in the name of consent claim that the choice to bear a child for pay is not as

---

[13] Matter of Baby M, 537 Atlantic Reporter, 2d series, 1227 (New Jersey 1988).

[14] Ibid., p. 1248.

voluntary as it seems. They argue that surrogacy contracts are not truly voluntary because the birth mother is unlikely to be fully informed. Since she cannot be expected to know in advance the strength of the bond she will develop with her child during pregnancy, it is unfair to hold her to her bargain once the baby is born.

In the Baby M case, the lawyers for the Sterns argued that Mary Beth Whitehead's consent was informed because she had had previous children of her own. But it is not clear that previous pregnancies supply the knowledge relevant to a surrogacy contract. The distinctive feature of such a contract is that it requires a woman to bear a child and then relinquish it. Bearing a child to love and raise as one's own does not necessarily inform a woman about what it would be like to bear a child and give it up for money.

The second objection to surrogacy contracts does not depend on finding a flaw in the act of consent. It holds that even a truly voluntary, fully informed agreement to sell a baby lacks moral force because certain things should not be bought and sold. This was the position of the New Jersey Supreme Court, which stated, "There are, in a civilized society, some things that money cannot buy."[15] This argument maintains that we should not regard ourselves as free to assign whatever values we want to the goods we prize. Certain modes of valuation are appropriate to certain goods. Treating children as commodities degrades them by using them as instruments of profit rather than cherishing them as persons worthy of love and care. Contract pregnancy also degrades women by treating their bodies as factories and by paying them not to bond with the children they bear.

Elizabeth Anderson advances a compelling version of this argument. "By requiring the surrogate mother to repress whatever parental love she feels for the child," Anderson writes, surrogacy contracts "convert women's labor into a form of alienated labor."

[15] Ibid., p. 1249.

The surrogate's labor is alienated "because she must divert it from the end which the social practices of pregnancy rightly promote— an emotional bond with her child."[16]

Anderson's argument brings out a controversial feature of the corruption argument against commodification. To object that market valuation and exchange of a good corrupts its character is to assume that certain things are properly regarded and treated in certain ways. Thus Anderson invokes a certain conception of the proper end of pregnancy and childbearing. To know whether a good should be subject to market exchange, according to this view, we need to know what mode of valuation is fitting or appropriate to that good. This is different from knowing how much the thing is worth. It involves a qualitative, not just a quantitative judgment.

Such judgments are bound to be controversial, even threatening. Part of the appeal of markets is that they do not pass judgment on the intrinsic worth of the things people buy and sell. Different people evaluate goods differently, and the market leaves them free to act on their own valuations. It is sometimes thought to be an advantage of consent-based objections to commodification that, unlike the argument from corruption, they avoid passing judgment on the intrinsic worth of the things being exchanged or the modes of valuation appropriate to them.

Despite this apparent advantage, however, the consent-based argument fails to address the most morally troubling features of commercial surrogacy. For it is precisely the deliberate, voluntary character of contract pregnancy that makes it worse than some instances of baby-selling. Dr. Hicks's black market in babies responded to a problem that arose independent of market considerations. He didn't encourage the unwed mothers whose babies he sold to become pregnant in the first place. Had he done so, had he advertised and recruited the women to become pregnant, bear a

---

[16] Elizabeth S. Anderson, "Is Women's Labor a Commodity?" *Philosophy & Public Affairs* 19 (Winter 1990): 81, 83.

child, and give it up for money, then his baby-selling business would be far more objectionable than it was. It would be as objectionable as the commercial surrogacy business carried on today in full public view.

The argument from corruption, which draws our attention to modes of valuation appropriate to certain goods and social practices, may also prompt us to reconsider the moral implications of the analogy between surrogacy and sperm-selling. This analogy is typically invoked in defense of surrogacy. If men should be free to sell their reproductive capacity, the argument goes, shouldn't women also be free to sell theirs? Isn't it unfair, isn't it discriminatory, to allow one but not the other?

Here may be a case where, on reflection, the moral force of the analogy works in the other direction. If, prompted by the surrogacy case, we conclude that certain modes of valuation are proper or fitting to certain kinds of goods, we may come to question the moral permissibility of sperm sales. Such qualms are heightened by the brazen way in which the market for sperm has become commercialized.

From time to time, there appears in the Harvard student newspaper, the *Crimson,* an advertisement stating that "the largest sperm bank in the United States is looking for donors." Those who qualify are promised thirty-five dollars per specimen, up to three times a week. For relatively little effort, eligible Harvard men can make $105 per week selling sperm.

It is no accident that Cryobank, Inc., locates its sperm banks near Harvard and MIT in the east and Stanford and Berkeley in the west. Its marketing materials play up the prestigious source of its sperm. A monthly catalog offers customers a physical and ethnic profile of each donor, including his major field of study. "It's not the Sears, Roebuck catalog," a company manager told the *Boston Globe,* "but it's a place to start."[17]

17 Sally Jacobs, "Wanted: Smart Sperm," *Boston Globe,* September 12, 1993, pp. 1, 39.

The marketing of Ivy League sperm commodifies the male reproductive capacity in much the way commercial surrogacy commodifies pregnancy. Both treat procreation as a product for profit rather than a human capacity to be exercised according to norms of love, intimacy, and responsibility. A further example illustrates the point.

Several years ago there was a scandal surrounding a doctor named Cecil Jacobson, an infertility specialist in Virginia. He didn't have a donor catalog. Unknown to his patients, all of the sperm he used to inseminate his patients came from one donor— Dr. Jacobson himself. Genetic testing proved that at least fifteen of the babies conceived at his clinic bore his genetic imprint. Columnist Ellen Goodman described the bizarre scenario: "Had his patients known what was happening between the time the doctor left the examining room and his return with a vial of sperm, I suspect they would have leapt off the table. At least one woman who testified in court was unnerved at how much her newborn daughter 'looks just like him.'"[18]

It is possible, of course, to condemn Dr. Jacobson for failing to inform the women in advance. But Goodman glimpsed another moral of the story: "The clamor over this case comes in part from a change in attitudes towards fathers. We are, finally, uneasy, about the disconnection between men, sperm, and fatherhood. We are trying to strengthen the lines between male sexuality and responsibility, fathers and children. Dr. Jacobson gave his infertility business the, uh, personal touch. Now the rest of us are in for a round of second thoughts on sperm donation." Perhaps, Goodman concludes, fatherhood should be something you do, not something you donate.[19]

---

[18] Ellen Goodman, "The Father of Them All," March 3, 1992, reprinted in Goodman, *Value Judgments* (New York: Farrar Straus Giroux, 1993), pp. 309–11.

[19] Ibid., p. 311.

4. PLURALITY AND COMMENSURABILITY

The argument from corruption has a distinctive feature that holds consequences for the way the debate about commodification should proceed. Unlike the argument from coercion, the argument from corruption will be different in each case. The reason is as follows: The argument from coercion always appeals to the ideal of consent, whereas the argument from corruption appeals to the character of the particular good in question. In the cases of surrogacy, baby-selling, and sperm-selling, the ideals at stake are bound up with the meaning of motherhood, fatherhood, and the nurturing of children. Once we characterize the good at stake, it is always a further question whether, or in what respect, market valuation and exchange diminishes or corrupts the character of that good.

Although the goods at stake will vary, it is nonetheless possible to identify one general feature of arguments from corruption that are leveled against commodification: All call into question an assumption that informs much market-oriented thinking. This is the assumption that all goods are commensurable, that all goods can be translated without loss into a single measure or unit of value.

The thesis that all goods are commensurable is familiar from at least some versions of utilitarianism, notably Benthamite utilitarianism. All arguments from corruption against commodification resist this claim. It does not seem to me possible, in general, to prove or refute the thesis of commensurability, which is one of the reasons that arguments by analogy play such an important role in debates about commodification. But it is reasonable to question the idea that all goods can be captured in a single measure of value, and to illustrate this doubt, I would like to close this lecture with one other story that I remember from the days, over two decades ago, when I was studying here in Oxford.

Back in those days, the men's colleges and the women's colleges were not yet mixed. And the women's colleges had rules against overnight male guests. These rules were rarely enforced and easily violated, or so I was told. But by the late 1970s, pressure grew to relax these rules and it became a subject of debate among the faculty at St. Anne's College. The older women on the faculty were traditionalists. They were opposed to change on conventional moral grounds. But times had changed, and they were embarrassed to state the real grounds for their objection. So they tried to translate their argument into utilitarian terms.

If men stay overnight, they argued, the costs to the college will increase. How, you might wonder? Well, they said, they'll want to take baths, and that will use up hot water. Furthermore, they argued, we'll have to replace the mattresses more often. (This is a true story.) The reformers met these arguments by adopting the following compromise: Each woman could have a maximum of three male overnight guests a week, provided that the guest paid fifty pence a night to defray the costs to the college. The day after the compromise was adopted, the headline in the *Guardian* read, "St. Anne's Girls: Fifty Pence a Night." It wasn't long before the parietal rules were waived altogether, and so was the fee. But the story calls into question the thesis that all goods are commensurable, that all values and virtues can be translated without loss into monetary terms. That is a thesis that the argument from corruption also rejects.

LECTURE II.
MARKETS, MORALS, AND THE PUBLIC SPHERE

1. OBJECTIONS TO THE ARGUMENT FROM CORRUPTION

The argument that commodification corrupts or degrades certain goods raises two difficulties that do not confront the argument from coercion. One is that the argument from corruption has to be made in a different way, case by case. It must be shown how, in each case, market valuation and exchange degrades or corrupts important values or ends that non-market practices may embody. The argument from coercion, by contrast, does not have to be defended in a different way each time. It points to a single ideal—the ideal of consent—not a plurality of ideals. The form of the argument is always the same: What seems like a free exchange of goods or services for money is not truly voluntary, because economic coercion, or economic necessity, is operating in the background.

The second difficulty follows readily from the first: Since the argument from corruption points not to consent but to the moral worth of particular human goods, the question arises how the case for these goods can be established, especially in the face of competing moral and religious convictions. Recall the argument against commercial surrogacy advanced by Anderson. She claims that certain modes of valuation are "fitting" or "proper" to certain kinds of goods. This argument has, at least to some, a worryingly Aristotelian aspect, for it depends on attributing to certain social practices a characteristic purpose or end. Arguments of this kind are subject to two familiar objections: If we derive the fitting or proper way of regarding goods from the social meanings that prevail in a given society at a given time, we run the risk of lapsing into conventionalism. If, for example, there are fewer and fewer things that money can buy these days, we might simply conclude that the meaning of our social practices is changing in this respect. The critical role of an appeal to proper modes of valuation is lost. If, however, we derive the fitting or proper way of regarding goods from some notion of the essential nature of the practices in questions, we run the risk of essentialism—the idea that the purposes and ends of social practices are fixed by nature.

Is it possible to argue that markets corrupt or degrade certain goods, without lapsing into conventionalism or essentialism?

How can such arguments proceed in the face of disagreement about purposes and ends? One way of proceeding, as I suggested above, is to argue by analogy—to begin with moral intuitions we have about certain practices, and to see whether or not the practices in question are relevantly similar. We considered, for example, whether commercial surrogacy was more like baby-selling or more like sperm-selling. The argument by analogy was saved from conventionalism by the fact that moral intuitions functioned as starting points for reflection, subject to revision as the argument unfolded. The initial intuitions against baby-selling and for sperm-selling were called into question in the course of reflecting on the similarities and differences between those practices and commercial surrogacy. Another way of proceeding is to begin with a certain conception of the good and then to explore its consequences for morally contested cases of commodification, and also commonly accepted ones. In the course of reflecting, we may find reason to revise our judgments about the cases or about the conception of the good that provides the starting point.

2. REPUBLICAN CITIZENSHIP

I turn now to three cases that concern markets and the public realm. Rather than begin with analogies and then tease out the conception of the good at stake, as in the surrogacy case, I'd like to proceed in the opposite direction—to begin by describing a certain conception of the good and then to explore its consequences for certain familiar market-oriented policies and practices. The cases I have in mind are: (1) military service, (2) voting, and (3) the distribution of income and wealth. I would like to argue that there is reason to limit the role of markets in governing these three practices more severely than we are accustomed to do. In each case, an excessive role for markets corrupts an ideal the practices properly express and advance—namely, the ideal of citizenship as the republican tradition conceives it.

According to the republican conception of citizenship, to be free is to share in self-rule. This is more than a matter of voting in elections and registering my preferences or interests. On the republican conception of citizenship, to be free is to participate in shaping the forces that govern the collective destiny. But in order to do that, and to do it well, it is necessary that citizens possess or come to acquire certain qualities of character, or civic virtues.[1]

The emphasis on civic virtue sets republican political theory apart from two other familiar theories of citizenship. One such theory is interest group pluralism, which conceives citizens as persons who are free to identify their interests and to vote accordingly. A second theory is the liberal conception of citizenship, which emphasizes toleration and respect for the rights of others. The liberal conception of citizenship allows for the inculcation of certain civic virtues, but only those necessary to liberal principles themselves, such as the virtues of toleration and equal respect. The republican conception of citizenship, by contrast, seeks to cultivate a fuller range of virtues, including a moral bond with the community whose fate is at stake, a sense of obligation for one's fellow citizens, a willingness to sacrifice individual interests for the sake of the common good, and the ability to deliberate well about common purposes and ends.

What justifies the republican conception of citizenship? There are two versions of republican political theory, and each gives a different answer. Modest versions of the republican conception hold that civic virtue matters instrumentally; unless citizens attend to the public good, it is not possible to maintain a political society that accords each person the right to choose and pursue his or her own ends. More robust versions of the republican tradition,

---

[1] For a fuller discussion, see Sandel, *Democracy's Discontent: America in Search of a Public Philosophy* (Cambridge, Mass.: Harvard University Press, 1996), pp. 4–7, 25–28.

by contrast, view self-government and the virtues that attend it as an essential part of human flourishing. According to this view, to participate in politics is not just a means to securing a regime that enables people to seek their own ends; it is also an essential ingredient of the good life. For strong republicans, deliberating about the common good under conditions where the deliberation makes a difference calls forth human capacities—for judgment and compromise, for argument and reflection, for the taking of responsibility—that would otherwise lie dormant. On this view, the purpose of politics is to call forth and cultivate distinctive human faculties that other pursuits, such as work or art, do not cultivate in the same way. With this conception of citizenship in mind, we can now consider how commodification corrupts the good of self-government in three domains of public life.

3. MILITARY SERVICE

Military service can be allocated in different ways, some involving the market, others not. Conscription allocates service without the use of markets. In its simplest version, it fills places according to a lottery of eligible citizens. A second way of allocating places in the military was employed by the Union during the American Civil War. It introduced market principles, but only to a point. In the first American draft, enacted in 1863, those who were called but who did not want to serve could hire a substitute to take their place. Many draftees advertised for substitutes in the newspapers, offering amounts from a few hundred dollars up to fifteen hundred dollars. The system was less than a resounding success. There were widespread protests. In the New York draft riots a thousand people died. Congress tried to quell the protest by amending the policy by setting a flat fee for exemption. If you were drafted and didn't want to serve, you could pay a three-hundred-dollar fee to the government. You didn't have to bother finding someone else. Three hundred dollars in those days was equivalent to one year's wages for a laborer.[2]

A third way of filling the ranks of the military carries market principles one step further. Rather than draft people and then allow the market to operate, the present-day American all-volunteer army uses market principles from the start. The term "volunteer" is something of a misnomer. Soldiers do not volunteer in the way that people volunteer to work in the local soup kitchen on Thanksgiving—that is, to serve without pay. The volunteer army is a professional army, in which soldiers work for pay. It is voluntary only in the sense that all paid labor is voluntary. No one is conscripted, and the job is performed by those who agree to do so in exchange for money and other benefits.

Compare these three ways of allocating military service—conscription, conscription with a buy-out provision (the Civil War system), and the market system. Which is most desirable? From the standpoint of market reasoning, the Civil War system is preferable to a system of pure conscription because it increases the range of choice. Those who are conscripted but who do not want to serve have the option of buying their way out, and those who are not conscripted but who want the job can buy their way in. From the standpoint of market reasoning, however, the volunteer army is better still. Like the Civil War system, it enables people to buy their way into or out of military service. But it is preferable to the Civil War system because it places the cost of hiring soldiers on the society as a whole, not just on the unlucky few who happen to be drafted and must therefore serve or hire a substitute to take their place.

So from the standpoint of market reasoning, the volunteer army is best, the Civil War system second best, and conscription

---

[2] On the Civil War draft, see James M. McPherson, *Battle Cry of Freedom* (New York: Oxford University Press, 1988), pp. 600–611; and Guido Calabresi and Philip Bobbitt, *Tragic Choices* (New York: W. W. Norton, 1978), pp. 158–67.

the least desirable way of allocating military service. But there are at least two objections to this line of argument. One is that we cannot prefer the volunteer army without knowing more about the background conditions that prevail in the society. The volunteer army seems attractive because it avoids the coercion of conscription. It makes military service a matter of consent. But some of those who serve in the all-volunteer army may be as averse to military service as those who stay away. If poverty and economic disadvantage is widespread, the choice to serve may simply reflect the lack of alternatives. This is the problem of the poor persons' army. According to this objection (an instance of the objection from coercion), those who buy their way in, or fail to buy their way out, are conscripted by the lottery of economic necessity.

The difference between conscription and the volunteer army is not that one is compulsory, whereas the other is not; it is rather that each employs a different form of compulsion—the state in the first case, economic necessity in the second. Only if people are similarly situated to begin with can it be said that the choice to serve for pay reflects people's preferences, rather than their limited alternatives.

The actual composition of the American all-volunteer army seems to bear out this objection. Thirty percent of the U.S. army troops who were sent to fight the Gulf War were African Americans, almost three times the percent of African Americans in the population as a whole. The enlistment rates for children of the richest fifteen percent of the population are one-fifth of the national average.[3] So it is easy to appreciate the force of the objection that the volunteer army is not as voluntary as it seems.

It is worth pointing out that this objection can in principle be met without doing away with the all-volunteer army. It can be met by making the background conditions of the society sufficiently equal so that people's choice of work reflects meaningful

[3] Larry Tye, "All-Volunteer Force No Mirror of Society," *Boston Globe*, February 2, 1991, pp. 1, 3.

consent rather than dire economic necessity. In this case as in others, the argument from coercion is not an objection to the commodification of military service as such, only to commodification that takes place under certain unfair background conditions.

A second objection to letting people buy their way into and out of military service is independent of the first. It holds that, even in a society where the choice of work did not reflect deep inequalities in life circumstances, military service should not be allocated by the labor market, as if it were just another job. According to this argument, all citizens have an obligation to serve their country. Whether this obligation is best discharged through military or other national service, it is not the sort of thing that people should be free to buy or sell. To turn such service into a commodity—a job for pay—is to corrupt or degrade the sense of civic virtue that properly attends it. A familiar instance of this argument is offered by Jean-Jacques Rousseau: "As soon as public service ceases to be the chief business of the citizens and they would rather serve with their money than with their persons, the state is not far from its fall. When it is necessary to march out to war, they pay troops and stay at home. . . . In a country that is truly free, the citizens do everything with their own arms and nothing by means of money; so far from paying to be exempted from their duties, they would even pay for the privilege of fulfilling them themselves. . . . I hold enforced labor to be less opposed to liberty than taxes."[4]

Rousseau's argument against commodifying military service is an instance of the argument from corruption. It invokes the republican conception of citizenship. Market advocates might defend the volunteer army by rejecting the republican conception of citizenship, or by denying its relevance to military service. But doesn't the volunteer army as currently practiced implicitly acknowledge certain limits to market principles, limits that derive from a residual commitment to the ideal of republican citizenship?

---

[4] Jean-Jacques Rousseau, *The Social Contract* (1762), trans. G. D. H. Cole, book 3, ch. 15 (London: J. M. Dent & Sons, 1973), p. 265.

Consider the difference between the contemporary volunteer army and an army of mercenaries. Both pay soldiers to fight. Both entice people to enlist by the promise of pay and other benefits. The U.S. army runs television commercials that make the job seem as attractive as possible. But if the market is an appropriate way of allocating military service, what is wrong with mercenaries? It might be replied that mercenaries are foreign nationals who fight only for pay, whereas the American volunteer army hires only Americans. But if military service is just another job, why should the employer discriminate in hiring on the basis of nationality? Why shouldn't the U.S. military be open to citizens of any country who want the work and possess the relevant qualifications?

The logic of the market could be extended to challenge the notion that armies should be run by the government. Why not subcontract military functions to private enterprise? In fact, the privatization of war, like the privatization of prisons, is a growing trend. Private corporations that hire mercenary forces play an increasing role in conflicts around the world. Sandline International is a London-based company registered in the Bahamas. It was hired by Papua New Guinea last year to put down a secessionist rebellion. Papua New Guinea's prime minister hired Sandline for $32 million to crush rebels his own army was unable to defeat. "I am sick and tired of our boys coming back in body bags," he said.[5]

Sandline, in turn, subcontracted with a South African–based company euphemistically named Executive Outcomes, which supplies and trains the soldiers. "Executive Outcomes has racked up an impressive record of military victories for its customers," reports the *Boston Globe.* "Equipped with Russian attack helicopters, heavy artillery, and battle-hardened veterans recruited from the troops that defended South Africa's former white supremacist

[5] Colum Lynch, "Soldiers for Hire Tempt War-Weary," *Boston Globe,* March 8, 1997, pp. A1, A12. See also Raymond Bonner, "U.S. Reportedly Backed British Mercenary Group in Africa," *New York Times,* May 13, 1998; and David Shearer, "Outsourcing War," *Foreign Policy* (Fall 1998): 68–80.

government, Executive Outcomes has waged war on behalf of the governments of Angola and Sierra Leone."[6]

In 1989, the United Nations proposed the International Convention against the Recruitment, Use, Financing, and Training of Mercenaries. But only ten nations have signed it, and two of them, Angola and Zaire, have already violated it. The United States did pressure the South African government to restrain the role of Executive Outcomes in Angola. But the American principled position was complicated by the fact that the United States then lobbied the Angolan government to hire a competing U.S. firm, Military Professional Resources Inc., to train the Angolan armed forces.[7]

The cases we have considered pose the following challenge to the commodification of military service represented by the all-volunteer army: If the Civil War system is objectionable on the grounds that it allows people to buy their way out of a civic obligation, isn't the volunteer army objectionable on similar grounds? And if military service is just another job to be allocated by the labor market, is there any principled distinction between the volunteer army and the mercenary forces recruited by Sandline, Executive Outcomes, and other firms? All three policies—the Civil War system, the volunteer army, and the mercenary forces—offend the republican conception of citizenship. Our unease in each case is best articulated and justified by the argument from corruption, which presupposes in turn the republican ideal of citizenship.

4. Voting

The commodification of military service is controversial in a way that the commodification of voting is not. No one defends the out-

---

[6] Lynch, "Soldiers for Hire."

[7] Ibid.

right purchase and sale of votes. But why is it objectionable? And if it is, what are the consequences for commonly accepted electoral practices that come perilously close to the buying and selling of votes?

Reformers have long worried about the role of money in politics.[8] So also did George Washington Plunkitt, the boss of the Tammany Hall political machine in New York. The problem with money in politics, he said, is that there is never enough to go around.[9] In recent years, however, there has been plenty to go around, at least in American politics. The last U.S. presidential campaign cost $800 million. There have been attempts, of course, to reduce the power of money in politics. Underlying these attempts is the worry that the present system of financing American political campaigns comes close to bribery. But even the debate over campaign finance leaves untouched a deeper corruption, and that is the politics of self-interest itself.

Consider the widely accepted practice of conducting democratic politics as if it were about aggregating and responding to interests. If it is wrong for moneyed interests to bribe politicians with campaign contributions, isn't it also wrong for politicians to bribe voters with campaign promises directed at their pocketbooks? Some bribes are more explicit than others. In Plunkitt's day, ward heelers distributed money, meals, and favors to bring the people to the polls. These days, it is more respectable to buy votes wholesale than retail. Retail vote-buying is bribery, but wholesale vote-buying is commonly accepted in the name of interest group politics.

The following example lies somewhere between the two: In the state of Washington a few years ago, casino promoters had a ballot measure seeking public approval of casino gambling. The measure

---

[8] I draw in this section on Sandel, "Votes for Sale," *New Republic,* November 18, 1996, p. 25.

[9] See William L. Riordon, *Plunkitt of Tammany Hall* (New York: E. P. Dutton & Co., 1963), p. 76.

provided that, if the referendum passed, ten percent of the profits from the casinos would be paid to those who voted in the election.[10] Was this a bribe, or was it a legitimate instance of interest group politics? Proponents argued that state governments often receive a portion of casino profits, and for that matter the profits of any industry that operates in a state; the Washington measure simply cut out the middleman and offered the money directly to the people.

Candidates' campaign promises often work in a similar way. In the early eighties, the U.S. Supreme Court heard a case involving a candidate for county commissioner in Kentucky. The candidate had promised that, if he were elected, he would lower the salary of his office. His opponent charged that this pledge violated a state law barring candidates from offering constituents a financial inducement for their vote.[11]

The Supreme Court rejected the challenge. It ruled that the promised salary reduction did not constitute a bribe. Why not? The reasoning of the court displays the moral confusion at the heart of the politics of self-interest. Justice William Brennan wrote the opinion. A state "may surely prohibit a candidate from buying votes," he sated. "No body politic worthy of being called a democracy entrusts the selection of leaders to a process of auction or barter." Brennan then asserted but did not defend a sharp distinction between buying votes and appealing to voters' self-interest. Our "tradition of political pluralism" assumes "voters will pursue their individual good through the political process," he wrote. Personal benefit "has always been, and remains, a reputable basis upon which to cast one's ballot."[12]

But what is the moral difference between a politician who buys

---

[10] Timothy Egan, "Hedging Bets on Democracy, Casinos Offer Cash to Voters," *New York Times,* August 18, 1995, pp. A1, B7.

[11] *Brown v. Hartlage,* 456 U.S. 45 (1982).

[12] Ibid., pp. 54, 56.

votes and a politician who panders to voters' self-interest? Both offer a financial reward in exchange for a vote. If it is disreputable to
sell my vote to a party boss for $500, why is it reputable for me to
cast my vote for the sake of a $500 tax cut? There are at least three
possible answers to this question, three ways of distinguishing the
bribe from the promise of a tax cut:

(1) It might be argued that the tax cut comes from public
funds, whereas the bribe comes from private funds, or from party
coffers. But this makes the tax cut worse. At least those casinos in
Washington were offering their inducements from private profits,
not from state funds. If voters must be paid off, isn't it better that
it be done with private money than with taxpayer dollars?

(2) Perhaps the difference is that a campaign promise may not
be kept, and so will exert a lesser influence on voters than an outright bribe. But this suggests, perversely, that the moral superiority of the campaign promise consists in the fact that the politician
who makes it cannot be relied upon to keep his or her word. In any
case, if voters are skeptical that the promise will be kept, they can
simply assign it a discounted value that reflects their degree of un-
certainty. The promise of a $500 tax cut with a fifty percent chance
of being enacted would be worth $250. But this would not make
it any more justifiable.

(3) Or maybe the difference is that a campaign promise is public and available to everyone, while a bribe is secret and offered
only to certain people. But many campaign promises are also tar-
geted at particular groups or have highly differential effects. In
any case, if bribes are wrong just because they are offered to some
and not to others, then why not universalize them? If votes could
be bought and sold openly, if there were an open market in votes,
then the secrecy would fall away, and everyone would be free to sell
at the going rate. The $800 million that Bill Clinton and Robert
Dole squandered on bumper stickers and attack ads could go directly to the people.

The reason that none of these distinctions succeeds is that they share the mistaken view that the purpose of democracy is to aggregate people's interests and preferences and translate them into policy. According to this theory, citizens are consumers, and politics is economics by other means. If this theory of democracy is right, then there is no good reason to prohibit the buying and selling of votes. Our reluctance to treat votes as commodities should lead us to question the politics of self-interest so familiar in our time. It should also lead us to acknowledge and affirm the republican ideals implicit but occluded in contemporary democratic practice.

5. THE GAP BETWEEN RICH AND POOR

The third example has to do with a condition that increasingly afflicts public life in a great many Western democracies, including the United States. It is a condition that partly reflects and partly deepens the tendency toward thinking of politics in market terms. The condition is the growing gap between rich and poor. In the 1990s, the gap between rich and poor in the United States has approached levels unknown since the 1920s. From 1979 to 1996, the bottom 40 percent of the population experienced a net loss in household income, while the top 5 percent gained almost 50 percent.[13]

The distribution of wealth also displays increasing inequality. In 1992, the richest 1 percent of the American population owned 42 percent of total private wealth, up from 34 percent a decade earlier, more than twice the concentration of wealth in Britain.[14]

[13] Richard B. Freeman, "Unequal Incomes," *Harvard Magazine* (January–February 1998): 64.

[14] David R. Francis, "New Figures Show Wider Gap between Rich and Poor," *Christian Science Monitor,* April 21, 1995, p. 1, citing a study by economist Edward N. Wolff. See also Edward N. Wolff, *Top Heavy* (New York: Twentieth Century Fund Press, 1995).

Someone recently calculated that the total wealth of the entire bottom 40 percent of the American population equals the wealth of one man, Bill Gates—over $40 billion.

What, if anything, is wrong with the growing gap between rich and poor? The answers to this question illustrate the different moral concerns lying behind the two objections to commodification. The argument from coercion, which derives from consent-based theories of politics, views the problem as one of distributive justice. From this point of view, too much inequality in the basic structure of society undermines the fairness of agreements people make—to undertake certain jobs, for example, at a given wage. In a sharply unequal society, people are not truly free to choose and pursue their values and ends.

But there is another objection to the growing gap between rich and poor. This objection, an instance of the argument from corruption, draws on the republican conception of freedom. The republican tradition teaches that severe inequality undermines freedom by corrupting the character of both rich and poor and destroying the commonality necessary to self-government.[15] The argument goes back to Aristotle. He held that persons of moderate means make the best citizens. The rich, distracted by luxury and prone to ambition, are unwilling to obey, while the poor, shackled by necessity and prone to envy, are ill suited to rule. A society of extremes "lacks the spirit of friendship" self-government requires. "Community depends on friendship," he wrote, "and when there is enmity instead of friendship, men will not even share the same path."[16] Rousseau argued, on similar grounds, that no citizen should "be wealthy enough to buy another, and none poor enough to be forced to sell himself." A

[15]   I draw in this discussion on Sandel, *Democracy's Discontent*, pp. 330–32.

[16]   Aristotle, *The Politics*, trans. and ed. Ernest Barker, book 4, ch. 11 (1295b) (London: Oxford University Press, 1946), pp. 180–82.

democratic state should "allow neither rich men nor beggars," for these two estates "are equally fatal to the common good."[17]

The argument from corruption directs our attention to the civic consequences of the gap between rich and poor so pronounced in our time. From the standpoint of the republican conception of citizenship, the danger is this: The new inequality does not simply prevent the poor from sharing in the fruits of consumption and choosing their ends for themselves; it also leads rich and poor to live increasingly separate ways of life. As Robert Reich has pointed out, affluent professionals gradually secede from public life into "homogeneous enclaves," where they have little contact with those less fortunate than themselves.[18] The children of the prosperous enroll in private schools, or relatively homogeneous suburban schools, leaving urban public schools to the poor. Public institutions cease to gather people together across class and race and instead become places for the poor, who have no alternative. As municipal services decline in urban areas, residents and businesses in upscale districts insulate themselves from these effects. They hire private garbage collectors, street cleaners, and private police protection unavailable to the city as a whole.

The commodification of policing offers a dramatic instance of the trend toward privatization. By 1990, the U.S. Labor Department found that, for the first time, more Americans were employed as private security officers than as public police officers.[19] The *Economist* reports that Americans now spend about $40 billion a year on public police, and $90 billion a year on private security services. In Britain, the number of private guards has grown from about 80,000 in 1971 to 300,000 today, about twice the number

[17] Rousseau, *Social Contract,* book 2, ch. 11, p. 225.

[18] Robert B. Reich, *The Work of Nations* (New York: Alfred A. Knopf, 1991), pp. 249–315.

[19] Ibid., p. 269.

of public police officers. Similar proportions obtain in Canada and Australia.[20]

On the republican conception of citizenship, the public realm is not only a place of common provision but also a setting for civic education. The public character of the common school, for example, consists not only in its financing but also in its teaching. Ideally, at least, it is a place where children of all classes can mix and learn the habits of democratic citizenship. Even municipal parks and playgrounds were once seen in this way—not only as places of recreation but also as sites for the promotion of civic identity and community. Today, even children's recreation is subject to the relentless forces of privatization and commodification. Instead of investing in public parks, parents can now make use of franchised "pay-per-use" playgrounds. For $4.95 per hour, they can take their children to private play centers in suburban shopping malls. "Playgrounds are dirty," said the owner of one such firm. "We're indoors; we're padded; parents can feel that their child is safe."[21]

Growing inequality is a problem from the standpoint of fairness, as theories of distributive justice explain. But it also does damage to the sense in which democratic citizens share a common life. This damage, this loss, is best captured by the argument from corruption. Here is a case where shifting the terms of philosophical argument may suggest new political possibilities. A politics that emphasizes the civic consequences of inequality may hold greater promise of inspiring the reconstruction of class-mixing public institutions than a politics that focuses on individual choice.

My argument in these lectures has been directed primarily against those who think that freedom consists in the voluntary

---

[20] "Policing for Profit: Welcome to the New World of Private Security," *Economist*, April 19, 1997, p. 21.

[21] Elizabeth Rudolph, *Time*, November 4, 1991, p. 86. See also Mickey Kaus, *The End of Equality* (New York: Basic Books, 1992), p. 56.

exchanges people make in a market economy, regardless of the background conditions that prevail. Libertarian philosophers and political theorists, rational choice economists, and adherents of the "law and economics" movement are the most obvious targets of my investigation. Also implicated, however, are a group of unindicted co-conspirators. These are the liberal consent theorists who think that the commodification and privatization of public life can be addressed simply by adjusting the background conditions within which markets operate. According to the co-conspirators, there is nothing wrong with commodification that fair terms of social cooperation cannot cure; if only society were arranged so that people's choices to buy and sell things were truly voluntary, rather than tainted by unfair bargaining conditions, the objection to commodification would fall away. What that argument misses are the dimensions of life that lie beyond consent, in the moral and civic goods that markets do not honor and money cannot buy.

Revealing Nature amidst Multiple Cultures:

A Discourse with Ancient Greeks

WALTER BURKERT

The Tanner Lectures on Human Values

Delivered at

University of Michigan
October 30 and 31, 1998

WALTER BURKERT is professor of classics emeritus at the University of Zurich. He studied classics, history, and philosophy at the universities of Erlangen and Munich, and received a Ph.D. from the University of Erlangen. He was a junior fellow at the Center for Hellenic Studies, and has been a visiting professor at Harvard, UCLA, and the University of California at Berkeley. He is a member of the Berlin Academy of Sciences, a corresponding fellow of the British Academy, and a foreign member of the American Philosophical Society and the American Academy of Sciences. In addition to his numerous publications in German many of his books have appeared in English, including *Creation of the Sacred* (1996), *Ancient Mystery Cults* (1987), *Greek Religion* (1985), and *Structure and History in Greek Mythology and Ritual* (1979).

A paradox of present times is the growing unpopularity of science amidst its overwhelming triumph. Thousands of citizens can be mobilized at any time, at least in Europe, against nuclear industry, against chemistry, and against genetic engineering, the very fields in which science has made its greatest advance in this century. What is especially disquieting about these conflicts is that they apparently cannot be settled by rational discussion of facts. Moral, yet irrational, impulses motivate aggression, alarmed by suspicion of hidden interests of money and power. The old idea that science is revealing facts of nature is lost in the turmoil.[1]

Parallel, I find, is the established tendency to stigmatize the concept of nature in social sciences. "There is no human nature apart from culture." "Humanity is as various in its essence as it is in its expression."[2] In the midst of mass communication and mass mobility, culture is found to speak with many voices, with many souls, as it were. Fixed standards are waning away within the multicultural conglomerate of the global village. No wonder even science has been declared a social construct.[3]

As cultural unanimity has been lost, cultural tradition is under attack, especially the one that has been dominant so long, our so-called Western tradition. Hostility from outside is met by bad conscience from inside. In the United States the accusations against dead white males have gained prominence, challenging "European cultural arrogance," which in turn is said to be based

---

[1] Bibliography is limited in this essay to a few basic references and some indications *exempli gratia.* For an apology of science on the background of modernist disputes, see R. G. Newton, *The Truth of Science: Physical Theories and Reality* (Cambridge, Mass., 1997).

[2] C. Geertz, *The Interpretation of Cultures,* (New York, 1973), pp. 35f.; cf. W. Burkert, *Creation of the Sacred: The Truth of Science* (Cambridge, Mass., 1996), pp. 1–4.

[3] Cf. Newton, pp. 23–44; Th. Nagel, "The Sleep of Reason," *New Republic,* October 12, 1998, pp. 32–38.

on ancient cultures of conceit.[4] Europe is hit by similar problems in a different key, as it is more the proximity of Islam than the thrust from Africa that is being felt.

What has been affected most of all amidst such controversies is the idea of progress.[5] Even history of science nowadays hesitates to retell the great story of the linear ascending progress of science, society, and culture; one rather asks for "contextualization" of theories and theses. The "change of paradigms" has become a key word to characterize the ruptures and inconsistencies of the routes taken by science.[6] The idea of objective truth is becoming an endangered species as it were, all the more in social sciences and *Geisteswissenschaften*. And yet we should acknowledge that in science at least there are not just fads and fashions to change paradigms, not just social games of power and influence: Something exists to prove or disprove statements and theories in general and in particular, and it is in relation to such criteria that science has been on the winning side, including its practical branch, technology. This success is not to be held against science, as if it were the result of arrogance and power; it is the very mark of its legitimacy. There has been an evolution toward increasing "fitness" of theories, fitness in relation to something we cannot but call "reality" or "nature."

The orientation of science toward "nature" or "reality" does not mean permanent possession of stabilized truth, but ongoing approximation. Progress of science has meant evolution of the mind too. Models have been constructed in unforeseeable ways, revealing unexpected features of reality, such as the wave-particle duality or the non-Euclidean geometry of the universe. Our imagination, trained by the continuous natural evolution, has to be trained

[4] See the overview of C. Stray, *Journal of Hellenic Studies* 117 (1997): 229–31, referring especially to M. Bernal, *Black Athena* (London, 1987); the quotation is from Bernal, p. 73. See also B. Knox, *The Oldest Dead White European Males and Other Reflections on the Classics* (New York, 1993).

[5] Cf. A. Burgen, P. McLaughlin, and J. Mittelstra, eds., *The Idea of Progress* (Berlin, 1997).

[6] Th. S. Kuhn, *The Structure of Scientific Revolutions,* 2d ed. (Chicago, 1970).

afresh. Traditional prejudice may halt progress for centuries, but finally has to yield to factual refutation. Heavenly bodies do not move in perfect circles, as platonizing astronomers had held for about 2,000 years; even if Galileo Galilei still refused to be convinced by Johannes Kepler's ellipses, the postulate had to be given up in the end.

Advance means change, and change is dangerous for the homoeostatic system we call life. Ruptures in the social system and corresponding anxieties will often be the consequence of progress. This is just "natural." Yet if the relation of science to natural reality should be lost from view, to be replaced by social interactions made absolute, this would be more than strange. It is true we are living in a social world; amidst infinitely multiple impulses of social dynamics, pressures, obligations, and evasions, we are forced to play social games with changing rules incessantly. It has been shown that nonhuman primates are using practically the whole of their intelligence for their social games. Why should it be different with humans? We are caught in the webs of our social world. In a certain way religion has succeeded in providing some openings of the closed system by suggesting the prospect of some nonempirical x to solve or to alleviate the paradoxes of existence,[7] at the cost of creating further dependence on nonobvious authorities. In another form science is proposing a theoretical world, independent of social differences, games, and pressures, to be acknowledged as what is just the case. Whether we do need this is not clear to everybody. The proposition, however, originated in ancient Greece.

Lost unanimity in contemporary culture has radically questioned traditional "humanism" too, which claimed that our specific "Western" tradition was implementing mankind's progress toward an ideal of "humanity." Thus the comforting concept of antiquity as the cradle of our culture and the starting point of such

---

[7] Cf. Burkert, *Creation of the Sacred,* pp. 26f.

progress has become controversial. If the Greeks are the oldest, they should be the deadest of those "white males." And yet, as we cannot and should not abandon the continuity of our own culture, the faint and distant voices of ancient Greeks may hold some message about our own position. The ancient world does present some simpler models for more complicated later developments, with the advantage of a more comprehensive perspective. The memories of antiquity may show the route that has been taken, the detours, the accidents, and the steps of success.

The Greek heritage, as is well known, has worked its compelling spell in at least three different parts of our culture, in art, in poetry, and in the compartment shared by science and philosophy. It is with this part that I shall take issue here. I would suggest that the crisis of science, the crisis of "nature," and the crisis of tradition are interconnected.

Traditionally the "great story" of ancient Greece has been a hymn to progress, progress both toward rationality and toward humanity; the two appeared connected in their contrast to brute primitivity. The slogan had been the momentous step from "Mythos to Logos,"[8] from fantastic tales about gods and the heroic past to a reasonable account of permanent nature, which is fundamental for "modern" consciousness. We are less secure today about the essence of such progress. The traditional praise of Greece has proved to be flawed, at least on three accounts:

(1) The originality of the "Greek miracle" is crumbling, as the older civilizations of the Near East have become better known. There are strata of high civilization that reach far beyond the pageant of Greece.[9]

(2) The focus of interest has shifted from "classical" to

---

[8] This is the programmatic title of a less interesting book by W. Nestle, *Vom Mythos zum Logos,* 2d ed. (Stuttgart, 1942).

[9] See W. Burkert, *The Orientalizing Revolution* (Cambridge, Mass., 1993); M. L. West, *The East Face of Helicon* (Oxford, 1996).

"wild."[10] That has rekindled a special interest in myth, be it nostalgic or critical; this has ousted the concept of "primitive mentality." Myth is no longer viewed as an inferior genre, but as a central and persistent phenomenon of culture. This also means that the superiority of *logos* is becoming less clear.

(3) The "rationality" of the Greek achievement has been found questionable;[11] the *logos* claimed by Greeks, the "reasonable account" of Greek philosophy and science, can be criticized for various kinds of prejudice and blunder, within a society dominated by machos and slaveholders. Modern doubts about rationality find their reflection in the ancient evidence and cast their shadow on the rising sun of the Greek miracle.

Take as an example the book on the "Sacred Disease," attributed to Hippocrates, a doctor of the fifth century B.C. This is a polemical treatise on epilepsy, which fervently advocates a "natural" explication of this illness, with vigorous polemics against the traditional characterization as a "sacred disease," to be tackled by religious rituals. This is enlightenment versus superstition, we are prone to judge: Epilepsy, the author writes, is not at all "sacred" but "has its nature and its cause"; it is a natural phenomenon. So far we acclaim the birth of natural science as the foundation of medicine. But when the author goes on to set out his own explanation, which is that phlegm should enter blood vessels and thus cause the convulsive attacks of epilepsy, this is so arbitrary, so contrafactual, nay ridiculous that "science" is not an applicable qualification. The consequences from this theory for treatment would be zero, if not detrimental; a traditional "purifier" or witch doctor, we imagine, might easily come up with better results. So where is

---

[10] The keyword comes from C. Lévi-Strauss, *La pensée sauvage* (Paris, 1962); see also R. G. Hamerton-Kelly, ed., *Violent Origins* (Stanford, 1987), pp. 149–76.

[11] See especially G. E. R. Lloyd, *Magic, Reason, and Experience* (Cambridge, 1979, and *The Revolutions of Wisdom* (Berkeley, 1987); R. Buxton, ed., *From Myth to Reason?* (Oxford, 1999).

the progress, but for the arrogance of polemics? This is not new knowledge, but rather a new kind of rhetoric, Geoffrey Lloyd has stated.[12] This new rhetoric indeed is contemporary with the political and judicial rhetoric that arose with emerging "democracy" just then. We see the social context in the evolution of media; we fail to see the triumph of science. We may still acknowledge that the author is dealing with a problem of excessive complication, which even today, after all the undeniable progress of brain specialists with most sophisticated equipment, lacks definite explanation. It is important to state that the interaction of phlegm and blood is a phenomenon that should be generally accessible, and refutable, whereas the reference to gods shifts the explanation "toward the obscure," as already Herodotus (2,23) would formulate. The cry of triumph was premature; but the route toward "nature" was promising.

It is easy to adduce examples of less controversial progress at the same epoch, "classical" discoveries from the crucial fifth century B.C., new chapters indeed of emerging natural science. A simple one is the statement that the moon shines by reflected light, light that comes from the sun. You can realize this if only you care to observe the moon regularly and realize how a globe's surface is lit by light from the side. It is still detracting from the charms of moonlight and flatly contradicts the Greek name *"Selene,"* which means the "shining torch" of night.

One step further is the explanation of the moon's eclipses as produced by the shadow of the earth in the sky. This demands some exertion of imagination to understand the interrelation of what is below with what is above the horizon: the sun standing somewhere beneath, opposite the full moon in the sky . . . Both theses, reflection and eclipse, were findings of Anaxagoras, about 450 B.C. "A view of hidden things [comes by] the things that ap-

[12] Lloyd, *Magic,* pp. 24–27, 86–98.

pear," Anaxagoras said.[13] Note that the sun's eclipse is easier to understand, though it is a much rarer phenomenon: You can recognize the moon covering the sun's face; this discovery is attributed to Thales, back in the sixth century.[14]

Let us note: These are discoveries of natural facts, explanations that are simply true, even if they were not accepted by everyone at the time, and some dissent was to remain for centuries. Statements of this kind are not dependent on personal or social issues. Of course there were conflicts, conflict with the traditional conviction that an eclipse is a "sign" that has some "meaning" for king and country, conflict with the seers whose prestige and livelihood depended on their competence to interpret such signs and to direct appropriate religious rituals. One could disregard the discovery of Anaxagoras, as general Nikias did to his doom at the siege of Syracuse, when he relied on the purported sign of the eclipse of August 27, 413 B.C., and led his army into catastrophe.[15] Still Anaxagoras's findings were and remained true; they could be learned and verified afresh by subsequent generations: This is the case. Hélas, it no longer signifies anything; the theoretical world disregards the interests of our social world.

More radical is the thesis that the earth is a globe. Nowadays we can see a satellite's view of our spherical earth every night on TV. We shall still have some difficulty imagining that right down here, at Ann Arbor, is the Indian Ocean some 600 miles west of Australia, where ships are moving upside down. We do not know for certain who was the first to pronounce the thesis of the spherical earth in the fifth century; Plato, in the fourth century, knew about it, and Aristotle had proofs both from theory and from

---

[13] H. Diels and W. Kranz, *Die Fragmente der Vorsokratiker,* 6th ed. (Berlin, 1952), 59 B 21a (henceforth DK).

[14] See W. Burkert, "Heraclitus and the Moon: The New Fragments in *P. Oxy.* 3710," *Illinois Classical Studies* 18 (1993): 49–55.

[15] Thucydides 7,50,4.

observation;[16] he knew about an attempt at measurement—it was about 75 percent too large,[17] but still remarkably correct as to the order of size. Eratosthenes, 150 years after Aristotle, had the "correct" number; Christopher Columbus, following Ptolemy, chose a smaller number, better suited to strengthen his own optimism. Already Aristotle had written that there should be one ocean stretching from Gibraltar to India. One proof for the sphericity of the earth came right from the moon's eclipse: If it is the earth's shadow that is seen in the eclipse, it always appears circular, whether the full moon is high in the sky or just at the horizon; it would be different if the earth were a flat disk. More persuasive was the change of height of the polar star, as one went south or north.[18] But remember that for about 2,000 years this insight about the spherical earth could not be proved directly, nor put to any practical use. Ancient ships were not equipped to sail around the globe; this first happened in 1522 of our era. One could discuss the problem of antipodes: some could express their disbelief; intellectuals would accept the proofs. There had been the discovery of a fact that is not obvious in direct experience, to be transmitted, to be learned by future generations—irrespective of personal or social interests.

Yet if Greek cosmologists agreed on the sphericity of the earth, they equally agreed, with negligible exceptions, on the thesis that the earth is immobilized at the center of the universe. There were arguments for this thesis, collected by Ptolemy the astronomer, physical arguments most of all;[19] it needed the new physics to be developed from Galileo to Newton to dispel those arguments and to make the earth circling around the sun a "physical" reality. Yet even the erroneous theory about the earth at rest is different from

---

[16] Cf. W. Burkert, *Lore and Science in Ancient Pythagoreanism* (Cambridge, Mass., 1972), pp. 303–6; Aristotle, *De caelo* 2,14, esp. 197b23ff.: arguments "through that which appears to the senses."

[17] 400,000 *stadia* = ca. 72,000 km circumference.

[18] Aristotle, *De caelo* 197b30.

[19] Ptolemy, *Syntaxis* 1,7.

the pronouncement that Earth is the Mother of humans, or of gods and humans, or of the local polis. This is rhetorically effective, even "existentially" relevant, as it may justify patriotic war and heroic death; this is the power of myth, as against any scientific hypothesis.

It is only our present state of knowledge that makes the distinction between discoveries such as the earth's sphericity and errors such as the earth's immobility. Both assumptions had been equally persuasive, well argued, and persistent in earlier epochs. There has been progress, but it appears only in retrospect. There is no criterium within the actual *status quo* to distinguish correct from wrong theories; there is no reliable indication where doors may open for future progress.

The discovery or rather the program of Greeks, of certain Greeks in their grand century, was still the revelation of independent and persistent reality, to be made a subject of intelligent discourse. It is the very concept of "nature" that has thus been created. The Greek word is *physis,* translated as *natura* by the Romans. Heraclitus, about 500 B.C., was the first to use the word in a prominent way. *Physis,* by etymology, is a form of "being"—the verbal root is identical with English "be"; it mainly meant the growth of plants in Greek. "Nature likes to hide," one of the most quoted sayings of Heraclitus,[20] refers precisely to this: Plants grow in secrecy; if you try to "see" this, digging up roots or unfolding buds, you will destroy the plant. Growth occurs on its own, undisturbed, but according to a predetermined course that repeats itself again and again: *Physis* is the opposite of manipulation. In contrast to all those conscious efforts of people—their decrees, conventions, actions, coercions—there is a basic department of reality that keeps to its course and makes sense by doing so, that develops by its own intrinsic laws, and that sustains life and ourselves. You may observe it with discretion; you cannot influence it

[20] DK 22 B 123.

directly, though you can hinder or destroy it. And you can put its essentials into speech, you can give an account, *logos,* you can show by *logos* what is the fact.[21] This is the *condicio sine qua non* of discoveries, of statements that will just be true: The world of nature is independent from the social world, though it forms a basis even for that. It is represented in all phenomena that we have come to call biological, but also in the greater frame of the universe, which appears to exhibit some "order," *kosmos,* to put it in Greek. This concept too goes back to Heraclitus.[22]

The contrasting concept was termed *nomos* by the Greeks, meaning "law" in the sense of "convention" or "custom": This refers to the inescapable integration of every person into the thrust and the limitations of traditional values and commandments. Such rules, *nomoi,* are dominant though limited in scope.[23] They make persons differ in language, customs, and character. Thus *nomos* approaches our concept of "culture." Theoretical descriptions of "society" and its functioning have occurred since the fifth century, in Protagoras, in Thucydides, and of course in Plato.[24] *Nomos* seemed necessary to counteract egoistic interests and unlimited private profit; but one could argue that there were so many different variants of *nomos* that none could be obligatory in general. This is graphically illustrated in the work of Herodotus, who is particularly concerned about the diversity of religious belief and practice. He approvingly hints at tendencies to find the divine in *physis,* the universe and its phenomena, such as the sky and the sun.[25] A free and disinterested view will keep hold of the reality of *physis.*

[21] Heraclitus, *DK* 22 B 1: "[I am] distinguishing each thing according to *physis* and declaring how it is."

[22] See J. Kerchensteiner, *Kosmos* (Munich, 1962).

[23] See F. Heinimann, *Nomos und Physis* (Basel, 1945).

[24] Important texts are Plato, *Protagoras* 323a–28d; Pericles' speech in Thukydides 2,34–46; Plato, *Republic.*

[25] Cf. W. Burkert, "Herodot als Historiker fremder Religionen," in *Hérodote et les peuples non grecs: Entretiens sur l'antiquité classique XXXV* (Vandoeuvres/Geneva, 1990), pp. 1–32.

Antiphon, a so-called sophist of the fifth century, impressively denounces *nomos:* [26] "In this we are made barbarians, the ones against the others; for by nature we are all organized in a similar way in all respects, barbarians and Greeks. You can observe the necessities of what is organized by nature in all humans, as it is provided by the same faculties for all of them; and in this there is neither barbarian nor Greek discriminated among us: We all breathe into the air by mouth and nostrils, we laugh when we are glad in our mind, and we weep when we are feeling distress; and by hearing we accept the sounds, and through brightness we see with our eyesight; and we are active with our hands, and we walk with our feet. . . . " Well, this is just "natural," this is simple and evident, and still it must give pause to all forms of xenophobia: Note how humans weep and laugh. The distinction between Greeks and barbarians had long been popular: We, the Greeks, are the center and peak of humanity, with all the others around, who are incomprehensible and inferior. Antiphon, with a clever language game, inverts this: We ourselves are made barbarians by such discrimination, in contrast to nature, which determines what is necessary, and which does not make such difference. The necessities of nature are not to be discussed or negotiated: How to breathe, to eat, to hear, and to see, these are just facts of nature, constituting the community of humankind.

I like even better a scene of Aristophanic comedy. In Aristophanes' *Clouds,* the comic hero Strepsiades, refined by the teachings of Socrates, is approached by his banker, who wishes to collect the interest for a loan he has made to Strepsiades. Strepsiades, however, tells the banker: "Look [at the sea]: Do you have the impression that the sea is more now than before?" No, the banker says, "it would not even be just for the sea to be more." "Behold,"

[26] DK 87 B 44. Wendy Doniger reminds me how close this is to the speech of Shylock in Shakespeare's *Merchant of Venice,* III 1: "Hath not a Jew eyes? hath not a Jew hands . . . if you prick us, do we not bleed? if you tickle us, do we not laugh? . . . " Note that the Antiphon text was published from a papyrus in 1916: the coincidence with Shakespeare is due to nature, not to literature.

Strepsiades says, "the sea does not become any more, even if the rivers are flowing into it. But you postulate that your money should become more and more [every day]?"[27] It would be good to remember this justice of nature when looking at the Dow Jones Index. Nature is homoeostatic; so is life. Data of "nature' are outside social and economic strife. The discovery of "nature" presents a basis for insight and for sensible discourse, free from the snares of greed and profit, the limitations of which become apparent.

The discovery of "nature" in the fifth century was felt to be a kind of triumph and a source of joy. Once more we meet Anaxagoras. What is the sense of human life? he was asked; "to look at the sky, the stars, the moon, the sun," was his response.[28] The Greek word for such a "look," a comprehensive, interested, yet noncommittal look, is *theoria*. With slight changes of meaning, this word *theoria* has remained another keyword in the wake of ancient Greeks: "theory." Primarily *theoria* meant to observe a festival. At Olympia, for example, there are the toiling athletes, there are businessmen making money, but there are also those who just enjoy the free look at what is going on.[29] A play of Euripides praised the happiness of the man who manages "to see the not-aging order [*kosmos*] of immortal *physis*"; such a man will definitely be above disreputable money affairs.[30] For Aristotle, too, a "theoretical life" seems to be the most perfect form of human existence.[31] So this is, I suggest, a decisive discovery of classical Greece, the proposition of a "theoretical world," which has become the "world of science,"

----

[27] Aristophanes, *Clouds* 1290–95. This banker unhesitatingly discovers social values in nature: the "justice" of the sea.

[28] Iamblichus, *Protrepticus* 51,11 = Aristotle, *Protrepticus* Fr. 11 Ross, and *Eudemian Ethics* 1216a11 = DK 59 A 30.

[29] This simile is attributed to Pythagoras by Heraclides Ponticus, Fr. 88 Wehrli; cf. W. Burkert, "Platon oder Pythagoras? Zum Ursprung des Wortes 'Philosophie,'" *Hermes* 88 (1960): 159–77.

[30] Euripides fr. 910 (= DK 59 A 30).

[31] Aristotle, *Nicomachean Ethics* 10; cf. W. Jaeger, "Über Ursprung und Kreislauf des philosophischen Lebensidals," in *Scripta Minora I* (Rome, 1960), pp. 347–93.

independent yet understandable; and the satisfaction of understanding can become an overwhelming personal joy. The happiness of a contemplative life is well known, and praised, in other
forms in other civilizations; today most will think of India in such
a context. The peculiarity of the Greek program is the view at ver-
ifiable reality, a *kosmos* of *physis*.

If this was inaugurated by Greeks in the fifth century, the question of the historical and social context comes back, including the
problem of an "Oriental" background. Classical antiquity was not
a new beginning; nor was Homer the first poet rising from the un-
contaminated dawn of humanity. The Greeks were at the Western
fringe of Asiatic high cultures.[32] As the direct knowledge about
the Ancient Near East has been regained in the last two centuries,
we know about Egypt, Mesopotamia, Syria/Palestine, and Asia
Minor as high cultures with writing, with literature, with a high
level of sophistication, of discussions and reflections, including
forms of science and mathematics, long before the Greeks.

Take a cuneiform tablet from the house of a family of conjurer-
priests at Assur in Iraq, about 650 B.C.[33] This text, as a comment
on older myths and rituals, describes how the god Marduk constructed the universe: "On the Upper Earth he established the
souls of men, in the center; on Middle Earth, he made sit his father
Ea, in the center" (Ea is the god of subterranean water); "In Nether
Earth, he included the 600 gods of the dead [*Annunaki*], in the
center." So far this states three stories of our world, the earth on
which we live, the water below—just as Thales had the earth rest-
ing on water—and farther down, at the lowest register, the Neth-
erworld with its appropriate gods. Heaven, by correspondence, has
three registers too: The highest story belongs to the God Heaven

[32] See n. 9 above.

[33] A. Livingstone, *Mystical and Mythological Explanatory Works of Assyrian and Babylonian Scholars* (Oxford, 1986), pp. 78–91; cf. W. Burkert, "Orientalische und griechis-
che Weltmodelle von Assur bis Anaximandros," *Wiener Studien* 107/8 (ΣΦΑΙΡΟΣ,
Festschrift Hans Schwabl, 1994/95): 179–86.

himself, called Anu with his Sumerian name, together with 300 heavenly gods; Middle Heaven, made of resplendent stone, is the throne of Enlil, the active ruling god; the lowest story, made of jasper-stone, darker but transparent, is the place of constellations: Marduk "designed the constellations of the gods on that."[34] The text does not bother to explain why we see alternately the resplendent sky at day and the jasper-sky with stars at night.

Compare what Anaximandros from Miletus wrote about one hundred years later: There are three skies, formed from the Infinite—Anaximander indeed uses a plural, "skies" (οὐρανοί), which is quite unusual in Greek.[35] These "skies" take the form of wheels circling around the earth, while the earth, a column-drum in shape, is suspended at the center. The wheels, from fiery openings inside, produce the stars, the moon, and the sun, at growing distances. If the stars belong to the smallest wheel, this agrees with the constellations in the lowest register according to the Assur system. Even closer is the agreement with Iranian religious lore: In Iranian texts, a sequence of "steps" marks the ascent of the soul after death toward the god Ahura Mazda, via Stars, Moon, and Sun, in this sequence, up to the "endless lights." For Anaximander, there is "the Infinite"; it is "the Divine" that encompasses and steers everything. But one should equally take account of the Hebrew Bible: A construction of four heavenly wheels is found in Ezekiel (1:15–18), when he describes his vision of the throne of god, the *merkavah;* the four wheels are constructed "like a wheel inside a wheel . . . and the rims of the wheels were full of eyes all round." This is uncannily close to Anaximander's cosmos, though dated about fifty years

[34] A very similar formulation occurs in the Platonic *Epinomis,* 983Af.; cf. P. Kingsley, *Ancient Philosophy, Mystery, and Magic: Empedocles and Pythagorean Tradition* (Oxford, 1995), p. 203.

[35] Anaximandros, DK 12 A 9, A 10, partially misunderstood in later doxography. "Three steps" in Iranian tradition: W. Burkert, "Iranisches bei Anaximandros," *Rhein. Museum* 106 (1963): 97–134.

earlier, while god's resplendent throne recalls Marduk's throne in the earlier text from Assur.[36]

Undoubtedly Anaximander's speculation stands within a context of similar picturesque drawings of the universe, competing with Mesopotamian, Iranian, and Hebrew constructions. What does mark the "progress"? The disappearance of the "underworld," as the earth shrinks to become a column-drum? What is more important, Anaximander does not refer to specific theology, to groups of recognized gods, as the Assyrian priest does—nor was he a member of a priestly family, for all we know, or a prophet such as Ezekiel. He does not speak of the throne of god, be it Enlil, Jahwe, or Ahura Mazda. Babylonian gods such as Anu and Enlil, Igigi and Annunaki, would have been meaningless to him as to his public. But even a Greek pantheon would have been just a local pantheon, one city's pantheon, with limited scope and limited obligations. Anaximander spoke of "the divine" in neutral form, encircling and steering the universe. The ruling power of a religious world has turned into an object within a theoretical world. In the segments of his world Anaximander arranged just the generally known and visible heavenly bodies in a spatial, technical construction, in "wheels," instead of divine categories. This was evidence accessible to others; this should constitute "consensible knowledge."[37] The "wheels" introduce a mathematical element into the model: The earth cannot fall, because it is at the center, at equal distance from all sides. The figures Anaximander gave for heavenly distances are absolutely arbitrary, derived from Hesiod's mythical poem.[38] Anyhow, his construction was wrong, especially as to the sequence

[36] Ezekiel 6; cf. M. L. West, *Early Greek Philosophy and the Orient* (Oxford, 1971), pp. 88ff. Note that the redaction of Genesis 1 and 2 might be about contemporary with Anaximander.

[37] For this concept, see Newton, *Truth of Sciences,* p. 120, referring to J. Ziman, *Reliable Knowledge* (Cambridge, 1978).

[38] Hesiod, *Theogony* 720–25: a nine days' fall from Heaven to earth, the same from earth to Tartaros; hence Anaximander uses multiples of nine.

of heavenly bodies. But that could be corrected, and this was rapidly done: Anaximander's construct was an adequate basis for subsequent emendations. Anaximander has "discovered the account [*logos*] of sizes and distances" in astronomy, as Eudemus, Aristotle's pupil, was to formulate.[39]

To what degree the decisive difference from the Assyrian priest or Ezekiel would have been recognizable for Anaximander's contemporaries is another question. Just then Phercydes of Syros invented a new mythical story in Greek about the universe, as did "Orpheus" in another key.[40] A supreme god to "shake" the universe is heralded by Xenophanes; a *daimon* or goddess recurs in Parmenides to arrange the heavenly circles and to procreate gods; Empedocles has Aphrodite creating our world of living creatures in her workshop.[41] If there was progress in the reduction of religious elements, in keeping clear of pantheons, the step was made reluctantly by the Greeks themselves, and it could be taken back. Aristotle contrasts "those who give an account of nature" with "those who give an account of gods," *physiologoi* with *theologoi*,[42] but his "first philosophy" tends to become "theology," and his own physics culminates in a theological concept, the "unmoved mover" of the universe; Plato introduced the term "craftsman," *demiourgos,* to create the universe, a concept the Christians were eager to take over. It was the subsequent progress of science that fixed Anaximander's status, as against "Orpheus" or Pherecydes; but there was not one line of uninterrupted progress. And yet improvement of unwarranted constructs was possible because there was discussion, not authority, there was a high degree of freedom within the social system, and there was the reference to generally accessible reality that made "consensible knowledge."

[39] Eudemus Fr. 146 Wehrli; cf. Burkert, *Lore and Science,* pp. 308–11.

[40] See H. S. Schibli, *Pherekydes of Syros* (Oxford, 1990); A. Laks and G. W. Most, eds., *Studies on the Derveni Papyrus* (Oxford, 1997).

[41] DK 21 B 25, 28 B 12/13, 31 B 73, 95–98.

[42] Hesiod and his like are *theologoi,* Aristotle *Met.* 1000a9; Empedocles is a *physiologos, Poet.* 1447b19.

History of philosophy is more interested in general principles than in the details of astronomical constructs. A decisive voice in the Greek concert, widely heard in the discourse on nature, was that of Parmenides. His simple thesis that "Being is, not-being is not" seems too abstract to raise emotions; still it was to become a basic tenet of Greek natural philosophy. It is the negative complement of the thesis of Parmenides that makes it a resounding paradox: There is no coming to be or passing away, since there is Being.[43]

There is some "Oriental" background and context for Greek forms of speaking and thinking even here. Already in Akkadian cosmogony we find the three concepts of "becoming" or "creating" (*banû*), "destroying" (*halaqu*), and "being there" (*bashû*) combined into a system; everything is bound to that pattern. In the epic of creation, *Enuma Elish,* the primeval god Anshar is addressed: "You are of wide heart, destiner of destinies; whatever is created or annihilated, exists with you."[44] "Everything" is found to be there within the borderlines of creation and destruction: "To become and to be destroyed, to be and not to be": this is a verse of Parmenides, formulating the same concepts in Greek.[45]

The specialty introduced by Parmenides is to isolate "being" within the tripartite system and to set it in opposition to both "becoming" and "being destroyed." This, in turn, reflects basic categories of the Greek language, the marked contrast of "aspect," the durative versus the punctual aspect. In the case of "being," language presents two roots, *es-* (it is) for the durative, and *phy-* (become), semantically related to *gen-* (generate), for the punctual

---

[43] The huge literature on Parmenides, with many conflicting interpretations, cannot be discussed here. I am especially indebted to E. Tugendhat, "Das Sein und das Nichts," in *Durchblicke: Martin Heidegger zum 80. Geburtstag* (Frankfurt, 1970), pp. 132–61; Ch. Kahn, *The Verb "BE" in Ancient Greek* (Dordrecht, 1973); A. Mourelatos, "Heraclitus, Parmenides, and the Naïve Metaphysics of Things," in *Exegesis and Argument: Studies in Greek Philosophy Presented to G. Vlastos* (Assen, 1973), pp. 16–48.

[44] *Enuma Elish* 2, 65; S. Dalley, *Myths of Mesopotamia* (Oxford, 1989), p. 241.

[45] DK 28 B 8,40.

aspect; in English both verbal roots have been mixed up to form one irregular paradigm, "is" alternating with "be." For Greeks, there is opposition: "if it became, it is not," Parmenides wrote (B 8,20), as if doing an exercise in Greek grammar; there is no *physis,* in the sense of "coming to be," Empedocles agreed.[46] The Indo-european background of Greek is the reason why very similar formulas do appear in Indian speculation. "Not-being cannot arise, being cannot pass away": this comes from the *Bhagavad Gita.*[47]

And this gives the linguistic exercise its special relevance, both in India and with Parmenides: As "being" becomes absolute, there is no birth and there is no death. "Coming to be extinguished, and perishing not to be heard of ": this is the statement of Parmenides.[48] Death does not happen. As reality is pronounced absolute, the reality of death is made to disappear. Should we say that Parmenides is using a pseudo-argument arising from the accidents of Indo-european language to annihilate death?

Yet Parmenides' thesis is about "reality," and it proved successful right at this level. Neoplatonists made Parmenides an idealist; moderns are prone to see him rather as a materialist.[49] His followers at any rate began to explain the natural world with all its changes, the multiple phenomena of coming to be and passing away, through the postulate of uncreated and imperishable constituents. This was argued with varying hypotheses by Anaxagoras, by Empedocles, and by Democritus. Anaxagoras held that "everything" is just there and was there all the time, one thing contained within the other in infinitely small quantums; Empedocles thought he could do with four elements, four "roots" and their "mixture," whereas Democritus went further in abstraction and

---

[46] Empedocles, DK 31 B 8.

[47] *Bhagavad Gita* 2,16 (using the same two roots; interpretation is controversial).

[48] Parmenides, DK 28 B 8,21, inverting expressions like "he perished not to be known, not to be heard of"; *Odyssey* 1,242.

[49] J. Burnet, *Early Greek Philosophy,* 4th ed. (London, 1930), p. 182.

stripped the basic constituents of qualities such as color, in order to derive everything from different geometrical forms of very small, indivisible particles, his "atoms." We need not go into details. Once more it is the following evolution that makes the status of Parmenides—and of Democritus—more than the authentic text of Parmenides' verses that happen to survive. And once more it is a judgment from our state of knowledge that we see the success as well as the shortcomings of, for example, Anaxagoras: It is true that the baby gets everything it needs for growing from its mother's milk, so all that stuff has been contained in the milk before: Anaxagoras was right to state this; but he was wrong to deny that flesh or bones could not arise from different constituents;[50] Empedocles, in turn, suggested a quantitative formula for the constitution of bones, which, of course, was by far too simple.[51] The route to natural science had been envisaged, but for the moment it did not lead very far; the difficulties were much greater than expected.

But the really strange and surprising fact is that the central thesis of Parmenides, the formula of indestructible being beyond birth and death, as taken up by his followers, makes a principle that still dominates our physical worldview: the principle of conservation, conservation of mass on the one side and of energy on the other, as it appeared in the last century, conservation of the duality of mass and energy, as it has become the thesis since Albert Einstein. Nothing can come from just nothing, and nothing can simply disappear—hence our problems with all kinds of refuse that cannot be annihilated; so far Parmenides is simply right.

The Parmenidean postulate is by no means trivial, nor is it evident in a general way. Myth will tell a different story. In the Babylonian *Enuma Elish,* for example, the gods say to Marduk: "Command destruction and creation: it will be so."[52] A king

[50] DK 59 B 10.

[51] DK 31 B 96.

[52] *Enuma Elish* 4,22; Dalley, *Myths,* p. 250.

has the power of "life and death"; at least his power to kill is undisputed. All the more, a god can "command destruction," and it will be so. Christian theology, guided by ancient cosmogonic myth, has taken a similar view; it introduced a god creating from nothing, *ex nihilo,* and also prone to destroy his world in the end. No, Parmenides had protested, even a god cannot work absolute annihilation, nor could he start with nothing. Our understanding of science largely agrees with Parmenides.

But there is more: Parmenides sees "being" in strict relation to speech and cognition. He insists that language is directed toward "being." Language may have, nay language should have, a specific content, or else it would be "nothing": "you say nothing," οὐδὲν λέγεις, is an expression of colloquial Greek to criticize and to put aside what the partner has just said. To speak with sense means "to speak being," τὰ ὄντα λέγειν. This is not "grooming talk,"[53] not speech as a social act, which articulates agreements and disagreements, sympathies and antipathies, supremacy and obedience. There is "objective" speech; it implies cognition. "Not without 'being' (in which it has been made speech) will you find cognition," Parmenides wrote (B 8,35). The intent toward "being" also means toward truth in an absolute sense, beyond personal, social, or political concerns. The revelation pronounced by Parmenides concerns the "well-rounded heart of *Aletheia* [truth]." This contrasts with the "opinions" of normal humans, βροτῶν δόξαι.[54] In fact mortals are not only mistaken in many respects: their intelligence largely consists in hiding their thoughts, emotions, and interests, and thus tricking others. Parmenides insists on the relation of speech to "being." The Parmenidean enquirer has embarked on a lonely road—"far indeed does it lie from the steps of men" (B 1,27)—but the findings can be publicized in a poem that claims truth. A new kind of communicative group

---

[53] A term introduced by D. Morris, *The Naked Ape* (New York, 1967), comparing social "small talk" with monkeys grooming their partners' fur.

[54] DK 28 B 1,29 f; cf. Kahn, *The Verb "BE" in Ancient Greek.*

should form, controlling what they say with regard to "being," free from the others' opinions. Is this discovery or just a postulate? It often fails in reality; and still this is quite a remarkable new form of rhetoric. Some may assume Parmenides received his paradoxical message through a kind of mystical revelation; but in his words there are "ways of enquiry" (ὁδοὶ διζήσιος) and their "signposts." His followers attempt to pursue such a way with varying success.

There is one field where such pursuit hardly fails: mathematics. One may consider Euclidean mathematics the gist of the Greek heritage.[55] Mathematics is a very special form of *logos,* indeed the most successful and stable one, even if mathematics will always remain the option of a minority. It does not depend on authority; nor must it be negotiated between conflicting interests. It is independent from specific cultural patterns, from language, race, or origin. All will agree, once they have decided for consistency. When measuring circles. Westerners and Chinese must end up with the same approximative value for π.

Once more there is an "Oriental" prelude to Greek science. In Mesopotamian astronomy, significant astronomical numbers were recorded and used for prediction of astronomical events. This was developing with important steps precisely in the sixth and fifth centuries.[56] Contacts with Greece, within the common Persian empire, cannot be denied. The concept of the zodiac as the "path of the moon" and the "path of the sun" in the sky, followed by five more planets, and divided into twelve "signs," seems to be one piece of transferable knowledge between East and West at that time.[57] There also was the problem of the inequality of seasons—

[55] See Einstein, as quoted by Newton, *Truth of Science,* p. 9.

[56] See B. L. Van der Waerden, *Die Anfänge der Astronomie* (Groningen, 1966); F. Rochberg-Halton, "Babylonian Horoscopes and Their Sources," *Orientalia* 58 (1989): 102–23.

[57] We know about a sixth-century poem on the zodiac by Kleostratos, DK 6; the first horoscopes in cuneiform are dated to 409 B.C.: Rochberg-Halton, "Babylonian Horoscopes."

summer, in our hemisphere, is a few days longer than winter—
which troubled Greek as well as Babylonian astronomers, down to
the final solution through Kepler's ellipses; the difference was
duly integrated in the Babylonian calculations.

In fact the Babylonians developed quite successful mathematical methods to describe the heavenly phenomena, including the
movements of the planets, methods that work with great precision, though without a three-dimensional cosmic model and also
without formulation of principles, even without demonstration, it
seems.[58] If natural science means the precise description of phenomena with the use of mathematics, the Babylonians are the
inventors. The first Greek attempt at natural science in mathematical form, the planetary system of Eudoxus, which uses the
complicated geometry of homocentric spheres, came in the fourth
century. Thus the Babylonians should get a "first" in natural science. They did not care about a geometrical model, but their figures were precise; theirs might even be called the more modern
position. Eudoxus's system is a spatial construct, visible to the
mind and even constructible as a machine: Ever since the Greeks
we are accustomed to imagining a cosmic machinery, already inti-
mated in Anaximander's "wheels." Eudoxus's system was wrong,
but it was improved soon, leading to Ptolemy's elaborate cosmos,
which became canonical for 1,400 years, to be replaced by the he-
liocentric world machine of Nicolaus Copernicus.

Deductive-demonstrative mathematics in the form of Euclidean geometry seems to have taken its essential form by the fifth
century. We encounter its first elaboration with Hippocrates of
Chios, about 430 B.C.; he was already tackling the frontiers of classical geometry, the problem of cubic roots and the squaring of the

---

[58] For deductive proof as a Greek discovery, see B. L. Van der Waerden, *Science
Awakening* (New York, 1961); qualifications in H. J. Waschkies, *Anfänge der Arthmetik
im Alten Orient und bei den Griechen* (Amsterdam, 1989), esp. pp. 302–26. See also Newton, *Truth of Science*, pp. 137–39.

circle.[59] The "classical" elaboration of geometry, the *Elements* of Euclid, was composed about 300 B.C.

Archimedes—about 220 B.C., when he discovered the formulas for the surface and the volume of the sphere—wrote: "By nature, these properties had existed before for these figures, . . . but it happened that all missed this and nobody realized this."[60] So he experienced the overwhelming joy of discovery of what he called a "natural" fact. Since Archimedes, and thanks to him—though with less joy—every schoolchild is taught these formulas. Progress in mathematical knowledge is undeniable. Archimedes holds that mathematical facts are just there all the time. Moderns may criticize him for underestimating the role of construction in mathematics; he did not envisage non-Euclidean geometry. But there are modern mathematicians who still will say that numbers with their strange properties have been created by God.

I wish to confront the sentence of Archimedes with what Francis Crick wrote about the great achievement of this century's science, the discovery of the genetic code, the structure of the "double helix": "All the time the double helix has been there, and active, and yet we are the first creatures on earth to become aware of its existence."[61] Crick in all probability did not know the text of Archimedes. Still there is the same happiness of discovery, of spelling out and representing in a model what had been there all the time. Such is "nature." Well, we are now beginning to manipulate the double helix, and this creates all sorts of anxieties and controversies. This does not invalidate science; we may respect or even share the feeling of overwhelming wonder at what has been discovered.

[59] The evidence in DK 42. Cf. W. Burkert, "ΣΤΟΙΧΕΙΟΝ: Eine semasiologische Studie," *Philologus* 103 (1959): 167–97.

[60] Archimedes, *De sphaera et cylindro* 1, pp. 2f. Heiberg; Cf. W. Burkert, "Konstruktion und Seinsstruktur: Praxis und Platonismus in der griechischen Mathematik," *Abhandlungen der Braunschweigischen Wissenschaftlichen Gesellschaft* 34 (1982): 125–41.

[61] F. Crick, *What Mad Pursuit* (New York, 1988), p. 62.

In this discourse with ancient Greeks, we have concentrated on the "glorious fifth century," on the so-called Presocratics or rather pre-Platonics. It is true that Plato has made an ambivalent intervention in this perspective. Apparently it was Socrates who, in his protest against Anaxagoras, insisted on reinstalling the social world with its practical values, instead of the world of *theoria*. A poignant criticism was that the "theoretical" view, the ideal of reasonable, disinterested discourse, did not solve any problems of real life. "What is above ourselves is nothing for ourselves," *quod supra nos, nihil ad nos*, "Socratic" moral philosophers held. Plato achieved a momentous synthesis of both "theory" and practical philosophy. Yet granting precedence to the "Good" even above "Truth," he also opened the way to ideological dogmatism and even to "totalitarian" systems.[62] Plato brought enormous advance at the level of argument; he made mathematics a decisive element in the theory of knowledge; yet his daring consequence of developing the metaphysics of mind—mind as the bearer of knowledge, prior to matter, embedded in an immortal soul—this construct of Platonic philosophy is becoming less and less acceptable in our natural worldview. A special synthesis occurred when Christianity adopted Platonism, stressing the independent, responsible "soul" as against the body, which meant freedom from needs and desires, from social constraints and political power, but still obedience to supreme authority, down to "the sacrifice of intelligence," *sacrificium intellectus*.

We are experiencing the breakdown of these postulates and constructs. Several factors, not directly related to each other, are contributing to enforcing the change. I would mention

- Darwin's theory of evolution, refined in contemporary biology, which placed humans in a continuous series with the other forms of life,

[62] This was the accusation of K. Popper, *The Open Society and Its Enemies I: The Spell of Plato* (London, 1945; 4th ed. 1962).

- the spectacular success of molecular physics and chemistry, which analyzes the processes of life in exact and minute details. By consequence, thinking is seen in its corporeal dimension, as "preparation for motion," a process in the brain.
- the presence of the computer, which gives a model of "thinking without mind." This goes together with more and more complex theories of self-organization.

I think we cannot and we should not try to rebuild the old Platonic house for soul and mind. To assume that mind prescribes the forms of reality is no less off course than the Parmenidean thesis that the inherent logic of Indo-european language excludes death. Nostalgic feelings, though, can hardly be eliminated. Should whole libraries of philosophical texts be judged antiquated? Even an obituary on book culture seems to be called for: Books in the Greek style, to be read, to be judged and criticized by the autonomous individual reader, books with their rhetorical and personal appeal, may rapidly become obsolete. In fact literacy started with lists, not with literature, in the ancient Near East; now we are back to accumulating growing series of information, handled by intelligent programs but also subject to fortuitous "attractors" that make dominating trends. We are close to a state when six billion individuals can simultaneously crisscross a jungle of competing and conflicting informations, pursuing their interests without acknowledged guidelines, but for the trivial fact that both financial and sexual interests stand out as dominating attractors—still reflecting nature's design of the basic needs of food and procreation. It seems especially strange how distinctions between "virtual" and "real" seem to disappear; "virtual reality" is the slogan of the day. We are caught within the World Wide Web, while the science of nature has become so complicated that nobody can "know" about it without gross simplifications. And research has become so costly that it is completely dependent on private or public financing, which necessitates all sorts of political and economic strategies to precede and to determine research. Nature goes into hiding again. No wonder the theoretical world of natural science is becoming unpopular, while the social sciences have turned away from "nature" to delight in their own autonomy. The social-economic world, in its virtual expansion, is finally about to englobe the theoretical world.

I hope that in this respect the discourse with ancient Greeks has been illuminating. There remains the fact that we cannot get rid of the "necessities of nature," as Antiphon said, to breathe, to eat, to hear, and to see, that we remain earth-dwellers on one globe from which we cannot escape. And whether we speak of the "universe" or of "nature," we are using Greek names and concepts. Of course, names are not important. But reality makes itself felt. "Nature" as a basic concern, as a power not to be disregarded, has come back with the environmental movement; this entrains vigorous sympathies for all that is "natural." Still the "environmental" perspective remains anthropocentric, nay egocentric: Here we are: the rest is arranged around ourselves in positive or negative relations, "environmental." The theoretical world picture should be different.

There remains the ideal of an intelligent look at realities, and of sensible discourse, of "consensible knowledge." This also means to expect continuing revelations of "nature." Neither these endeavors nor their success are dependent on special varieties of race, gender, or social systems. There remains the experience and the postulate of individual, self-responsible minds, of conscious and independent personality. This finally leads back to a sentence of Plato: "Every soul has seen 'Being,' or else it would not have come into human shape."[63] The chance to catch sight of reality constitutes human dignity. I would call this the legacy of the ancient "theory of nature." I do not think this is just Western cultural arrogance. If the Greek outlook has fertilized European style, if this

---

[63] Plato, *Phaedrus* 249E.

has become world style, it cannot be forced to hide as opposed to different cultural approaches or aspirations. It rather means a chance of freedom versus social and economic pressures. It includes the postulate of free discussion, of free roads toward truth. Pleading, and hoping, for intellectual culture is not advocating the ivory tower as opposed to the street parade; it rather means pleading for an essential section of human rights.

Text and Spirit

GEOFFREY HARTMAN

THE TANNER LECTURES ON HUMAN VALUES

Delivered at

University of Utah
April 13 and 14, 1999

GEOFFREY H. HARTMAN is Sterling Professor Emeritus of English and Comparative Literature and senior research scholar at Yale University. He was educated at Queens College of the City of New York, and received his Ph.D. from Yale University. He is the recipient of fellowships from the Guggenheim Foundation, the National Endowment for the Humanities, and the Woodrow Wilson Center, has been a visiting scholar at numerous universities in the United States, Europe, and Israel, and is a member of the American Academy of Arts and Sciences and the Academy of Literary Studies. Early in his career he produced an impressive body of literary criticism, including *The Unmediated Vision* (1954), *Wordsworth's Poetry, 1787–1814* (1964), *The Fate of Reading* (1975), and *Criticism in the Wilderness* (1980), among others. More recently he has begun to explore the topics of witness and historical memory, and the cultural and political implications of the Holocaust. His books on those subjects include *Bitburg in Moral and Political Perspective* (1986), *Holocaust Remembrance: The Shapes of Memory* (1994), and *The Longest Shadow: In the Aftermath of the Holocaust* (1996).

The face-to-face with the text has replaced the face-to-face with God.

—EDMOND JABÈS[1]

Even a casual observer of the worldly scene, or of news that besieges ears and eyes, and becomes increasingly a confusing talk show with endlessly extemporized sense and nonsense, even you and I, who are that casual observer, cannot fail to notice how often the supernatural turns up as a topic. Let me excerpt a moment close to Christmas 1997. "In Books, It's Boom Time for Spirits," runs a headline of "The Arts" section of the *New York Times* (Tuesday, November 11, 1997, E 1). The very next week, this same section, devoted to Robert Gobert's installation piece in the Los Angeles Museum of Contemporary Art, features a Madonna standing on a drainage grate with a cruciform pipe through her belly, which elicits the curious headline "Religion That's in the Details" (not only entrails) and adds "A Madonna and Drain Pipe Radiate an Earthy Spirituality." The number of best sellers on near-death or out-of-body experiences is well known; spirit raptors proliferate; and the recovered memory syndrome has not only insinuated devastating suspicions about family values but also made stars of obscure people who claim to have lived previous lives as saints, warrior-heroes, and amazonian queens.

Serious scholars too have turned from their literary preoccupations to write, as Harold Bloom has done, on *The American Religion* and, with the approach of the millennium, on omens, angels, avatars, and such. Bloom's survey of Christian and heterodox movements since 1800 envisions the year 2000 as the triumph of an unacknowledged, specifically American religion, "in which . . . something deeper than the soul, the real Me or self or spark is

---

[1] *Le Parcours* (Paris: Gallimard, 1985), 84.

[155]

made to be utterly alone with . . . a free God or God of Freedom"
who loves every American with a personal love. Bloom would like
to stand aloof, but finds he too is part of this scene—as American
as Ralph Waldo Emerson or Walt Whitman. "Religious criticism," he says, "even if it seeks to banish all nostalgia for belief,
still falls into the experience of the spiritual, even as literary criticism cannot avoid the danger of falling into the text."[2] Though
there is nothing new in the antics of hucksters and televangelists,
or meeting the Lord in the air (in a spaceship, no less, according to
Louis Farrakhan), or weeping statues, or miracles on Broadway
(Tony Kushner, *Angels in America*), or the amazing ease with which
both preachers and skinheads claim to have heard the call of God,
it is time to reflect on this bullishness in the spiritual market.

Does the mere approach of the year 2000 act as a magnet? My
initial thought is that there is enough craziness in traditional religion itself, I mean imaginative, poetic craziness, so that this sort of
human circus is unnecessary. At the same time I agree with William Blake that imagination is religion's birth mother, always trying to free its unorthodox offspring, the poets, from the strictures
of positive religion. But then, of course, one remembers a different
aspect of the spiritual impulse, that it is never entirely disinterested: it often breaks through as the compulsive side of those
whose disgust with the human condition—with themselves or
others or politics—becomes intolerable, and who tend to advocate
purgative schemes of reform.[3]

---

[2] My two quotations come from *The American Religion: The Emergence of the Post-
Christian Nation* (New York: Simon & Schuster, 1992), pp. 15, 256–57. See also Bloom's
Omens of Millennium: The Gnosis of Angels, Dreams, and Resurrection (New York: Riverhead
Books, 1996).

[3] I omit entirely, here, the issue of spirituality in politics, except to recall the damage done by the Christian anti-Jewish polemic focusing on the enmity of spirit to the
letter of the (divine) law. Carl Schmitt is not wrong when he writes in *Der Begriff des Poli-
tischen* [The Concept of the Political] (1932): "All concepts in the spiritual sphere, including the concept of spirit, are intrinsically pluralistic and can only be understood by
studying their concrete political circumstances [sind . . . nur aus der konkreten politis-
chen Existenz heraus zu verstehen]. . . . If the center of spiritual life in the last four centuries has constantly displaced itself, then, as a consequence of that, all concepts and

To write adequately about spiritual experience—or what is named such—would need the tolerance and comprehensiveness of a William James. The task of distinguishing between spirituality and spiritism seems endless. The question of where spirituality is today is complicated by the increasing predominance of visual texts, of the movies. How "spiritual" is a film like *Seven,* written by Andrew Walker? It is one of many staging the city as an evil place that requires purification through a punisher or avenger. Based on the Christian typology of the Seven Deadly Sins, it tracks a murderer's grisly serial killings in pursuit of a spiritual quest. The killer himself imposes the scheme of the Seven Deadly Sins on randomly chosen victims, and the surprise is that, though outwitting the police, he allows himself to be killed at the end as a sacrifice to his own scheme—because he embodies one of those sins. There is no spiritism here of the supernatural kind; but there is a borderline sense of the uncanny, as in so many detective stories, where a fiendish force seems to outmaneuver human reason. The rational wins only because the murderer (or author) wants it to, in order to save the concept of motivation. *Seven* cannot be dismissed as the gothic exploitation of religious mania: it is a ghastly hyperbole demonstrating how sinister that mania becomes when the spiritual life runs amok, when its claim to mark and fight evil is seized by a despairing intensity that leads to flamboyant acts of proclamation.[4]

In general, the detective story format of looking for clues that do not yield easily to looking, and mock in their cunning character the noisy, clumsy pursuit of the police, points to the need for a different kind of *attention.* In such films there is a glut—gluttony—of sight that cuts across all attempts to render these moral

---

words have constantly changed their meaning, and it is necessary to remember the plurisignification of each word and concept" (my translation).

[4] The criminal as artist (and artist as criminal) is not a rare theme in modern literature. See Joel Black, *The Aesthetics of Murder: A Study in Romantic Literature and Contemporary Culture* (Baltimore: Johns Hopkins University Press, 1991).

fables spiritual.[5] Perhaps the spiritual can only be caught at the margin, glimpsed, not focused on: it evades being incorporated, or fixed as a purely visual event. In *Seven,* there is a short moment in a police station where, quite implausibly, strains of classical music are heard—an allusion, probably, to a more striking scene in another film, *The Shawshank Redemption,* where music of that kind transports the prisoners in the yard to a world they have not known and may never know.[6] Brushed by the wings of that music, they stand still, in their inner space, attentive; then the miraculous notes evaporate into the grim round of their daily existence.

My aim is to cover only one aspect of spiritual experience, that which involves "listening" to texts. This aspect of spirituality is linked to my previous examples through the quality of attention that texts, canonical or noncanonical, foster.

Many have claimed that something read, even as fragmented as a single sentence come upon by chance, has made a radical difference and set them on a new course with spiritual implications. This happened most famously to Augustine; the *tolle lege* (take up and read) episode from his *Confessions* recalls the magical practice of the *sortes Virgilianae* or *sortes Biblicae,* in which you opened the sacred book and decided on a course of action by taking the verse that met your eye as an oracle. The practice survived into Methodism and was known to George Eliot, whose Dinah Morris in *Adam Bede* seeks divine guidance "by opening the Bible at hazard."[7] Saul Lieberman, a distinguished scholar of the Talmud, speculated that

---

[5] Only Ingmar Bergman's late TV film, *The Blessed,* has the courage to portray a religious *folie à deux* culminating in a self-mutilation, the eyes being literally put out. More than Baruch Spinoza, adduced by Bloom, this film presents a love of God that is the opposite of "The American Religion."

[6] Strains of music like that are also heard in Jean-Luc Godard's *Weekend* and in Roberto Benigni's *Life Is Beautiful.*

[7] Eliot, *Adam Bede* (Harmondsworth: Penguin, 1980), p. 82. (I am told that this kind of divination was still practiced—at least into the 1960s—in Methodist circles of the American South.) Efraim Sicher's important essay "George Eliot's Rescripting of Scripture: The 'Ethics of Reading' in *Silas Marner,*" *Simeia* 77 (1997): 243–70, links biblical interpretation of this kind to the larger issue of the relation of chance and design in both secular and sacred texts.

this sort of divination was also behind the curious notion of *bat kol,* echo, literally "daughter of the voice [of God]," heard in an era when He was no longer audible, or, as the Bible puts it, open vision had ceased—the era of post-prophetic teachers who between the third century B.C.E. and the fifth C.E. were the founding fathers of orthodox Judaism.

The perplexed soul would go out of the house of study and the first sounds heard were to be a deliverance, indicating the path to be followed. Some of these sounds must have penetrated the scholar's house; but perhaps his devoted attention, his *kavanah,* kept them out. The celestial *bat kol* could also "appear" in dreams or daydreams.[8] This audism has something desperate about it; it is clear, from such incidents, that "the spirit blows where it lists," or that, to cite Bob Dylan, the answer is blowing in the wind.

In order to respect secular experience, to see in it a potential hiding-place of the spirit—not unlike the way that art after Marcel Duchamp values trashy occasions—we eavesdrop everywhere. Chance mingles inextricably—as so often in novelistic plots— with a potential ethics. The surrealists say that such encounters reveal an *hasard objectif.* Today we don't necessarily consult the

---

[8] See Saul Lieberman, *Hellenism in Jewish Palestine* (New York: Jewish Theological Seminary, 1950). One of the voice's most famous manifestations is recorded in *Berakhot* 3a of the Babylonian Talmud, where Rabbi Yose is said to hear it in the ruins of Jerusalem, cooing like a dove and lamenting: "Woe to me for I have destroyed my house and burned my temple and have exiled my children." The scene here is clearly an elegiac one, and the *bat kol* generally is mild rather than a cause for panic or fear. According to the *Encyclopedia Judaica,* the *bat kol* was already on occasion heard in the biblical period: midrashic sources gave it a role, for example, in Solomon's judgment of the two women claiming the same child. The episode, in book 8 of Augustine's *Confessions,* is especially remarkable in that the voice is both external ("'Take up and read'") and textual ("I seized, opened, and in silence read that section, on which my eyes first fell . . . "). Augustine mentions the case of Saint Antony, who, entering the room where the Gospel was being read, "received the admonition as if what was being read was spoken to him." (I quote from the Pusey translation of *The Confessions.*) Antony was the first of the desert fathers, and Augustine must be referring to an aural episode recounted in *The Life and Affairs of Our Holy Father Antony* ascribed to Athanasius of Alexandria (mid fourth century). We are told that Antony, entering the church just as the Gospels were being read, "heard the Lord saying to the rich man, *If you would be perfect, go, sell what you possess and give to the poor, and you will have treasure in heaven.*" Athanasius continues: "It was as if by God's design he held the saints in his recollection, and as if the passage were read on his account."

"bouche d'ombre" of Virgil or the Bible and turn them into a lottery; but the world, the very world from which we seek refuge, still opens to divulge accidental epiphanies. Modern Age spiritism of this kind may have begun with Charles Baudelaire's *Fusées* (Fireworks): it describes a type of trance that parallels a depth experience also yielded by hashish, but extends it like a magical varnish over anything and everything, including "la première phrase venue, si vos yeux tombent sur un livre" (the first-come phrase, if you happen to look into a book).[9] Poetry itself, Baudelaire suggests, is the product of an intelligence lit up by an intoxication of this kind.

Indeed, for both orthodox scholars and psychedelic adventurers the act of emerging from a period of concentration, of isolated study or brooding, into the promiscuous clamor of the street or the sad variety of books one admires and cannot make one's own seems to hide a sensuous need, the wish for a coup de foudre, a choice as absolute as Emily Dickinson's

> The soul selects her own society
> Then shuts the Door—
> To her divine Majority—
> Present no more—(303)[10]

Love too amazes, akin to Grace, because it occurs involuntarily among the impossible diversity of human beings with whom one wishes to be intimate. As we have seen with the Jonestown sui-

[9] He also uses the word "spirituel" to describe it, which connotes in French both spiritual and witty (the latter word reinforcing the intellectual character of the experience) and evokes a sense of strange "correspondences" between different events or perceptual phenomena (sounds and colors, for instance). Swedenborgianism (Balzac, for instance, made it in the early 1830s the subject of *Serafita* and *Louis Lambert*), Thomas de Quincey (his *Opium Eater,* which Baudelaire translated), and Edgar Allan Poe contributed their influence throughout the nineteenth century: in fact, the attempt to view poetry as a highly conscious hallucinogenic gateway came close to being programmatic in French symbolism. In the United States too, spiritistic phenomena, including Turning Tables, assumed fashionable proportion from the 1850s on.

[10] *The Complete Poems of Emily Dickinson,* ed. Thomas H. Johnson (Boston: Little Brown and Company, 1960), p. 143.

cides, the need to love, or to cleave to a strong, ordering voice, whether that of the guru or the text he claims to embody, is essential to this kind of spirituality. We too easily neglect the fact, however, that the promise of life, of rebirth, can produce its own rigor mortis: in Dickinson's words, a closing of the valves of attention "Like Stone."

Myself, I have never graduated beyond fortune cookies; and even those lost their charm when I opened one and received the all too probable message: "What you have eaten isn't chicken." But I admit that, being a student of literature, and reading a lot, in the canon as well as miscellaneously, there are times when a passage has taken my breath away: when I have been tempted to call the impact of such a text spiritual and supposed that others would also call it such. The first case I will take up is perhaps too good, in that the subject-matter is already in the religious realm. I read Cardinal Newman's *Dream of Gerontius* again, a play structured as a *viaticum* or ultimate rite of passage: it describes the individual soul passing from the instant of death to the judgment seat. It was not so much Newman's daring conception that held me, as he shows the dying man moving like a somnambulist along that fatal path, accompanied by the voices of the funeral mass and the intercession of orders of angels. What held me was an early moment in this process, when Gerontius expresses his terror: terror of dying, *timor mortis,* but also of God's judgment closing in. Newman places heroism at life's end, as it is overwhelmed by pangs related to the physical agony of death, pangs that contain an intuition of damnation:

> I can no more; for now it comes again
> That sense of ruin, which is worse than pain,
> That masterful negation and collapse
> Of all that makes me man. . . .

In this prayerful monologue Gerontius does not address himself to God, Christ, Mary, or other intercessors—till he is seized once more by a spasm of fear. The comfort of address, of being called or being able to call upon, is removed, as he begins a free fall, dying alone, without steadying hand or voice:

> as though I bent
> Over the dizzy brink
> Of some sheer infinite descent;
> Or worse, as though
> Down, down for ever I was falling through
> The solid framework of created things. . . .

Like Gerontius, at that moment, we realize how ordinary life bears us up; so that if the term "spiritual" can enter appropriately here, it also refers to the gratitude we owe created or material things for their support. The earth generally does not give way; and we trust our body, for a time. There are intimations, however, that this confidence cannot last: either at the end of our life, or at the end of days, or indeed at any time in the course of individual existence, we are deserted, a trapdoor opens, the pit yawns. Then spirits enter or reenter, and the immediate frontier is death.

In considering the colorful aspects of free-floating spirituality, as well as that closely linked to an organized religion like Catholicism or Judaism, I will try to avoid cornering myself into a decisive definition of the phenomenon itself. Like Nathaniel Hawthorne in "The Celestial Railroad," I am anxious not to become a Mr. Smooth-it-away. I suggest, then, that we often seize on one event, whether disturbing or exhilarating or both, that cuts across a relatively careless, wasteful, or ignorant life. We focus on what was revealed: on what turned us around, not necessarily from bad to good but toward a sense of purpose and identity. The quality of attention so aroused is not inevitably the outcome of a religious exercise: it can involve acts of attention described by Nicolas de Malebranche as "the natural prayer of the soul."[11] Or there is John

---

[11] Cf. Simon Weil: "L'attention absolument sans mélange est prière," in *La pesanteur et la grâce,* intro. by Gustave Thibon (Paris: Librairie Plon, 1948), p. 135.

Keats's wonderful analogy: "I go among the Fields and catch a glimpse of a stoat or a fieldmouse peeping out of the withered grass—the creature hath a purpose and its eyes are bright with it."[12]

These accidental and defining events can be textual. Readers, poetically inclined, yet also distracted by passages that seem to stand out, must find a way to go where these lead. Such readerly absorption is, I think, becoming rarer, not just because books have multiplied and the World Wide Web is there to be manipulated, but also because film has become a major art form; and film is panoramic, requiring a more diffused as well as demanding attention, or one that hypnotizes through a variable zooming and focusing. The tyranny of the eye, the simple pleasure of filmic omnipotence, combines distraction with a faux-semblant of concentration.

Of course, some intensity of the visual has always existed: the use of religious icons or the meditative "exercises" of Ignatius of Loyola tell us how important images, inner or outer, have been. Or, as in D. H. Lawrence's "Bavarian Gentians," written a few months before his death, the coming darkness renders the visible more visible, counterpart of a kindly light purely and intensely nature's own and that acts as a *psychopompos:*

> black lamps from the halls of Dis, burning dark blue
> giving off darkness, blue darkness, as Demeter's pale
>   lamps give off light,
> lead me then, lead the way.[13]

Yet unless the discipline of reading has first come about, without being routinized by print culture, it is doubtful we could even approach an analysis of "spiritual value," at least in our civilization.

---

[12] To the George Keatses, March 19, 1819.

[13] There are two versions of "Bavarian Gentians" (as well as related drafts with the title "Glory of Darkness"). I am quoting from *The Complete Poems of D. H. Lawrence,* ed. Vivian de Sola Pinto and Warren Roberts (New York: Viking Press, 1971), p. 697.

In many conversion experiences, as William James has shown, terror and turmoil are aroused or allayed when a voice is heard uttering Scripture words.[14] Poetry's dense or enigmatic phrases have a parallel effect; they often induce a contemplative mood, asking to be carried longer in the womb of the mind, and do not bring a premature and disenchanting clarity to birth.

Is spirituality, then, linked to the sense of the individual as such being found, or found out? That those affected feel directly called or addressed is probably more important than recognizing whose voice it is, or the exact content of the call. A sudden, mysterious utterance outflanks our resistance to being identified, or known too well. Is not the oldest—and youngest—game that of hide-and-seek? Shock, surprise, self-consciousness, unanticipated arousals of guilt or joy, even a negative correlative of these, "Blank misgivings of a Creature / Moving about in worlds not realized" (William Wordsworth, "Ode. Intimations of Immortality.")— such radical moments, not always verbal, though demanding a verbal response, or a temporal, sustained act of consciousness, may not constitute the spiritual as such or bind it to the ordinary life we lead. Yet they furnish a disruption from which we date a conscious birth.

The individual is always singled out, is always one of three stopped by an Ancient Mariner, transported by a musical phrase, "looked at" by a work of art, as when the archaic torso of Apollo admonishes Rainer Maria Rilke: "You must change your life." There is often a heightened sense of place or virtual embodiment. The spiritual in those moments approaches ecstasy, but does not leave the body except to enter, at the same time, a specific visionary expanse. So Jacob at Beth-el: "How full of awe this place!" (Genesis 28:17). Or the flashbacks of trauma: "I think I would have no trouble even now locating the spot on the median strip of Commonwealth Avenue [in Boston] where they [the repressed ex-

---

[14] James, *The Varieties of Religious Experience* (1902), Lecture IX, "Conversion."

periences of many years ago] emerged out of that darkness. . . . "[15]
Krzysztof Kielslowski's film *The Double Life of Veronique* intimates
how strong and sensuous the pull is toward union with a second
self, which is always in another place, and whose absent presence is
felt as a loss, even a disembodiment. This ghostly, complementary
other becomes the obscure object of desire: it is endlessly imagined, mourned, pursued. Aesthetics classifies such feelings as sublime; religion generally as full of awe. They exalt, terrify, and
humble at the same time.

The torment of individuation seems to be essential even when
the newly minted person flees from it into the arms of a brother-
hood, sisterhood, or God. It is notoriously difficult, as we all know,
to distinguish the sense of election from mania. Then how do we
get from such instances of spiritual experience to a communal
bond without betraying or falsifying them? To hear voices is a
form of madness; random textual surprises are borderline cases
that interpellate the reader and can be amplified as inner quotations, cryptomania, or internalized commands. Yet once we have
redeemed that madness by turning to methodical exegesis, are we
still in the precarious domain of being singled out, or do we simply confirm what we already know through doctrine or doxis? Has
astonishment or awe turned into dogmatic faith?[16]

We should not underestimate the importance, negative or positive, of hermeneutics in religion: an activity that flexes the meaning of a canonical text, as we seek wisdom or, more dangerously, an
altered identity. The methodical character of hermeneutics tries to
minimize eccentric responses by establishing a true, authoritative,
original meaning. Yet everyone who has ventured into the field of
interpretation, even when it represents itself as a discipline or a

---

[15] Brooke Hopkins, "A Question of Child Abuse," *Raritan Review* (Winter 1993):
35.

[16] Cf. A. J. Heschel in *God in Search of Man* (New York: Jewish Publication Society
of America, 1955), who goes so far as to assert: "Awe rather than faith is the cardinal at-
titude of the religious Jew" (p. 77). He identifies awe with *Yir'at shamayim,* or what philosophers of religion after Rudolf Otto call the *tremendum.*

science, knows the polyphony if not cacophony of exegesis, and how endlessly interesting it is to try to meet the challenge of texts. Though we take for granted that the voice of God is no longer heard in the way the boy Samuel heard it, or which would make the interpreter reply "Here I am," a part of us returns to certain texts as to vestiges in which strength of spirit condenses itself and could achieve what Robert Frost memorably called "counter-love, original response."

I have given my talk the title "Text and Spirit" because it has always puzzled me how dependent spirituality is, not only on books—necessary for cultural transmission, once there is dispersion, or as the oral tradition becomes too complex—but on textual issues. The rivalry of religion with religion could not continue without systems of interpretation that activate in specific ways the faith-community's Scripture, which may be a book shared by several religions.

It must already be clear, in any case, that there is a link between text and spirit when textual incidents, in the form of fragments or citations, are like a voice falling into us, taking hold of us. Though elaborated and restored to their first or another context, such audita remain snatches from a ghostly conversation or a more absolute book. I have represented this receptivity to spiritualized sound, to "the secret that has become audible in language,"[17] as a psychic and existential fact. Moreover, I have stressed its contingency, as religion itself often does, when it depicts a divine intervention: a prophet is unexpectedly called, a commanding voice is heard, a rebus or inscription appears.

---

[17] "[D]as hörbar gewordene Geheimnis in der Sprache" is one of Gershom Scholem's formulations. Scholem does not mean that the secret is revealed or directly expressed in language: it becomes perceptible *as* a secret, or, as Sigrid Weigel says, it points to the "Bedeutungspur eines Bedeutungslosen," which transcends "Mitteilung and Ausdruck." See Scholem, *Judaica III: Studien zur jüdischen Mystik* (Frankfurt/M: Suhrkamp, 1970), p. 271; and Weigel, "Scholem's Gedichte und seine Gedichtstheorie: Klage. Adressierung, Gabe und das Problem einer Sprache in unserer Zeit," *Deutsche Vierteljahrsschrift für Literaturwissenschaft und Geistesgeschichte,* Sonderheft (1999): 49. Walter Benjamin's well-known fascination with the quotational form, his wish to write a book consisting only of citations, is also relevant here.

But I have also said that the orthodox hermeneutics we have inherited, while respecting life-changing responses to source-texts
with canonical status, seeks to limit these.[18] Though some passages are more astonishing than others, and though, through unknown mediations, even ordinary biblical pericopes can have a
startling effect, both religious and literary theories of interpretation take much pride in the doctrine of context—a predetermined
context, shielding the reader from subjectivity and speculative excess. Similarly, in evangelical or charismatic movements, where
startling conversions—even convulsions—are expected, what
takes place is, as it were, programmed in, and becomes a sacred or,
at worst, sacrilegious mimicry.

The force of the acoustic fragment, then, surprises, because it
comes from outside, even when that outside is within us. It does
not matter how we analyze the psychic fact; what is important is
that this metonymic textual condensation, this appearance of
word as vision, *leads back* to a source-text, or is the germ, as in creative writing, of a *leading forward,* a transformative moment that
creates its own narrative support.[19]

[18] The opposite is true of the Kabbalah, which often "relativizes" the letters in
Scripture, claiming the Torah was originally, as one mystic claimed, "a heap of
unarranged letters" combining in different forms according to the state of the world. See
Gershom Scholem, *On the Kabbalah and Its Symbolism,* tr. Ralph Manheim (New York:
Schocken Books, 1965), pp. 74–83. It is Emmanuel Levinas's distinction that he sees in
non-Kabbalistic midrashic calls to "seek and decipher" an orthodox hermeneutics that
does not sacrifice multiplicity of meaning: "That the Word of the living God may be
heard in diverse ways does not mean only that Revelation measures up to those listening
to it, but that this measuring up measures up the Revelation: the multiplicity of irreducible people is necessary to the dimensions of meaning; the multiple meanings are multiple people" (*Beyond the Verse: Talmudic Readings and Lectures,* tr. Gary D. Mole [London:
Athlone, 1994], p. 134). This is reminiscent of Isaac Luria's development of the conception that the 600,000 souls that received the Torah at Sinai are disseminated by transmi-
gration into "sparks" present in every generation of Israel, and that "[i]n the Messianic
age, every single man in Israel will read the Torah in accordance with the meaning peculiar to his root" (Scholem, *On the Kabbalah,* p. 65).

[19] Jacques Lacan, seeking to define the action of the unconscious, disputes the
Christian commonplace that the letter kills while the spirit gives life. He would like to
know "how the spirit could live without the letter." "Even so," he adds, "the pretensions
of the spirit would remain unassailable if the letter had not shown us that it produces all
the effects of truth in man without involving the spirit at all." In short, Freud discovered
that this "spiritual" effect of the letter points to the existence of an unconscious process.

In talking of spirit, we have an obligation to go first to where the word *ruach* appears in the Hebrew Bible.[20] After "In the beginning God created the heaven and the earth," Genesis discloses that "the earth was unformed and void, and darkness was upon the face of the deep." The *ruach elohim* that "hovered over the face of the waters" is close to that darkness on the face of the deep. But this might suggest that chaos, the *tohuvabohu* of unformed earth and water, may have preexisted; in which case the creation would not be *ex nihilo,* out of nothing, but only a form-giving event. The Bible's opening phrasing defeats that thought; and the "spirit of God," with the formless darkness mere backdrop, manifests itself as a commanding voice instantly originating light. Yet even here, in this place of power, "Light is called, not torn forth."[21]

In the second chapter of Genesis, there is a subtle parallel to the spirit hovering over the face of the waters: "there went up a mist from the earth, and watered the whole face of the ground" (2:6). This is a transitional sentence that could be joined either to the previous verse describing the barren, soon to be fertile, earth or to the next verse that retells the creation of humankind: "Then the Lord God formed man of the dust of the ground, and breathed into his nostrils the breath of life; and man became a living soul." The words for breath and soul are not *ruach* but respectively *neshamah* and *nefesh.* As a picture, then, of the creative act, there is some-

---

[20] There is a wonderful feeling on reading that ancient text, which Buber and Rosenzweig capture in their translation of it: a feeling of the sheer impress of each word, as if it were newly created. We never quite lose the sense that reading the original aloud and understanding it remain parallel yet separate activities, despite generations of effort to have sound and sense converge. At the same time, what is communicated by the Hebrew Bible is, to borrow Goethe's phrase, an "open mystery." Or, as Levinas remarks, transcendence is intelligible.

[21] John Hollander, *The Work of Poetry* (New York: Columbia University Press, 1997), p. 37. (No wonder the Gospel of John, with its more ecstatic quest for union with God, identifies logos and light.) Hollander suggests two things in his chapter on "Originality" from which I take this: that comparative religious (cosmogonic) texts could make us expect a cataclysmic account of creation, and that perhaps such an account, revised, may have been the original version. What matters, though, is that the text as it stands does not entirely efface this suppositious trace of a "more" original account of the origin.

thing gentler here and more intimate: a proximity of divine to human one does not feel in the first creation-of-man account (Genesis 1:26–29), despite the theme of *zelem elohim,* of being created in God's image. In fact, where we might expect the *ruach* to reappear, as in Genesis 3:8, we find instead a voice, "the voice of the Lord God walking in the garden." The earlier depiction showed the spirit of God as a hovering force in the formless darkness; in the later picture, however, the mist rising from the ground and watering the face of the earth is an image taken directly from nature, and the creation that follows is distinctly anthropomorphic, in that its subject is literally the shaping of a man, while the very art of description is friendly and naturalistic. Genesis 3:8, moreover, augments the idea of a relation between *ruach elohim* and voice, the voice that generates light. Without, to be sure, a definite body, that *ruach*-voice now addresses and interpellates the lapsed human being, an act that can be said to call it to consciousness or conscience.

If my analysis is correct, *ruach* is not anthropomorphic (it is, if anything, closer to theriomorphic), though as a speaking and intelligible voice it moves toward a pathos at once human and sublime. *Ruach* never forfeits its quality as a *tremendum.*[22] This is borne out when we enter the later, more historical era of Judges, where the voice of God, while still manifest, often escapes those who search for it. The episodes that focus on the relation between Samuel, Saul, and God are particularly disturbing: indeed, here the verb *lidrosh,* the root of "midrash," meaning to seek out the voice, appears.[23]

The episodes are disturbing because while God's relation to Samuel remains familiar, allowing responsive words of obedience,

[22] On that notion in the history of religion, see Rudolf Otto, *The Idea of the Holy* (1917), trans. John W. Harvey (Harmondsworth: Pelican Books, 1959).

[23] See First Samuel 9:9, perhaps interpolated; but Saul's name in the Hebrew suggests asking, most clearly after Saul's death in Samuel 1:28:6: "When Saul inquired of the Lord [*vajish'al Shaul be-adonai*], the Lord answered him not, neither by dreams, nor by Urim, nor by prophets," which leads into the episode of the ghost-seer of Endor.

the pressure on Saul is terrifying. Saul is an *am ha'aretz,* going to the seer for a mundane, bumpkin-like purpose—"Can you give me guidance where my asses are?"—and being confronted by a fearful demand, a question that is not a question at all but an astonishing, exalting imposition: "And on whom is all the desire of Israel? Is it not on thee, and on all thy father's house?" (Samuel 1:9:20). Samuel then predicts Saul's journey home, which culminates in his joining a band of prophets: "And the spirit of the Lord will come mightily upon thee, and thou shalt prophesy and be turned into another man" (Samuel 1:10:1–7), where "come mightily upon" translates *zalachat,* "seize" thee or "fall upon" thee (cf. Samuel 1:11:6 and 1:16:13). A power of transformation is evoked, akin to that of the *ruach* in the first lines of Genesis.[24]

Clearly, the open vision and voice are passing from Israel. The presence of God returns in the prophets, but with more violence, ambivalence, chanciness, and—in Abraham Heschel's sense—pathos: so the *devar-adonai* is like a burning fire consuming Jeremiah's heart and bones (Jeremiah 20:9). God's *ruach* reverts to something of its aboriginal appearance: we are made to feel its incumbent mystery and transforming violence more than its intimacy.

It is well known that the sealing of the canon of Hebrew Scripture is linked to a recession, if not disappearance, of prophetic voice and vision. With the destruction of the First Temple, then decisively with the destruction of the Second and Bar Kochba's defeat, inquiry of God must go through "midrash." The Sages may still be looking for asses, but these include the Messiah's donkey. Those rabbis are not shy; they assert on the basis of Deuteronomy 30:11–15 that the Law is not "in heaven" but among them in the earthly tribunal; indeed, they abjure the authority of the *bat kol* and seek to shut down the prophetic impulse, even as Saul banished the witches whom he was nevertheless forced to consult.

---

[24] In Saul's fits of anger against David, when he seeks to kill him, the *ruach* is cited as a cause, and the English translation has to parse it as "an evil spirit from the Lord."

This means, in effect, that spirit has become textualized; inquiry of the Lord, in the post-prophetic and post-priestly era, is mediated by the recitation, reading, and contemplative study of Talmud Torah.

This multilayered commentary continues to call itself an oral tradition, however, and claims descent from Sinai; the image of direct transmission, through the voice of God or daughter of that voice,[25] is never entirely given up. To read in the Talmud, or to extend its inquiry, becomes a religious experience itself. Priest and prophet are replaced by the figure of the rabbi of exemplary learning who walks with the Law (*halakhah*, the path), even as the righteous of old had walked and conversed with God.[26]

The rabbinic revolution, as it has been called, seals the canon and draws the consequences of that closure.[27] In the Sages' own hyperbole God is made to say of an errant Israel, "Would that you forsake me, and keep my Torah!" (*Lamentations Rabbah*, Introduction, chap. 2). This expresses, of course, a fear that *God* has forsaken the community; in captivity and dispersion, only the Torah remains.[28] But whatever dryness of spirit ensues, whatever constriction and

[25] No one has explained why it should be "daughter" of the voice: in the masculine atmosphere of rabbinic religion the Shechinah is another instance of the feminine as a figurative religious influence. It is possible to speculate that the rabbinic founders recognized that, in a normal human context, voice had a distinctly feminine inflection, and in most cases tried to guard against that "profane" element. How strongly the metaphor of voice persists, even where there is no sacred text, and can be none, is shown when Emil Fackenheim adds to the revealed commandments or the 613 *mitzvot* the "Commanding Voice of Auschwitz" forbidding Jews to give Hitler a posthumous victory by abandoning Judaism, or escaping from the "intolerable contradictions" of historical existence after Auschwitz. See his *The Jewish Return into History: Reflections in the Age of Auschwitz and a New Jerusalem* (New York: Schocken Books, 1978).

[26] In the *Zohar* this peripatetic notion becomes a technical expression "to illuminate the path [*derech*]." For an interesting discussion of how prophecy becomes exegesis, see Emmanuel Levinas, *Transcendance et intelligibilité* (Geneva: Labor et Fides, 1996), pp. 63–67.

[27] The best account of what that closure meant is found in Moshe Halbertal, *The People of the Book: Canon, Meaning and Authority* (Cambridge, Mass.: Harvard University Press, 1997).

[28] One other aspect of divinity, however is imaginatively discovered and developed: the Shechinah or "dwelling" of God, closely linked to Torah. The Shechinah becomes a complex and consolatory personification elaborated by the Kabbalah into the feminine aspect of the divine.

narrowness of purpose, the act of reading strengthens and takes on a quality of prayerful recitation: of a crying to God in words of the canonized text—in His own voice, as it were—as well as a listening for His response.

This sort of feeling may even be discerned in the exegetical method of Midrash. It is true that its tendency to atomize Scripture is the historical result of an editing process that conveys with great economy the interpretive wisdom of generations of rabbis. But does not this style of exposition have something unique? One might think that how Midrash usually atomizes Scripture would diminish the latter's eloquence. Its divisions of Scripture certainly sin against plot or story, the very features that entice us to look at the Bible as literature. What matters in Midrash is the verse, or part of the verse, even a single word or letter. Meaning is achieved by the montage of biblical patches. Gershom Scholem once called the "mosaic style" of the great halakhists "poetic prose in which linguistic scraps of sacred texts are whirled around kaleidoscope like."[29] Yet a sense remains that these are written voices accumulating, though fragmented, as one voice.[30]

---

[29] Scholem goes on: "and are journalistically, polemically, descriptively, and even erotically profaned"—but this part of his sentence must refer to Karl Kraus's style, which he sees as being derived from "the Jews' relationship to language." See *Walter Benjamin: The Story of a Friendship,* trans. Harry Zohn (Philadelphia: Jewish Publication Society, 1981), p. 107.

[30] By now we accept the atomism of Midrash as the natural form of Jewish commentary; a good way of collecting and ordering the combined wisdom of generations of rabbis and learned readers to the present day. Yet its methodical segmentation, which tears a seamless robe or exposes the stitching, and even sows contradictions (though only to resolve them), equalizes all verses and sharpens concentration. It is as if *bat kol* were still at work, allowing disjunct fragments and phrases to circulate and catch us. There is, to be sure, sustained symbolism and story-telling in the Kabbalah and, later, in Hasidism; and the genre of the retold Bible never dies. But a sense remains that each verse, phrase, word, letter (and letter-ornamentation) counts; the segmentation is a synoptic wager. Moshe Idel has emphasized that in Abulafia's prophetic Kabbalah (*kabbalah nevu'it*), the Hebrew of the Bible is considered as hiding the names of God, and knowledge of Him is revealed not by studying its language as a conventional human sign-system (an accommodated *lashon b'nei adam*) but by engaging in a contemplation that leads to so radical a deconstruction, or creation of new signifiers, that it engenders a striking metaphor: "Read the entire Torah, both forwards and backwards, and spill the blood of the languages."

What I have tried to do is sketch a minimalist theory of spirituality, influenced mainly by the Jewish commentary tradition. Some of you will be disappointed by this modest approach. Spirituality is a word with great resonance, yet I have not extracted for you large, exalted structures of sensibility or discourse. Were I to do so, on another occasion, I would have to respect an entire oeuvre or midrashic sequence and show how words dim the eyes as well as refresh them, insofar as visuality and idolatry may be linked. I would have to deal with the issue of anthropo/gyno/morphism—or divine pathos—as a fertile, if always disputed, wellspring of religious energy, and stay longer with the way *ruach* breaks into voice, or becomes voice-feeling, close to the heart of the throat, yet threatening to turn the human response into a stammer. The very word "spirituality," moreover, still seems somewhat foreign to traditional Jewish thinking and observance: it got preempted by Pauline Christianity. Only to Emmanuel Levinas might it be applied: his theology evokes a vigilance, even an insomnia, that keeps human finitude, traumatized by the infinite, from enclosing itself in "the hegemonic and atheistic self" for which life reduces to equanimity.[31]

There is one further generalization I want to venture. It returns to something almost as equivocal as dreams, namely the gift of speech and what Dante and Franz Rosenzweig both call its "grammar": voiced thinking that becomes writing and seeks a coincidence of spirit and letter. That coincidence is rare and demands a price—an engagement that takes time, perhaps a lifetime. For there is no guarantee that poetic words, ancient or modern, will

---

[31] See, e.g., *Nouvelles lectures talmudiques* (Editions de Minuit, 1996), pp. 28–29. Also: "[P]eut-être cette théologie s'annonce-t-elle déjà dans l'éveil même à l'insomnie, à la veille et à l'inquiète vigilance du psychisme avant que la finitude de l'être, blessé par l'infini, ne soit porté à se recueillir dans un Moi, hégémonique et athée, du savoir" (*Transcendence et intelligibilité*, p. 29). But the most difficult task would be to engage with issues of purity and impurity; not only to take up arms against the charge of Jewish literalism as a blind or imperfect reception of spirit but also to examine the emphasis on biblical and rabbinic Judaism on the efficacy, practical or mystical, or laws of purity that seek to bring Jews into the Presence as a holy people.

make sense, or the same sense, to different readers throughout history. In fact, the more earnest our attention to language, the more the conventional links dissipate, and a nakedness appears in the words as words, one that both arouses and threatens the process of intellection.

We often feel, then, that biblical words say too much to be received: their anagogical force, while helping to break what Rosenzweig calls the shell of the mystery ("die Schale des Geheimnisses"),[32] can make us feel as poor as Edward Taylor, the Puritan poet:

> In my befogg's dark Phancy, Clouded minde,
> Thy Bits of Glory, packt in Shreds of Praise
> My Messenger [i.e., his poetry] doth lose, losing his Wayes.[33]

We cannot presume to win spiritual coherence lightly, when the spirit itself is so often figured as a preternatural, disruptive intervention. The not-foundering of communication under that pressure is unusual, for speech could turn into nothing more than a contiguous mass of alien sounds.[34] Perhaps, then, shards, *klipot,* Edward Taylor's "Bits of Glory . . . Shreds of Praise," must suffice.

Let me end by recounting what happened to Martin Buber. His path to the great Buber-Rosenzweig translation of the Bible was

---

[32] Rosenzweig applies the expression to the creation that follows upon God's word. "Gott sprach. Das ist das zweite. Es ist nicht der Anfang. . . . Gott schuf. Das ist das Neue. Hier zerbricht die Schale des Geheimnisses" (*Der Stern der Erlösung* [Heidelberg: Lambert Schneider, 1954]), II.1.31.

[33] "Meditation Twenty-eight," in *The Poetical Works of Edward Taylor,* ed. Thomas H. Johnson (Princeton: Princeton University Press, 1971), p. 139.

[34] Another way of putting it is to say that its coherence, or sense, might disappear, and that the fallout from any false imposition of meaning could lead to a cosmic sort of skepticism: "If the sun or moon should doubt / They'd immediately go out" (Blake, *Auguries of Innocence*). Philology, when it becomes inspired criticism, senses the lacuna in a text or the wrong word that has filled it.

very complex, but one episode stands out.[35] Well-acquainted in early youth with the Hebrew original and then with several translations including Martin Luther's, he noticed shortly after his Bar Mitzvah that he read the Bible with literary enjoyment—which upset him so much that for years he did not touch any translation but tried to return to the *Urtext,* the original Hebrew. By then, however, the words had lost their familiar aspect and seemed harsh, alien, confrontational: "sie sprangen mir ins Gesicht."[36]

Thirteen years later (one thinks, therefore, of a second Bar Mitzvah), Buber attended Theodor Herzl's funeral and came home feeling oppressed. As he reached for one book after another, everything seemed voiceless and meaningless ("stumm"). Then, as if by chance, and without expectation, Buber opened the Bible—and happened upon the story of how King Jehoiakim had Jeremiah's scroll read and consigned piece by piece to a brazier's fire (Jeremiah 36:21ff.); this went to Buber's heart, and he began to face the Hebrew once more, conquering each word anew, as if it had never been translated. "I read [the Hebrew] aloud, and by reading it this way I got free of the whole Scripture, which now was purely *Migra'.*"[37] A few years later, while reading a biblical chapter aloud, the feeling came over him that it was being spoken for the first time and had not yet been written down, and did not have to be

---

[35] I am indebted for this example to Herbert Marks, "Schrift und Mikra," in *Logos und Buchstabe: Mündlichkeit und Schriftlichkeit in Judentum und Christentum der Antike,* ed. Gerhard Sellin and François Vouga (Tübingen: Francke Verlag, 1996), pp. 103–26. See also the same essay in English: "Writing as Calling," *New Literary History* 29, no. 1 (1998): 15–37.

[36] I am using both the German version as printed in the appendix to Anna Elizabeth Bauer, *Rosenzweigs Sprachdenken im* Stern der Erlösung *und in seiner Korrespondenz mit Martin Buber zur Verdeutschung der Schrift* (Freiburg dissertation), published in the series Europäische Hochschulschriften (Frankfurt a/M: Peter Lang, 1992), pp. 447–63, and the English translation (which I sometimes modify) found as appendix a in *Scripture and Translation: Martin Buber and Franz Rosenzweig,* tr. Lawrence Rosenwald and Everett Fox (Bloomington: Indiana University Press, 1994), pp. 205–19. Buber's "[The Hebrew words] sprang into my face" is ironic in the sense that what the religious seeker desires is precisely to "see" God, to diminish the *hester panim.*

[37] *Scripture and Translation,* p. 208.

written down. "The book lay before me, but the book melted into voice."[38]

Buber has not left us a reflection on why the "found" passage from Jeremiah affected him so powerfully, and he does not refer explicitly to the *bat kol.*[39] But his stated wish to "get free of" Scripture by first converting it into an aural experience is remarkably candid. The Hebrew root *gara'* in *migra'* may have helped as a first step toward a retranslation of the Bible that challenges Luther's strongly vernacular version.[40] *Qara',* as in *Q'ryat Sh'ma,* denotes the action of calling, of a crying out or reciting, as well as naming: the content of this prayer is, after all, a naming of God. *Qara'* as "reading" never loses its residual meaning of "calling out." Moreover, in the episode from Jeremiah, the verb *qara* (when spelled with ayin rather than aleph) is a near-homonym of "tearing"—a sacrilegious act on the part of the king, but one that recalls two distantly related events. First, the destroyed scroll is rewritten by Jeremiah's scribe Baruch, a doubling that could recall that of Sinai's tablets, as well as raise the issue of the relation of written to oral Torah. Both Buber and Rosenzweig try to express the link between text and spirit in a radical way, one that goes

[38] Buber writes typically, in 1936: "das biblische Wort ist von der Situation seiner Gesprochenheit nicht abzulösen, sonst verliert es seine Konkretheit, seine Leiblichkeit. Ein Gebot ist keine Sentenz, sondern eine Andrede . . ." ("Ein Hinweis für Bibelkurse," *Rundbrief,* quoted by Ernst Simon, in *Aufbau im Untergang: Jüdische Erwachsenbildung im nationalsozialistischen Deutschland als geistiger Wiederstand* [Tübingen: J. C. B. Mohr, 1959], 67).

[39] One should remark the similarity of this to Luther's experience on discovering through a "found" passage in the prophet Habbakuk the meaning of Romans 1:17: "Now I felt as if I had been born again: the gates had been opened and I had entered Paradise itself," quoted by Heiko O. Oberman, *Luther: Man between God and Devil* (New Haven: Yale University Press, 1982), p. 165. It is significant that this discovery may have come through a "fit" in Wittenberg tower (or its "cloaca"), as Luther came upon that passage in Habbakuk. Once again, and in the most humble or worldly circumstance, a found text leads to a startling inner event.

[40] In what follows I am indebted to Herbert Marks, "Schrift und Mikra," pp. 125–26. On Buber's "metanomianism," especially in comparison to that of Scholem and Rosenzweig, see Paul Mendes-Flohr, "Law and Sacrament: Ritual Observance in Twentieth-Century Jewish Thought," in *Jewish Spirituality: From the Sixteenth-Century Revival to the Present,* ed. Arthur Green (New York: Crossroad, 1987), pp. 317–45.

through the restitution of its oral or aural resonance, but otherwise does not seek to transform the Bible by any type of spiritualizing interpretation. *"Schrift ist Gift* [Script is poison]," Buber quotes Rosenzweig, from a letter shortly before their work of translation began, "holy *Schrift* included. Only when it is translated back into orality can I stomach it."[41]

The episode from Jeremiah, moreover, leads intertextually to Second Kings 22, in which Shaphan the scribe reads the newly discovered book of the law *(sefer hatorah)* to King Josiah; but there the king tears his clothes,[42] not the scroll, and—after instructing Shaphan to "inquire of the Lord" *(dirshu et adonai,* i.e., consult the oracle of the prophetess Hulda)—has it read aloud to the assembled people. This episode occurs in chapter 22 of Second Kings, whose chapter 2 had recounted the story of Elijah and Elisha: how Elijah ascends in a whirlwind and perhaps leaves to his disciple a "double portion of . . . *ruach.*" But when Elisha dies, there is no ascension and no mention of a *ruach* legacy. The fiery chariot and horses carrying Elijah away become, when Elisha is lamented (Second Kings 13:14–15), no more than a figurative allusion, an exclamation ("My father, my father, the chariots of Israel and the horsemen thereof!")[43] expressing the fear that the *ruach* will depart from Israel with Elisha's passing. This sequencing of episodes

---

[41]   Rosenzweig's audacious statement has a traditional root in the reluctance of the Sages to remove the written Torah from the context of an oral tradition, which, while it built fences around the Law, remained open to an awareness that the lava of the Sinaitic revelation had never entirely petrified—that words could be montaged, revoweled, redivided, recontextualized, even their letters (especially in the Kabbalah) permuted.

[42]   Elisha tears his clothes at the passing of Elijah (2:12), as does the king of Israel having read Naaman's letter (5:7), which might portend a disaster. The *g'ria* is to this day a ritual tearing of clothing on the death of a close relative or a public calamity. Another homonym, the word for "it happened," enters in 5:7. A question could be raised about the relation between the apparently neutral "it happened that" and the meaning bestowed by the other two homonyms.

[43]   Since King Josiah, as chapter 23:11 tells us, in his purifying of religious worship, takes away "the horses that the kings of Judah had given to the sun . . . and burned the chariots of the sun with fire," I would guess that this figure refers not only to Elijah's strength, by way of a military metaphor, but also to a strength that comes from a God who transcends the idolatry of the "constellations and all the host of heaven" (23:5).

in Kings suggests the transition from prophecy as open vision to a scroll that must provide vision by inquiry, by a midrashic process linked to recitation and learned research. Despite the sporadic persistence of prophecy, the spirit will now have to reside mainly within the temple of a text.

I leave the last word to Levinas, who suggests that talmudic and midrashic literature shows that "prophecy may be the essence of the human, the traumatism that wakes it to its freedom." Thought itself is said to be an elaboration of such a moment. "It probably begins through traumatisms to which one does not even know how to give a verbal form: a separation, a violent scene, a sudden consciousness of the monotony of time. It is from the reading of books—not necessarily philosophical—that these initial shocks become questions and problems, giving one to think."[44] Prophecy and the ethical coincide, where self-identity, challenged by otherness, instructed and roused by particular texts, becomes "la spiritualité de l'esprit."[45]

[44] From an interview of 1980, in *Ethics and Infinity,* trans. Richard Cohen (Pittsburgh: Duquesne University Press, 1985), p. 21. For Levinas's ambivalent relation to literature, see Jill Robbins, *Altered Readings: Levinas and Literature* (Chicago: Chicago University Press, 1999).

[45] *Nouvelles lectures talmudiques,* pp. 36–37

The Blank Slate, the Noble Savage, and the

Ghost in the Machine

STEVEN PINKER

The Tanner Lectures on Human Values

Delivered at

Yale University
April 20 and 21, 1999

STEVEN PINKER is professor in the department of brain and cognitive sciences and director of the McConnell-Pew Center for Cognitive Neuroscience at the Massachusetts Institute of Technology. He was educated at McGill University and at Harvard University, where he received his Ph.D. He was recently elected to the American Academy of Arts and Sciences, and is a fellow of the American Association for the Advancement of Science, the American Psychological Association, and the American Psychological Society. His publications include *Learnability and Cognition: The Acquisition of Argument Structure* (1989) and *The Language Instinct* (1994), which was named one of the ten best books of 1994 by the *New York Times,* the *London Times,* and the *Boston Globe.* His most recent book, *How the Mind Works* (1997), won the *Los Angeles Times* Book Prize in Science and the William James Book Prize from the APA, and was a finalist for the Pulitzer Prize and the National Book Critics Circle Award.

These are extraordinary times in the history of human knowledge. For hundreds of years the progress of science has been a story of increasing unification and coherence, which the biologist E. O. Wilson has recently termed *consilience,* literally "jumping together."[1]

In 1755, Samuel Johnson wrote that his *Dictionary* should not be expected to "change sublunary nature, and clear the world at once from folly, vanity, and affectation." Few people today understand his use of the word "sublunary," literally "below the moon." It was an allusion to the ancient belief that there was a strict division between the pristine, lawful, unchanging cosmos above and our grubby, chaotic earth below. The division was already obsolete when Johnson wrote; Newton had shown that a single set of laws described the forces pulling the apple toward the ground and keeping the moon in its orbit around the earth.

The collapse of the wall between the terrestrial and the celestial was followed by a collapse of the once equally firm (and now equally forgotten) wall between the creative past and the static present. Charles Lyell showed that today's earth was sculpted by everyday erosion, earthquakes, and volcanos acting in the past over immense spans of time. The living and nonliving, too, no longer occupy different realms. William Harvey showed that the human body is a machine that runs by hydraulics and other mechanical principles. Friedrich Wöhler showed that the stuff of life is not a magical, quivering gel but ordinary compounds following the laws of chemistry. Darwin showed how the astonishing diversity of life and its ubiquitous signs of good design could arise from the physical process of natural selection among replicators. Mendel,

Preparation of this paper was supported by NIH grant HD 18381.

[1] E. O. Wilson, *Consilience* (New York: Knopf, 1998). See also J. Tooby and L. Cosmides, "Psychological Foundations of Culture," in *The Adapted Mind,* ed. J. Barkow, L. Cosmides, and J. Tooby (New York: Oxford University Press, 1992).

and then Watson and Crick, showed how replication itself could be understood in physical terms.

But one enormous chasm remains in the landscape of human knowledge. Biology versus culture, nature versus society, matter versus mind, and the sciences versus the arts and humanities survive as respectable dichotomies long after the other walls dividing human understanding have tumbled down.

But perhaps not for long. Four new fields are laying a bridge between nature and society in the form of a scientific understanding of mind and human nature.

The first is cognitive science. Many thinkers believe there is a fundamental divide between human behavior and other physical events. Whereas physical behavior has *causes,* they say, human behavior has *reasons.* Consider how we explain an everyday act of behavior, such as Bill getting on a bus. No one would invoke some physical push or pull like magnetism or a gust of wind, nor would anyone need to put Bill's head in a brain scanner or test his blood or DNA. The most perspicuous explanation of Bill's behavior appeals instead to his beliefs and desires, such as that Bill wanted to visit his grandmother and that he knew the bus would take him there. No explanation has as much predictive power as that one. If Bill hated the sight of his grandmother, or if he knew the route had changed, his body would not be on that bus.

For centuries the gap between physical events, on the one hand, and meaning, content, ideas, reasons, or goals, on the other, has been seen as a boundary line between two fundamentally different kinds of explanation. But in the 1950s, the "cognitive revolution" unified psychology, linguistics, computer science, and philosophy of mind with the help of a powerful new idea: that mental life could be explained in physical terms via the notions of information, computation, and feedback. To put it crudely: Beliefs and memories are information, residing in patterns of activity and structure in the brain. Thinking and planning are sequences of transformations of these patterns. Wanting and trying are goal states that govern the transformations via feedback from the world about the discrepancy between the goal state and the current situation, which the transformations are designed to reduce.[2] This general idea, which may be called the computational theory of mind, also explains how *intelligence* and *rationality* can arise from a mere physical process. If the transformations mirror laws of logic, probability, or cause and effect in the world, they will generate correct predictions from valid information in pursuit of goals, which is a pretty good definition of the term "intelligence."

The second science bridging mind and matter is neuroscience, especially cognitive neuroscience, the study of the neural bases of thinking, perception, and emotion. Our traditional and most familiar conception of the mind is based on the soul: an immaterial entity that enters the fertilized egg at conception, reads the instrument panels of the senses and pushes the buttons of behavior, and leaks out at death. Neuroscience is replacing that conception with what Francis Crick has called the astonishing hypothesis: that all aspects of human thought and feeling are manifestations of the physiological activity of the brain. In other words, the mind is what the brain does, in particular, the information-processing that it does.[3]

Astonishing though the hypothesis may be, the evidence is now overwhelming that it is true. Many cause-and-effect linkages have a physical event on one side and a mental event on the other. If an electrical current is sent into the brain by a surgeon, the brain's owner is caused to have a vivid, lifelike experience. A host of

[2] S. Pinker, *How the Mind Works* (New York: W. W. Norton, 1997); H. Gardner, *The Mind's New Science: A History of the Cognitive Revolution* (New York: Basic Books, 1987); J. A. Fodor, *The Elm and the Expert* (Cambridge, Mass.: MIT Press, 1994).

[3] F. Crick, *The Astonishing Hypothesis: The Scientific Search for the Soul* (New York: Simon & Schuster, 1994); M. S. Gazzaniga, ed., *The New Cognitive Neurosciences* (Cambridge, Mass.: MIT Press, in press); M. S. Gazzaniga, R. B. Ivry, and G. R. Mangun, *Cognitive Neuroscience: The Biology of the Mind* (New York: W. W. Norton, 1998).

chemicals can find their way to the brain from the stomach, lungs, or veins and change a person's perception, mood, personality, and thoughts. When a patch of brain tissue dies because of trauma, poisoning, infection, or lack of oxygen, a part of the person is gone: he or she may think, feel, or act so differently as to become quite literally "a different person." Every form of mental activity—every emotion, every thought, every perception—gives off electrical, magnetic, or metabolic signals that are being read with increasing precision and sensitivity by new technologies such as positron emission tomography, functional magnetic resonance imaging, electroencephalography, and magnetoencephalography. When a surgeon takes a knife and cuts the corpus callosum (which joins the two cerebral hemispheres), the mind is split in two and in some sense the body is inhabited by two selves. Under the microscope, the tissues of the brain show a breathtaking degree of complexity—perhaps a hundred trillion synapses—that is fully commensurate with the breathtaking complexity of human thought and experience. And when the brain dies, the person goes out of existence. It is a significant empirical discovery that no one has found a way to communicate with the dead.

The third bridging discipline is behavioral genetics. All the potential for complex learning and feeling that distinguishes humans from other animals lies in the genetic material of the fertilized ovum. We are coming to appreciate that the species-wide design of the human intellect and personality and many of the details that distinguish one person from another have important genetic roots. Studies show that monozygotic (identical) twins separated at birth, who share their genes but not their family or community environments, are remarkably alike in their intelligence, personality traits, attitudes toward a variety of subjects (such as the death penalty and modern music), and personal quirks such as dipping buttered toast in coffee or wading into the ocean backward. Similar conclusions come from the discovery that monozygotic twins are far more similar than dizygotic (fraternal) twins, who share only half their genes, and from the discovery that biological siblings of any kind are far more similar than adoptive siblings. The past few years have also seen the discovery of genetic markers, genes, and sometimes gene products for aspects of intelligence, spatial cognition, the control of speech, and personality traits such as sensation-seeking and excess anxiety.[4]

The fourth bridging science is evolutionary psychology, the study of the phylogenetic history and adaptive functions of the mind. Evolutionary psychology holds out the hope of understanding the *design* or *purpose* of the mind, not in some mystical or teleological sense, but in the sense of the appearance of design or illusion of engineering that is ubiquitous in the natural world (such as in the eye or the heart) and that Darwin explained by the theory of natural selection.[5]

Though there are many controversies within biology, what is not controversial is that the theory of natural selection is indispensable to make sense of a complex organ such as the eye. The eye's precision engineering for the function of forming an image could not be the result of some massive coincidence in tissue formation like the appearance of a wart or tumor or of the random sampling of genes that can lead to simpler traits. And the human

---

[4] T. J. Bouchard, Jr., "Genes, Environment, and Personality," *Science* 264: 1700–1701; D. H. Hamer and P. Copeland, *Living with Our Genes: Why They Matter More Than You Think* (New York: Doubleday, 1998); S. E. Fisher, F. Vargha-Khadem, K. E. Watkins, A. P. Monaco, and M. E. Pembrey, "Localisation of a Gene Implicated in a Severe Speech and Language Disorder," *Nature Genetics* 18: 168–70; J. M. Frangiskakis, A. K. Ewart, A. C. Morris, C. B. Mervis, J. Bertrand, B. F. Robinson, B. P. Klein, G. J. Ensing, L. A. Everett, E. D. Green, C. Proschel, N. J. Gutowski, M. Noble, D. L. Atkinson, S. J. Odelberg, and M. T. Keating, "LIM-Kinase1 Hemizygosity Implicated in Impaired Visuospatial Constructive Cognition," *Cell* 86 (1996): 59–69; R. Plomin, J. C. Defries, G. E. McClearn, and M. Rutter, *Behavioral Genetics* 3d ed. (New York: W. H. Freeman, 1997).

[5] J. H. Barkow, L. Cosmides, and J. Tooby, eds., *The Adapted Mind: Evolutionary Psychology and the Generation of Culture* (New York: Oxford University Press, 1997); S. Pinker, *How the Mind Works* (New York: Norton, 1997); D. Buss, *Evolutionary Psychology: The New Science of the Mind* (New York: Allyn & Bacon, 1999).

eye's similarity to the eyes of other organisms, including many arbitrary and quirky design features, could not be the handiwork of some cosmic designer.[6]

Evolutionary psychology extends this kind of argument to another part of the body. For all its exquisite natural engineering, the eye is useless without the brain. The eye is an organ of information processing; it does not dump its signals into some empty chasm, but connects to complicated neural circuits that extract information about the depths, colors, motions, and shapes of objects and surfaces in the world. All this analysis of the visual world would itself be useless unless it fed into higher circuits for categorization: the ability to make sense of experience, to impute causes to events, and to remember things in terms of useful predictive categories. And in turn, categorization would be useless unless it operated in the service of the person's goals, which are set by motives and emotions such as hunger, fear, love, curiosity, and the pursuit of status. Those are the motives that tend to foster survival and reproduction in the kinds of environments in which our ancestors evolved.

Beginning with the eye, we have a chain of causation that leads to faculties, or modules, or subsystems of mind, each of which can be seen as an adaptation akin to the adaptations in the organs of the body. Recent research has shown that aspects of the psyche that were previously considered mysterious, quirky, and inexplicable, such as fears and phobias, an eye for beauty, family dynamics, romantic love, and a passionate desire for revenge in defense of honor, have a systematic evolutionary logic when analyzed like other biological systems, organs, and tissues.[7]

Cognitive science, neuroscience, behavioral genetics, and evolutionary psychology are doing nothing less than providing a sci-

---

[6] G. C. Williams, *Adaptation and Natural Selection: A Critique of Some Current Evolutionary Thought* (Princeton, N.J.: Princeton University Press, 1966); R. Dawkins, *The Blind Watchmaker: Why the Evidence of Evolution Reveals a Universe without Design* (New York: Norton, 1986).

[7] Pinker, *How the Mind Works.*

entific understanding of the mind and human nature. It is important to note that this understanding is not an alternative to more traditional explanations in terms of learning, experience, culture, and socialization. Rather, it aims at an explanation of how those processes are possible to begin with. Culture is not some gas or force field or bacterial swarm that surrounds humans and insidiously seeps into or infects them. Culture has its effects because of mental algorithms that accomplish the feat we call learning. And learning can be powerful and useful only if it is designed to work in certain ways. Both a parrot and a human child can learn something when exposed to speech, but only the child is equipped with an algorithm for learning vocabulary and grammar that can extract words and rules from the speech wave and use them to generate an unlimited number of meaningful new sentences. The search for mechanisms of learning animates each of the four new sciences.

A chief goal of cognitive science is to identify the learning algorithms that underlie language and other cognitive feats.[8] Similarly, a major goal of neuroscience arises from the realization that all mental activity, including learning, arises from the neurophysiology and neuroanatomy of the brain: when people learn, neural tissue must change in some way as the result of experience. The phenomenon is called neural plasticity, and it is currently being explored intensively within neuroscience. Behavioral genetics, too, is not aimed at documenting an exclusively genetic control of behavior. In most studies, only around half of the variance in intellectual or personality traits has been found to correlate with the genes; the other half comes from environmental or random factors. Behavioral genetics, by allowing us to subtract the resemblances between parents and children that are due to their genetic relatedness, and to partition the remaining causes into those operating within the family (such as the correlations between adoptive siblings reared together) and those outside the family (such as the

[8] S. Pinker, *Language Learnability and Language Development* (Cambridge, Mass.: Harvard University Press, 1984/1996).

lack of a perfect correlation between identical twins reared together), is essential to our understanding of the nature of the socialization process. Finally, according to evolutionary psychology human beings are not robotic automata or bundles of knee-jerk reflexes. Mental adaptations are what biologists call *facultative* adaptations: a crucial part of their design is to sense environmental variation and adjust to find the optimum behavioral strategy.

How will these new sciences bridge the gaps in human knowledge that I alluded to at the outset, completing the consilience that we have enjoyed so long in the physical sciences? The emerging picture is that our genetic program grows a brain endowed with emotions and with learning abilities that were favored by natural selection. The arts, humanities, and social sciences, then, can be seen as the study of the products of certain faculties of the human brain. These faculties include language, perceptual analyzers and their esthetic reactions, reasoning, a moral sense, love, loyalty, rivalry, status, feelings toward allies and kin, an obsession with themes of life and death, and many others. As human beings share their discoveries and accumulate them over time, and as they institute conventions and rules to coordinate their often conflicting desires, the phenomena we call "culture" arise. Given this continuous causal chain from biology to culture through psychology, a fundamental division between the humanities and sciences has become as obsolete as the division between the sublunary and supralunary spheres.

Does this picture deserve the dreaded academic epithet "reductionism"? Not in the bad, indeed, idiotic sense of trying to explain World War I in terms of subatomic particles. It *is* reductionist in the good sense of aiming for the deep and uniquely satisfying understanding we have enjoyed from the unification of sciences such as biology, chemistry, and physics. The goal is not to eliminate explanations at higher levels of analysis but to connect them lawfully to more fundamental levels. The elementary processes at one level can be explained in terms of more complicated interactions one level down.

Not everyone, needless to say, is enthralled by the prospect of unifying biology and culture through a science of mind and human nature. There have been furious objections from many quarters, particularly the academic left and the religious and cultural right. When E. O. Wilson and other "sociobiologists" first outlined a vision of a science of human nature in the 1970s and 1980s, critics expressed their reservations by dousing him with ice water at an academic conference, protesting his appearances with pickets, bullhorns, and posters urging people to bring noisemakers to his lectures, and angry manifestoes with accusations of racism, sexism, class oppression, genocide, and the inevitable comparison to the Nazis.[9] In their popular book *Not in Our Genes,* three prominent scientists, Richard Lewontin, Steven Rose, and Leon Kamin, felt justified in the use of nonstandard forms of scientific argumentation such as doctoring quotations and dropping innuendoes about their opponents' sex lives. When the psychologist Paul Ekman announced at an anthropology conference his discovery that facial expressions of basic emotions are the same the world over, he was shouted down and called a fascist and racist.[10] Though the worst of the hysteria has died down, ad hominem arguments and smears of racism and sexism are not uncommon in both academic and popular discussions of behavioral genetics and evolutionary psychology.

Alarms have been sounded not just by tenured radicals and commissars of political correctness. In a highly publicized article entitled "Sorry, But Your Soul Just Died," the left-lampooning author Tom Wolfe discusses the prospects of the new understanding

[9] See R. Wright, *The Moral Animal* (New York: Pantheon, 1994); E. O. Wilson, *Naturalist* (Washington, D.C.: Island Press, 1994).

[10] For documentation, see Pinker, *How the Mind Works,* pp. 45, 569*n*45, 366, 580*n*366.

of mind, brain, genes, and evolution with a mixture of admiration and dread. He predicts:

> . . . in the year 2006 or 2026, some new Nietzsche will step forward to announce . . . "The soul is dead." He will say that he is merely bringing the news, the news of the greatest event of the millennium: "The soul, that last refuge of values, is dead, because educated people no longer believe it exists." . . . Unless the assurances of [E. O. Wilson and his allies] also start rippling out, the lurid carnival that will ensue may make [Nietzsche's] phrase "the total eclipse of all values" seem tame.[11]

Farther to the right, the journalist Andrew Ferguson, writing in the neoconservative magazine *Weekly Standard,* is far less ambivalent. He reviewed a recent book by Francis Fukuyama, which argued that civility and social institutions always reassert themselves because of aspects of human nature recently revealed by the new sciences. The book "is sure to give you the creeps," Ferguson wrote, because "Whether [a] behavior is moral, whether it signifies virtue, is a judgment that the new science, and materialism in general, cannot make."[12] In another book review he characterizes the new sciences as saying that people are nothing but "meat puppets," in contrast to the traditional Judeo-Christian view in which "human beings were persons from the start, endowed with a soul, created by God, and infinitely precious. And this is the common understanding . . . the new science . . . means to undo."[13]

Clearly the new sciences of mind are widely seen as threatening, almost in the manner of a religious heresy. For observers such as Ferguson it is literally the religious doctrine of the immaterial

---

[11] *Forbes* magazine, 1996.

[12] A. Ferguson, "The End of Nature and the Next Man," *Weekly Standard,* 1999.

[13] A. Ferguson, "How Steven Pinker's Mind Works," *Weekly Standard,* January 12, 1998.

soul that he sees as threatened. For others it is a modern secular religion, which John Tooby and Leda Cosmides have called the Standard Social Science Model or SSSM.[14]

The ascendancy of the SSSM is a key event in modern intellectual history that began in the first decades of the twentieth century and was firmly entrenched by the 1950s.[15] The model embraces three beliefs, which give me the title of this paper.

The first is John Locke's doctrine of the tabula rasa, the Blank Slate: that the human mind is infinitely plastic, with all its structure coming from reinforcement and socialization. Here are two of the twentieth century's earliest and most vociferous defenders of the Blank Slate, the psychologist John B. Watson and the anthropologist Margaret Mead:

> Give me a dozen healthy infants, well-formed, and my own specified world to bring them up in and I'll guarantee to take any one at random and train him to become any type of specialist I might select—doctor, lawyer, artist, merchant-chief, and yes, even beggar-man and thief, regardless of his talents, penchants, tendencies, abilities, vocations, and race of his ancestors. (John B. Watson, *Behaviorism*, 1925)

> We are forced to conclude that human nature is almost unbelievably malleable, responding accurately and contrastingly to contrasting cultural conditions. . . . The members of either or both sexes may, with more or less success in the case of different individuals, be educated to approximate [any temperament]. (Margaret Mead, *Sex and Temperament in Three Primitive Societies,* 1935)

The second belief is Jean-Jacques Rousseau's doctrine of the Noble Savage: that evil comes not from human nature but from

---

[14] Tooby and Cosmides, "Psychological Foundations."

[15] For an excellent history, see C. N. Degler, *In Search of Human Nature: The Decline and Revival of Darwinism in American Social Thought* (New York: Oxford University Press, 1991).

our social institutions. We find the doctrine today in a particularly pure form in the "Seville Statement" of 1986, in which twenty social scientists, with the endorsement of UNESCO and several academic societies, declared that it is "scientifically incorrect" to say that "we have inherited a tendency to make war from our animal ancestors," that "war or any other violent behavior is genetically programmed into our human nature," that humans have a "violent brain," or that war is caused by "instinct." We see the doctrine as well in the popular image of native peoples living in peaceful coexistence with the ecosystem and with one another.[16]

The third doctrine is what Gilbert Ryle called the Ghost in the Machine: the belief that we are separate from biology, free to choose our actions and define meaning, value, and purpose. As Wolfe puts it,

> Meantime, the notion of a self—a self who exercises self-discipline, postpones gratification, curbs the sexual appetite, stops short of aggression and criminal behavior—a self who can become more intelligent and lift itself to the very peaks of life by its own bootstraps through study, practice, perseverance, and refusal to give up in the face of great odds—this old-fashioned notion (what's a boot strap, for God's sake?) of success through enterprise and true grit is already slipping away, slipping away . . . slipping away . . .
> . . . Where does that leave self-control? Where, indeed, if people believe this ghostly self does not even exist, and brain imaging proves it, once and for all?

Similarly, Ferguson writes that the scientific belief that our minds arise from neural activity

> runs counter to the most elemental belief every person has about himself. . . . Beyond this, however, the "scientific belief"

[16] "The Seville Statement on Violence," *American Psychologist* 45 (1990): 1167–68.

would also appear to be corrosive of any notion of free will, personal responsibility, or universal morality. . . .

The old myth of natural law had a means for making moral judgments, of course. But it took as fundamental the very concepts that the new science wants to render meaningless—that human beings are endowed with souls, for example.

At first it would seem that the Ghost in the Machine would be chained to religious thought; that secular thinkers would have nothing to do with an immaterial soul. Those who deny the existence of human nature would attribute behavior instead to the cumulative effects of socialization and conditioning. But in fact it is common for believers in the Standard Social Science Model to invoke an "I," a "we," a "you," or a "person" that somehow floats free of genetics, neurobiology, or evolution and can act as it pleases, constrained only by current environmental circumstances. Rose, an ardent foe of evolutionary psychology and behavioral genetics, repeatedly declares in a recent book that "we have the ability to construct our own futures, albeit not in circumstances of our own choosing"; the statement is intended as a refutation of "reductionist" biology.[17] But he never explains who the "we" is, if not highly structured neural circuits, which must get that structure in part by genes and evolution.

The Standard Social Science Model arose in part as a legitimate backlash against many deplorable events of the nineteenth and the first half of the twentieth century. These include pseudoscientific doctrines of racial and ethnic inferiority, coercive eugenic policies, the oppression of women, the maltreatment and neglect of children, the theory of "Social Darwinism," which tried to justify inequality and conquest as part of the wisdom of nature, policies of

---

[17] S. Rose, *Lifelines: Biology beyond Determinism* (New York: Oxford University Press, 1998).

racial discrimination, and outright genocide.[18] As a result, the precepts of the SSSM, which would appear to undermine any ideology that could permit such horrors, have acquired a moral authority and are felt to be the foundation for political and ethical decency.

The precepts, however, are factual claims, many of which are being refuted. Does this mean that we are forced to return to repugnant doctrines and horrific practices? My aim in this lecture is to convince you that the answer is no: the supposed conflict between the new sciences of mind and human nature and our ethical values is misconstrued. The habit of basing equality, dignity, and human rights on the doctrines of the Blank Slate, the Noble Savage, and the Ghost in the Machine is a product of fuzzy thinking about both ethics and science, and we can bid these doctrines good riddance without compromising human values at all. I will try to allay four fears that have surrounded the prospects of a science of mind and human nature.

The first fear is of the possibility of biological differences. If the mind has an innate structure, the worry goes, different people (or different classes, sexes, and races) could have different innate structures, and that would justify discrimination and oppression. But if there were no innate structure, there could be, by definition, no individual or group differences in innate structure, and thus no basis for discrimination. Therefore, according to this moral argument for the SSSM, there is no human nature. The argument, however, is fallacious both empirically and morally.

The empirical problem is that discoveries about a universal human nature—the bread and butter of cognitive science and evolutionary psychology—do not imply innate differences between individuals, groups, or races. Any page of *Gray's Anatomy* will show a complex design of systems, organs, and tissues that are qualitatively alike in every normal human being (though of course

18 Degler, *In Search of Human Nature.*

with numerous quantitative differences in size and shape). The same is likely to be true of the mental equivalents of systems, organs, and tissues. This is not because it would be nice if it were true, but because of particular properties of the forces that shaped human nature. Sexual recombination and natural selection (which adapts organisms to an environmental niche by weeding out variants that are less fit) are homogenizing forces, making the members of a species qualitatively alike.[19] And in the case of humans, the racial divisions in the family tree probably opened up only recently and are constantly being bridged by the fact that humans migrate and interbreed with gusto, which has resulted in a steady shuffling of genes across racial groups for tens of thousands of years. It is therefore unlikely that individuals or races differ qualitatively in any mental faculty, and indeed the striking universals in language, emotions, and cognitive categories that emerge from the ethnographic record suggest that in fact the differences are small to nonexistent.[20] All this means that research on human nature does not necessarily lead to invidious assertions about the mental traits of specific people or groups.

But of course there *could* be genetic variation, most likely quantitative, among people and races; it would be absurd to declare this outcome impossible a priori just because it would be uncomfortable if true. If such variation were discovered, what would follow? Would discrimination or oppression be justified? Of course not! Discrimination against an individual on the basis of the person's sex, race, ethnicity, or sexual orientation is simply wrong on moral grounds. Now, conceivably someone could argue on grounds of economic efficiency that a rational agent ought to factor in group statistics in making a decision about an individual (say, whether the person should be admitted to a university, or be

---

[19] J. Tooby and L. Cosmides, "On the Universality of Human Nature and the Uniqueness of the Individual: The Role of Genetics and Adaptation," *Journal of Personality* 58 (1990): 17–67.

[20] D. E. Brown, *Human Universals* (New York: McGraw-Hill, 1991).

released on parole), because that is what standard Bayesian inference demands: prior probabilities (such as the probability that people of a given race or sex will succeed in school or commit a crime) should influence the estimate of posterior probabilities (whether a *given* individual will succeed in school or commit a crime). But I think most people would agree that the rights of an individual to be considered on his or her individual merits and accomplishments trump any gain in overall accuracy of decision-making based on the use of the statistics of races, ethnic groups, or genders. It is one of many cases in which we willingly sacrifice a modicum of freedom and economic efficiency for a more general good. (Other examples include laws safeguarding individuals' privacy and those that outlaw the voluntary sale of one's vote, one's organs, or one's freedom.)

Crucially, the moral argument against discrimination can be made *regardless* of the existence or nonexistence of any empirically discovered biological differences among people or groups. And that is surely the way we want it. Is there *any* conceivable finding on group differences in any trait that would undermine our belief in the evil of racial or sexual discrimination against an individual? If not, we should not fear the study of human nature just because it may stumble upon some innate difference.

This is especially important to keep in mind when it comes to possible differences between men and women. When it comes to the sexes, the *Gray's Anatomy* argument breaks down. The difference between male and female anatomy is a vivid illustration that there *can* be important biological differences between members of the human race. Though some writers still insist that all sex differences are products of sexism or socialization practices, the argument requires standards of evidence worthy of the tobacco industry. The more honest of these writers admit that they are motivated by a fear that the discovery of any biologically influenced sex differences will compromise the ideals of feminism or gender equality. (Thus we have the strange situation in which some writers, under the banner of a dubious form of feminism, argue that women are identical to men in terms of their inherent propensity for promiscuity, infidelity, taste for pornography, and violence.) The assumption appears to be that *fairness* requires *sameness,* and that is absurd. Whether or not males are identical to females in some or all psychological traits, it is intolerable for public institutions to discriminate against individual men and women on the basis of their sex. We can all agree with Gloria Steinem when she said, "There are really not many jobs that actually require a penis or a vagina, and all the other occupations should be open to everyone."

The second fear is the possibility of evil instincts. The unstated assumption is that if deplorable behavior such as aggression, war, rape, clannishness, exploitation, xenophobia, and the pursuit of status and wealth is innate, that would make them "natural" and hence good. And even if we agree that they are not good, they are "in the genes" and therefore cannot be changed, so attempts at social reform are futile. Aggression is objectionable, and social reform is desirable; therefore, the argument seems to go, *Homo sapiens* must be a bunch of nice guys. Only "society" is at fault.

The lunatic version of this argument is, of course, the Seville Statement, with its fiat that all claims about biological propensities toward dominance, violence, and war are "scientifically incorrect." The signatories were at least clear about their motives. They alleged that the "incorrect" statements "have been used, even by some in our disciplines, to justify violence and war" (they gave no examples) and concluded that "biology does not condemn humanity to war, and that humanity can be freed from the bondage of biological pessimism and empowered with confidence to undertake the transformative tasks needed in the International Year of Peace and in the years to come."

The Seville Statement is a textbook example of what the philosopher G. E. Moore called the Naturalistic Fallacy: that whatever is found in nature is morally right. In this case, the fallacy is that if people are prone to violence, that would make it justifiable.

Hence the signatories' decision to legislate empirical claims about people's natural propensities was, in their minds, a tactic to bring about peace. Apparently it was inconceivable to these leading social scientists that there could be selection for violent behavior *and* that violent behavior is morally unjustifiable. Their manifesto is especially egregious because the legislated factual claims are a blatant kind of disinformation.

The notion that the human brain houses no inherent tendency to use violence, and that violence is an artifact of some particular culture at a particular time, has to confront an obvious fact about human history. Winston Churchill wrote, "The story of the human race is war. Except for brief and precarious interludes there has never been peace in the world; and long before history began murderous strife was universal and unending." Or as one biologist put it, "*Homo sapiens* is a nasty business."

For many years intellectuals tried to deny the significance of history with two myths. One is the myth of the peaceful savage, where "savages" or hunter-gatherers are thought to be representative of a human nature uncorrupted by the malign influences of civilization. According to this myth, among preagricultural peoples war is rare, mild, and ritualized, or at least it used to be before contact with Westerners. Recent books by anthropologists, biologists, and historians who have examined the factual record, such as Napoleon Chagnon, Richard Keeley, Jared Diamond, Martin Daly and Margo Wilson, Richard Wrangham, and Michael Ghiglieri, have shown that this is romantic nonsense; war has always been hell.[21]

It is not uncommon among preagricultural peoples for a third

---

[21] N. A. Chagnon, "Life Histories, Blood Revenge, and Warfare in a Tribal Population," *Science* 239 (1988): 985–92; J. Diamond, *Guns, Germs, and Steel* (New York: Norton, 1997); L. H. Keeley, *War before Civilization: The Myth of the Peaceful Savage* (New York: Oxford University Press, 1996); M. Daly and M. Wilson, *Homicide* (Hawthorne, N.Y.: Aldine de Gruyter, 1988); R. Wrangham and D. Peterson, *Demonic Males* (n.p., 1996); M. Ghiglieri, *The Dark Side of Man: Tracing the Origins of Violence* (New York: Perseus Books, 1999).

of the men to die at the hands of other men, and for almost half of the men to have killed someone. As compared to modern warfare, in primitive warfare mobilization is more complete, battles are more frequent, casualties are proportionally higher, prisoners are fewer, and the weapons are more damaging. Even in the more peaceable hunter-gatherer societies such as the !Kung San of the Kalahari desert, the murder rate is similar to that found in modern American urban jungles such as Detroit. In his survey of human universals gleaned from the ethnographic record, the anthropologist Donald Brown includes violent conflict, rape, envy, sexual jealousy, and in-group/out-group conflicts as traits documented in all cultures.[22]

A related romantic myth is the harmony and wisdom of nature. Many intellectuals still believe that animals kill only for food, that among animals war is unknown, and that, in the words of the Seville Statement, dominance hierarchies are a form of bonding and affiliation that benefits the group. The reality was summed up by Darwin: "What a book a devil's chaplain might write on the clumsy, wasteful, blundering, low, and horribly cruel works of nature!" The most chilling example is the one closest to home. The primatologists Jane Goodall and Richard Wrangham have documented behavior in our closest relatives, the chimpanzees, that would surely be called genocide if it had been observed in humans. In evolutionary terms, killing a member of one's own species is hardly an anomalous or puzzling event. As Daly and Wilson have pointed out, "Killing one's antagonist is the ultimate conflict resolution technique, and our ancestors discovered it long before they were people."[23]

Is any of this a "justification" for war or other violent conflict? Obviously not. As we used to say in the 1960s, war is not healthy for children or other living things. Nothing about the behavior of

[22] Brown, *Human Universals.*

[23] Daly and Wilson, *Homicide,* p. ix.

hunger-gatherers or primates could conceivably push us from ab-
horring war and trying to eliminate it.

But is war nonetheless inevitable, making attempts to prevent
it fruitless? Here too the answer is no. The human mind is a complex system with many parts. One may be an urge to neutralize ri-
vals by any means necessary. But another is a calculator that can
come to the realization that conflict has terrible costs and that everyone can come out ahead by dividing up the surplus that results
from laying down arms. According to Brown's survey, what is *also*
universal across human societies is the deploring of conflict, violence, rape, and murder and the use of mechanisms to reduce
them, including laws, punishment, redress, and mediation.

And another obvious empirical fact is that the human condition
can improve. For all the horrors of the past few centuries, they have
seen the disappearance of war, slavery, conquest, blood feuds, des-
potism, the ownership of women, apartheid, fascism, and Lenin-
ism from vast swaths of the earth that had known them for decades,
centuries, or millennia. Even at their worst, the homicide rates in
American cities were twenty times lower than those measured
among many foraging peoples. Modern Britons are twenty times
less likely to be murdered than their medieval counterparts.[24]

There are many reasons that war and aggression can decline despite a constancy of human nature. They include a knowledge of
the lessons of history and the use of face-saving measures, mediation, contracts, deterrence, equal opportunity, a court system, en-
forceable laws, monogamy, and limits on perceived inequality.
These are humble, time-tested methods that *acknowledge* human
nature and its dark side. They are likely to continue to be more hu-
mane and effective than attempts to re-engineer culture and redesign human nature, as we are reminded by the recent history of the
Soviet empire, Cambodia, and mainland China. Indeed, the
strongest argument against totalitarianism may be recognition of

[24] Daly and Wilson, *Homicide.*

a universal human nature: that all humans have innate desires for life, liberty, and the pursuit of happiness. The doctrine of the Blank Slate, which justifies the dismissal of people's stated wants as an artifact of a particular time and place and thereby licenses the top-down redesign of society, is a totalitarian's dream.

The third fear aroused by a science of human nature is the dissolution of free will and the resulting universal abdication of responsibility. If behavior is a physical consequence of ricocheting molecules in the brain shaped in part by genes that were put into place by natural selection, where is the "person" whom we hold responsible for his or her actions? If the rapist is following a biological imperative to spread his genes, the worry goes, it's a short step to saying that it's not his fault. This worry has been stated by voices of both the left and the right. When E. O. Wilson suggested that humans resemble most other mammals in the great male desire for multiple sexual partners, Rose accused him of really saying, "Don't blame your mates for sleeping around, ladies, it's not their fault they are genetically programmed."[25] Tom Wolfe writes in a similar vein (though with tongue partly in cheek):

> The male of the human species is genetically hardwired to be polygamous, i.e., unfaithful to his legal mate. Any magazine-reading male gets the picture soon enough. (Three million years of evolution made me do it!) Women lust after male celebrities, because they are genetically hardwired to sense that alpha males will take better care of their offspring. (I'm just a lifeguard in the gene pool, honey.) Teenage girls are genetically hardwired to be promiscuous and are as helpless to stop themselves as dogs in the park. (The school provides the condoms.) Most murders are the result of genetically hardwired compulsions. (Convicts can read, too, and they report to the prison psychiatrist: "Something came over me . . . and then the knife went in.")

[25] S. Rose, "Pre-Copernican Sociobiology?" *New Scientist* 80 (1978): 45–46.

But this argument is fallacious for two reasons. First, the apparent threat to the traditional notion of free will has nothing to do with genetic, neurobiological, or evolutionary explanations of behavior; it is raised by *any* explanation of behavior. In this century it has been far more common to excuse behavior because of putative *environmental* causes. Remember the gang members in *West Side Story,* who explained, "We're depraved on accounta we're deprived"?

> Dear kindly Sergeant Krupke,
> You gotta understand,
> It's just our bringing up-ke,
> That gets us out of hand.
> Our mothers all are junkies,
> Our fathers all are drunks.
> Golly Moses, naturally we're punks!

Stephen Sondheim's lyrics lampooned the psychoanalytic and social science explanations of behavior popular in the 1950s and 1960s. Since then we have seen the Twinkie Defense that mitigated the sentence of the mayor-murdering Dan White, the Abuse Excuse that led to a mistrial of the Menendez brothers, the Black Rage Defense offered to the Long Island Railroad gunman Colin Ferguson, and the Pornography-Made-Me-Do-It defense attempted by several attorneys for rapists. Clearly there is nothing specific to brains, genes, or evolutionary history that lends itself to bogus justifications for bad behavior; any explanation can be abused in that way.

And that leads to Rose's and Wolfe's second fallacy, the confusion of explanation with exculpation. The difference between them is nicely captured in the old saying "To understand is not to forgive." We would do well to keep the two separate. If some moral system identifies personal responsibility with a ghost in the machine, we ought to discard that moral system, because the ghost is being exorcised, but we still need the notion of individual responsibility, if for no other reason than to construct policies of effective deterrence and to satisfy people's sense of justice. A better moral system would separate causation from responsibility as two sets of rules played out over the same entities (humans and their actions). We don't want the morality of killing, raping, lying, and stealing to depend on what comes out of the psychology or neuroscience lab at the other end of town. The autonomous moral agent is an indispensable construct that makes judicial and moral reasoning possible. It allows us to distinguish voluntary from involuntary acts, intended from unintended consequences, and the acts of rational adults from those of children, animals, and the patently deluded. It does not literally require a ghost in the machine as an alternative to a causal explanation in biological terms.

What about the more practical worry that the exorcising of the ghost implies that there is no way to hold people responsible for their behavior, and hence no way to reduce bad behavior? If bad behavior results from biological urges, is it inevitable, no matter how much we may condemn it? The answer is the same as the one to the question of whether urges toward violent conflict imply that war is inevitable. Since the mind has more than one part, one urge can counteract another and prevent it from pressing the buttons of behavior. Together with motives to hurt, lie, philander, and crave status, the human brain houses motives to avoid punishment, condemnation, loss of reputation, loss of self-esteem, and mistrust or abandonment by allies and loved ones. These faculties of social reasoning and emotion are every bit as "biological" as the deadly sins, so an approach to behavior that is consilient with biology does not dissolve hopes of improving standards of individual behavior.

The final fear is that a scientific explanation of mind will lead to a dissolution of meaning and purpose. The worry is that if emotion and feeling are just biochemical events in our brains, and if emotions are just patterns of activity in circuits ultimately designed by natural selection as a way of propagating our genes, then our deepest ideals would be shams. Life would be a Potemkin village with only a facade of value and worth. For example, if we love our children because the genes for loving children are in the bodies of those children and the genes are thereby benefiting copies of themselves, wouldn't that undermine the inherent goodness of that love and the value of the self-sacrifice that parenting entails? If our empathy and good deeds toward others evolved, as evolutionary psychologists suggest, as ways of obtaining favors in the future, and if our sense of fairness and justice evolved as a way to avoid getting cheated when exchanging favors, wouldn't that imply that there is no such thing as altruism or justice, that deep down we're really selfish?

The worry reminds me of the opening scene of *Annie Hall* in which the young Alvy Singer is taken by his mother to a doctor:

Mother: He's been depressed. All of a sudden, he can't do anything.

Doctor: Why are you depressed, Alvy?

Mother: (Nudging Alvy) Tell Dr. Flicker. (Young Alvy sits, his head down. His mother answers for him.) It's something he read.

Doctor: Something he read, huh?

Alvy: (His head still down) The universe is expanding.

Doctor: The universe is expanding?

Alvy: (Looking up at the doctor) Well, the universe is everything, and if it's expanding, someday it will break apart and that would be the end of everything!

Mother: (Disgusted, she looks at him. Shouting) What is that your business? (She turns back to the doctor.) He stopped doing his homework.

Alvy: What's the point?

Mother: (Excited, gesturing with her hands) What has the universe got to do with it? You're here in Brooklyn! Brooklyn is not expanding!

Alvy's mother has a good point. Brooklyn is not expanding. What may seem depressing at the ultimate level of scientific analysis can be without consequence at the day-to-day scale on which we live our lives. The worry that our motives are "selfish" in an ultimate, evolutionary sense, and that therefore our supposedly selfless motives are really shams, is a confusion, a misreading of Richard Dawkins's metaphor of the selfish gene.

Dawkins pointed out that an excellent way to understand the logic of natural selection is to imagine that genes are agents with selfish motives.[26] The metaphor provides insight into complex processes of evolution and has led to countless successful empirical predictions. Unfortunately, the idea easily leads to a confusion, flowing from the assumption that the genes are our deepest hidden self, our essence. If genes are selfish, one might be tempted to think, then deep, deep down *we* must be selfish. The conclusion is a strange hybrid between evolutionary biology and Freud's theory of an unconscious self with ignoble motives.

The fallacy is that the *metaphorical* motives of the *genes* are different from the *real* motives of the *person*. Sometimes, the most selfish thing the genes can do is to help build a thoroughly unselfish person. For example, the love of children, at the psychological

[26] R. Dawkins, *The Selfish Gene* (New York: Oxford University Press, 1976/1989).

level of analysis at which we make sense of our own behavior, is obviously pure and heartfelt. It is only at a different level of analysis—the ultimate or evolutionary level at which we seek to explain *why* we have that pure emotion—that "selfishness" comes into the picture. The selfishness at one level does not contradict a selflessness at a different level, any more than the fact that the entire universe is expanding over billions of years undermines the fact that Brooklyn was not expanding in the 1940s.

A more general worry arises from the undisputed fact that experimental psychology has taught us that some of our experiences are figments. For example, the qualitative difference between the color red and the color green does not correspond to any qualitative physical difference in the light producing the sensation of red and green; wavelength, which gives rise to the perception of hue, is a continuous variable. The difference in kind between red and green is a construct of our perceptual system and could be different in an organism with slightly different chemistry or wiring (indeed, such organisms exist: people with red-green colorblindness). The new sciences of mind seem to be implying that the same is true of our perception of the difference between right and wrong—that the attainment of meaning and moral purpose may be just our way to tickle certain pleasure centers in the brain. They would have no more reality than the difference between red and green and could be meaningless to a person with a slightly different constitution.

But the analogy is imperfect. Many of our mental faculties evolved to mesh with real things in the world. Our perception of depth is the product of complicated circuitry in the brain, circuitry that appears to be absent in other species and even in certain impaired people. But that does not mean that there aren't real trees and cliffs out there or that the world is as flat as a cartoon. And this argument can be carried over to more abstract properties of the world. Humans (and many other animals) appear to have an innate sense of number, which can be explained by the utility of reasoning about numerosity in our evolutionary history. That is perfectly compatible with the Platonist theory of number believed by many mathematicians and philosophers of mathematics, according to which abstract mathematical entities such as numbers have an existence independent of minds. The number three is not a figment like greenness; it has real properties, which are discovered and explored, not invented out of whole cloth. According to this view, the number sense evolved to mesh with real truths in the world that in some sense exist independent of human knowers.

A similar argument can be made for morality. According to the theory of moral realism, right and wrong have an existence and an inherent logic that licenses some chains of argument and not others. If so, our moral sense evolved to mesh with the logic of morality; it did not invent it out of the whole cloth.[27] The crucial point is that something can be *both* a product of the mind *and* a genuinely existing entity.

Even if one is uneasy with the admittedly difficult idea that moral truths exist in some abstract Platonic sense, one can preserve the inherent value of our moral judgments in other ways. One could be agnostic about the realism of moral judgments and simply note that our moral sense cannot work unless it *believes* that right and wrong have an external reality. That is, we cannot reason other than by presupposing that our moral judgments have some inherent validity (whether or not one could ever determine that they do). So when we have a moral debate, we would still appeal to external standards, even if moral reasoning is a biological adaptation; we would not merely be comparing idiosyncratic emotional or subjective reactions.

CONCLUSION

As I mentioned at the outset, these are exciting times in the study of the human mind and in the state of human knowledge in general. Thanks to cognitive science, neuroscience, behavioral

[27] See R. Nozick, *Philosophical Explanations* (Cambridge, Mass.: Harvard University Press, 1981), pp. 317–62.

genetics, and evolutionary psychology, we are beginning to arrive at an understanding of human nature that will bridge the last remaining chasms of knowledge: between matter and mind, and between biology and culture. This promises to lead to a particularly satisfying depth of understanding of our own kind, fulfilling the ancient injunction to know thyself.

In addition, a better understanding of mind and brain holds out the promise of indispensable practical applications. To take just one example, Alzheimer's disease will surely be one of the leading causes of human misery in the industrial world over the next several decades, as we live longer and stop dying of other causes. The successful treatment of Alzheimer's will come not from treating memory and personality as manifestations of an immaterial soul or of some irreducible, dignified agent. It will come from treating memory and personality as phenomena of biochemistry and physiology.

But the coming of a science of mind consilient with biology is, I recognize, not an innocuous development. It challenges beliefs that are deeply held in modern intellectual life and that are, in the minds of many, saturated with moral import. The most fundamental of these beliefs are the doctrines of the Blank Slate, the Noble Savage, and the Ghost in the Machine.

I have argued that the new developments in the sciences of mind do not have to undermine our moral values. On the contrary, they present opportunities to sharpen our ethical reasoning and put our moral and political values on a firmer foundation. In particular, it is a bad idea to say that discrimination is wrong only because the traits of all humans are identical. It is a bad idea to say that war, violence, rape, and greed are bad because humans are not naturally inclined to them. It is a bad idea to say that people are responsible for their actions because the causes of those actions are mysterious. And it is a bad idea to say that our motives are meaningful in a personal sense only if they are meaningless in a biological sense. These are bad ideas because they imply that either scientists must be prepared to fudge their data or we must all be prepared to give up our values.

I argue that we do not have to make that choice. With a clearer separation of ethics and science, we can have our values and greet the new understanding of mind, brain, and human nature not with a sense of terror but with a sense of excitement. In the sixteenth century people attached grave moral significance to the question of whether the earth revolved around the sun or vice versa. Today it is hard to understand why people were willing to base moral beliefs on a plainly empirical claim, and we know that morals and values easily survived the claim's demise. I suggest that the same is true of the grave moral significance currently attached to the denial of human nature and of a materialist understanding of the mind.

The Problem with Purity

RICHARD WHITE

THE TANNER LECTURES ON HUMAN VALUES

Delivered at

University of California, Davis
May 10, 1999

RICHARD WHITE is Margaret Byrne Professor of American History at Stanford University. He was educated at the University of California at Santa Cruz and at the University of Washington, where he received his Ph.D. He is a former president of the Western History Association, and has served on the boards of the Forest History Association, the Institute of the North American West, and the Environmental History Association. His many publications include *Remembering Ahanagran: A History of Stories* (1998), *The Organic Machine: The Remaking of the Columbia River* (1995), and *The Middle Ground: Indians, Empires, and Republics in the Great Lakes Region, 1650-1815* (1991), which won the Francis Parkman Prize and was a finalist for the Pulitzer Prize. He is the recipient of a MacArthur Foundation Fellowship.

1

We have a problem with purity. By "we" I mean, in descending order, all of us, collectively, as Americans; I mean environmentalists, of whom I still consider myself one; and I mean American intellectuals, particularly academics, of whom I am certainly one.

Our problem with purity rises from a search for values that might give us a dependable guide to avoid the horrors that have marked the twentieth century. Whatever problems the future holds, it's nice to be pulling out of the twentieth century: two world wars, the Depression, the Holocaust, massive famines, repression, racism, murders on an industrial scale. Historians tend to resist nostalgia. Not that, all things considered, we are without problems now. There is, just to mention the environmental problems, global warming and the diminishing ozone layer; there is rapid and pronounced extinction of species. There already a lack of clean water for most of the world's population and the oceanic fisheries are crashing.

The instincts that lead us away from such horrors toward purity are admirable. We want rules, a set of values, that can both explain why human beings cause such things to happen and prevent them from happening again. What many of us have done, myself included, is to find the root of many of the horrors of our time in categorical mistakes, confusing one thing with another, and in transgressing forbidden boundaries. We have logically deduced that the solution is purity: keeping the categories separate, the boundaries intact.

This sounds abstract, an intellectual formulation, but I don't think it is. Two examples can show what I mean. Racism is, for example, a confusion of categories that has in the twentieth century cost tens of millions of people their lives and blighted the lives of hundreds of millions of others. In racism some physical marker such as skin color is taken as a sign of ineradicable qualities such as intelligence or morality so that a glance can tell you all you need to know about a person. We have confused biology with culture and society. We have looked toward nature when we should have been looking at culture. Similarly, many people regard our environmental problems as a transgression of boundaries. In Barry Commoner's famous formulation, "Nature knows best," and we have endangered the planet and ourselves by inserting our culture and our technology into realms like the ozone layer, or the climate, or the rain forest where they don't belong. The solution, again, is purity. Follow nature in nature's domain.

These are not silly positions. Culture is culture and biology is biology, and when we completely confuse the two, we do produce racism and sexism. Our interventions into the natural world for all their technical achievement have produced some very dangerous results. The boundaries seemingly must hold.

Yet we fear that the boundaries aren't holding, and some people believe, or profess to believe, that they have collapsed forever. These fears are particularly pronounced in regard to the environmental front, among both intellectuals and activists.[1] The battle is over, and Nature has lost. There is no more nature to defend: nature can't be saved because it has already disappeared. "Postmodernism," as Fredric Jameson writes, "is what you have when the modernization process is complete and nature is gone for good."[2] The quite literal eradication of the natural, the other-than-human, is not confined to academic theory; it also appears in best-selling books, such as Bill McKibben's *The End of Nature*.[3] What they

---

[1] Mary Douglas and Aaron Wildavsky, *Risk and Culture: An Essay on the Selection of Technological and Environmental Dangers* (Berkeley: University of California Press, 1983).

[2] Fredric Jameson, *Postmodernism, or The Cultural Logic of Late Capitalism* (Durham: Duke University Press, 1991), pp. ix, 170, 366.

[3] Bill McKibben, *The End of Nature* (New York: Anchor Books, 1989).

mean is that nature as other, nature as separate and alien, is dead, kaput, vanished. We have touched everything, our mark is everywhere; there is nothing left but us.

Most people are not postmodernists. Even postmodernists are not, for most of the day, postmodernists. And although enough people are willing to listen to Bill McKibben to make his book a best seller, they don't act as if they believe nature is dead. People go on preserving wild lands, planting gardens, hiking in the mountains, worrying about floods, wildfires, and earthquakes.

They also go on hoping for some standard that is clear and powerful enough—pure enough—to serve as a guide through a complicated and dangerous world. We live in an age where the human ability to shape nature, on scales that vary from individual genes to the entire globe, is both real and astonishing. We have seemingly perfected the ability to so calibrate control and danger that they increase in tandem. We are awed and frightened by our own power. We search for something to guide us, some pure entity ultimately distinct from us, yet which has our best interests at heart.

This is essentially a religious impulse, but it takes secular form; and while many people are willing to believe that the Force is with us, we have predictable problems agreeing on what secular form the Force takes. The favorite forms of the Force are usually Nature and the Market. The answer to our problems is either the Market knows best or Nature knows best. These are the pure entities that will lead us through a mixed and dirty world.

This is comforting as long as we don't think about it too much. I opened the newspaper in February to find President Clinton informing the nation that "[n]on-native plants and animals are upsetting nature's balance, squeezing out native species, causing severe economic damage and transforming our landscape." He was denouncing some real and expensive environmental nuisances such as star thistle and zebra mitten crabs that threaten such surprising marks of nature's balance in North America as cattle and irrigation works.[4] It is not that ecological invasions are not real and have not done real damage, but I wonder where President Clinton thinks he and those cows came from? Those of us whose ancestors have come from elsewhere over the last five centuries have long been softening up the continent for such laggards as start thistle and zebra mitten crabs. To denounce them for disturbing nature's balance is like General Custer denouncing the Seventh Cavalry for disturbing the Sioux. But more than that, denouncing ecological invasion and praising nature's balance at the end of the millennium is not shutting the barn door after the horse has left; it is shutting the barn door after the horse has died and the barn has fallen down. Appeals to nature and its balance are appeals to purity, but nature is not as reliable a guide if we have been for centuries so inextricably tangled in the natural world that traces of nature are everywhere in us and traces of us have infiltrated more and more of nature.

The market is no better. By its advocates' own definition, the market is a reflection of human desires, and so has some limits as the Force. In practice the market depends as much on manipulating human desires as on fulfilling them and, in any case, the natural world does not respond to advertising campaigns as eagerly as we might wish. At least publicly, our ability to think about what is going on seems trapped in ways that either fail to describe the world we live in or else rehearse versions of invisible hands or pristine balance that have little to do with the world we have made.

We cannot escape the paradox of control and danger by appealing to some larger force that will inevitably lead us to the best of all possible worlds. We may very well have arrived in Oz, because, in fact, the market never speaks and nature never speaks; instead various oracles claim to speak for them. We grant these oracles authority that they do not of themselves possess. Our various wizards are

---

[4] *San Jose Mercury News,* February 4, 1999, pp. 1A, 16A.

knock-offs of the Wizard of Oz, who explained his rise to wizardry after his balloon was blown off course and landed in Oz by telling Dorothy, in one of the movie lines that really resonates for the middle-aged, that times being what they were, he took the position.

2

"That times being what they were, I took the position" is a nice epitaph for the end of the twentieth century. It may be time to make the best of what we have, and if we are going to try to fool others, we should avoid fooling ourselves. I realize that any person whose favorite character in *The Wizard of Oz* is the wizard has some explaining to do if he is lecturing on human values. I am here to try to justify mixed and dirty worlds. It is not a position to which I expected my intellectual life or my disciplinary training as a historian would lead me.

I don't want to pretend my own intellectual life is some kind of epic journey. It has been concerned with issues such as race and nature, but at one end, it has the Navajo Tribal Archives, which, when I did research there, were housed in a doublewide in Window Rock. I slept in the parking lot. Someone (I was never sure who exactly he was) gave me the key and told me to answer the phone. I didn't see him again for three days. At the other end are the Walt Disney Studios. One building in the complex that houses the archives there is decorated to look like it is being held up by the seven dwarves, but the dwarves are forty feet tall. Forty-foot dwarves are not only architecturally disconcerting, they are conceptually disturbing. Is a forty-foot dwarf still a dwarf? Or is it now a giant disguised to look like a dwarf? Doublewides and forty-foot dwarves pretty much bracket my academic career to date. I mention them now to keep things in perspective, but I do think that important issues lurk in unlikely places.

I also think that since three zeros on the calendar tend to fix people's attention, this is a handy time for reassessment. There is reason to reassess. I have a favorite cartoon. It shows three stone-age guys trying to push a rock the size of this building. There is a fourth guy off to the side watching them. He is saying: "Wait a minute, this is getting us nowhere." The title of the cartoon is "The Dawn of Reason."

I think purity is getting us nowhere. I appreciate the instincts that push us toward it; I share a fear of the problems that it addresses. And I realize that when I attack purity, people can think that I am actually an advocate for the problems purity seeks to solve. I might be remembered as the guy who gave the Tanner Lectures and defended racism and global warming. I went to Catholic school. I was taught by nuns. I don't attack purity lightly.

My doubts about purity partly grew out of my own work. There is nothing like a failed project to concentrate your attention. I have spent the last three years, among other things, writing and rewriting and rewriting a set of essays that I had tentatively entitled "Thinking with Nature."

Thinking with nature is a habit of mind, and it is best explained by example. In the essays I look at Thomas Jefferson and Ralph Waldo Emerson, Henry David Thoreau and Susan Cooper and John Muir, but I'll draw my example from the most influential of twentieth-century Americans: Walt Disney.

The example that I have in mind is Bambi. You might think that a Stanford professor taking on Bambi is a bit much, but I'd argue that Walt Disney and his animals, cartoon and real, are probably the most significant influences on how Americans think about the natural world in the late twentieth century. And in any case, Disney is a wonderful example of thinking with nature because he did it so consciously and so explicitly. He sought in his films to portray a real nature, one true to life (as he emphasized in his True-Life Adventure films), but one that also communicated basic social values, usually without ever showing a human being, indeed often by making human beings threats to nature.[5] Disney's animals had feelings, hopes, families and friends, and most of all they had personality. And since they were quite consciously human analogues, the audience sympathized with them. But the message went farther than this. Bambi, for example, was not just a distinct member of a forest community. Bambi had to learn proper values; he had to learn American individualism. In dialogue cut from the final film but preserved pictorially in the scene where the Prince of the Forest arrived after the death of Bambi's mother, Disney himself summarized the message: "Why couldn't he say YOU'VE GOT TO LEARN TO WALK ALONE. . . . He believes you have to take things as they come and face facts. That's his philosophy—the philosophy of anyone who is going to survive in the forest."[6] But, of course, this is not the philosophy of the forest. This is the philosophy of Walt Disney and American individualism. What is happening here is indicative of the film's double nature and the habit of thinking with nature. The appeal is to a transparent "real" nature—the forest—while it is reflective of the audience's supposed emotions and values: individualism.

Bambi is an exercise in thinking with nature, and Disney is doing what thinking with nature trains us to do so well: embedding our basic social values in nature so that they seem universal expressions of the natural world itself. When we see nature, we read out culture. When we justify our culture, we ground it in nature. Disney's animals were allegorical characters standing in for humans; but his animals were also animals, and the characteristics that applied to them and to humans must be universal traits—rules of

[5] Walt Disney, "Why I Like Making Nature Films," reprinted from *Woman's Home Companion* (May 1954) in Kathy Jackson, *Walt Disney: A Bio-Bibliography* (Westport, Conn.: Greenwood Press, 1993), p. 122.

[6] Ollie Johnston and Frank Thomas, *Bambi: The Story and the Film* (New York: n. p., 1990), p. 174.

nature—that jump over the boundary that otherwise separates humans from animals.[7] This is thinking with nature.[8]

I began writing the essays because I thought that thinking with nature was bad. When we confuse the categories of the natural and the social, it becomes impossible to think clearly about either society or nature. I had no problem with cartoons. I just didn't want them becoming social policy. So starting with Thomas Jefferson and ending with Walt Disney, I was going to show the confusion of categories and the problems that it created. The problems were basic. We reduced gender—the cultural roles we ascribe to men and women—to biology. We naturalized them. We reduced race—a cultural construction in which certain intellectual and moral qualities are attached to physical markings, usually skin color—to biology. We naturalized it. We confused the social and the natural.

My attack was pretty conventional, and it had two blind spots. The first blind spot was predictable: I was condemning what I myself did. I, too, mixed together the cultural and the natural. The second was more disturbing, when I thought about it; what I was condemning—thinking with nature—might not always be such a bad thing.

There were two moments that caused me to reconsider my attempts to maintain the boundaries. The first came when I realized my left hand seemed serenely unaware of what my right hand was doing. On the one hand, I was working on a project that condemned the confusion of the cultural and the natural, but on the other hand I had just written another book, *The Organic Machine,* pointing out that the cultural and the natural were, in fact, mingled, confused, and increasingly impossible to separate.

---

[7] Disney, "Why I Like Making Nature Films," p. 122.

[8] It is close to what Simon Schaffer means when he writes "The natural and the social are hard to tease apart. Social relations are naturalized and nature appropriated by the social order" (Simon Schaffer, "The Earth's Fertility as a Social Fact in Early Modern Britain," in *Nature and Society in Historical Context,* ed. Mikuláš Teich, Roy Porter, and Bo Gustafsson [New York: Cambridge University Press, 1997], p. 124).

The Organic Machine was an attempt to escape from the declensionist narrative of environmental history. Most environmental histories tell a single story over and over again. It is really the Judeo-Christian story of the fall, sin, and the expulsion from Eden. Once, the story goes, human beings lived in paradise, but they sinned, and because of their sin they were expelled. In environmental history the sin was defiling paradise, and the defilers became Europeans and their descendants, who, not exactly learning from their mistakes, have spent the last half millennium finding new paradises inhabited by people who maintained their environmental innocence and mucking them up.

When deep cultural stories begin to pass as history, there is cause for suspicion, and *The Organic Machine* was an attempt to tell a different story. *The Organic Machine* is about the Columbia River, and its thesis is that the best way to understand the river is as an entity that has been in constant flux. Gradually human beings have modified it. They have created the illusion of conquering the river, of turning it, as the common phrase is in the Pacific Northwest, into a series of slackwater lakes. We apply social language to the river. We have raped it or killed it; but such language is deceptive. We have changed the Columbia to the detriment of some species and the benefit of others. Where once the Columbia said salmon, it now says shad and squawfish. The Columbia is not dead, as we may find out this spring when an immense snowpack in the Northwest melts. The dams depend on larger natural rhythms of snowfall and snowmelt, of rain and gravity and seasons, but we have created a system where what is natural and what is human becomes harder and harder to distinguish. Each intrudes on and influences the other. The river has become an organic machine. Denouncing thinking with nature on the one hand and describing organic machines on the other leads to some seeming inconsistencies.

The contradiction between condemning thinking with nature and writing *The Organic Machine* was only the first moment of doubt; the second came when I encountered people who were far ahead of me when it came to abjuring thinking with nature, and it caused me to question how far down this particular road I was willing to go. They not only didn't want to think with nature; they were ready to leave a world of nature entirely behind and turn themselves into very unorganic machines.

Katherine Hayles, a literary critic, gave a talk at the University of Washington several years ago on why it is important that human beings have bodies. The point was that being embodied was a critical part of our knowledge of, experience in, and thinking about the world. Our bodies are the nature in us. The talk was engaging and interesting, but I was puzzled as to who exactly formed the other side of this argument. Who thought human beings didn't need bodies? I found out. It was the guys in the front row (and they were all guys). They were from the virtual reality lab at the University of Washington. They were angry.

Bodies were in their view vestigial, nothing more than one large appendix that had outlived its usefulness. In the future, consciousness, which reduced down to electrical signals, would be systematically downloaded into a machine. We could, presuming no one pulled the plug, live forever free of sickness, aging, fat, balding, menstrual periods, arthritis, and all the pains of being embodied.

I like to think of myself as a progressive guy, but I don't think I want to go there even as I find myself with a middle-aged body that often refuses to do what I ask it to do. But if I insist that our having a body is essential to thinking about desirable forms of human culture and society, then it seems that I am opening the back door on thinking with nature even as I shut the front door. Who we are, how we act in the world, what we know about the world— all the things that I on the one hand wanted to ascribe purely to culture—seemed on the other hand to depend on our being embodied, to being ourselves to some degree natural.

I had hoped that my essays on thinking with nature would reduce the habit of mind to a categorical mistake; a mistake that you had only to reveal, as when Toto pulled the curtain on the Wizard of Oz, and it would lose its power. But our very embodied condition and the organic machines that we have created led me to think that I had oversimplified things. Thinking with nature was more complicated than I had thought. Purity presented far more problems than I had anticipated.

3

Having created a mixed and dirty world in which what is cultural and what is natural becomes less and less clear and as hybrids of the two become more and more common, what do we do? Having recognized that we ourselves—embodied as we are—are the ultimate hybrids of the cultural and the natural, how do we understand ourselves and the world that we shape? On the one hand, we cannot deny either the social horrors that come from deep confusions of the social and the natural or the problems that we have created by our increasingly powerful interventions into the natural world. On the other hand, we cannot deny that the social and the natural are inextricably mixed and that the natural world is, for better or worse, already a result of our past actions.

These are very late twentieth century problems, but for me they echo the thinking of a figure from the beginning of the republic: Thomas Jefferson. Jefferson thought with nature. This is not surprising. Jefferson and his contemporaries were immersed in nature. James Madison writing to Thomas Jefferson in 1788 kept a close eye on both the chances for the ratification of the constitution and spring frosts: "it does not appear that any thing less vulnerable than young cucumbers has been injured."[9] Madison was writing to a man who spent his life giving attention to weather,

[9] James Madison to Jefferson, April 22, 1788, in Julian Boyd, ed., *The Papers of Thomas Jefferson* (Princeton: Princeton University Press, 1950), 13:98–99.

orchards, dung, brick-earth, peas, peaches, firewood, clover, and soil washing off of hills.[10] In the wake of the constitution's ratification, the two future presidents happily botanized together.[11]

Jefferson's thinking with nature shows both the complexity of this habit of mind and its shifting valence. Jefferson thought with nature to argue for American independence—"the separate and equal station to which the Laws of Nature and Nature's God" entitled us—and for natural rights. But Jefferson also thought with nature to justify the inferior position of African Americans by arguing that "nature had been less bountiful to them" in intelligence and that nature demanded they be kept separate from whites.[12] Knowing as we know now about Jefferson's own relationship with his slave Sally Hemings, who was also his wife's half-sister, we realize that when he argued for the inferiority of African Americans, he was proclaiming the inferiority of his own lover and at least one of his children. This highlights not only Jefferson's own flaws and limits, but how tangled this habit of mind is. It does not always appear in purely progressive and reactionary packages that can be separated.

Jefferson, it seems to me, becomes only more useful to us as his own flaws, limits, and contradictions become apparent. Natural rights and racist claims for African American inferiority are the poles of Jefferson's thinking with nature. The meaning of these things for us (and for Jefferson) changes and becomes more tangled precisely because of Jefferson's own embodied being in the world. The sex he had with Sally Hemings, the labor of his slaves that he depended on, the children that he fathered: all of these rightly shape how we read his proclamations about nature and so-

[10] See Robert C. Baron, ed., *The Garden and Farm Books of Thomas Jefferson* (Golden, Colo.: Fulcrum, 1987).

[11] Jefferson to Thomas Randolph, June 5, 1791, in Baron, *The Garden and Farm Books of Thomas Jefferson*, p. 185.

[12] Jefferson, *Notes on the State of Virginia,* ed. William Peden (New York: W. W. Norton, 1954), p. 142.

ciety. The contradictions and the impurities don't negate his glittering abstractions: they illuminate them.

Direct appeals to nature to justify human social orders and values seem always to go wrong, just as attempts to preserve a pure nature by defining human beings as separate from nature seem to be hopelessly flawed. It is our bodies that are the problem. Attempts to reduce what we do and think to our bodies—our nature—don't work, but neither do attempts to ignore our embodied existence, the nature in us.

Jefferson in his less grandiose moments knew this. When Jefferson thought about society and the kind of republican values he wished to cultivate, he rarely did so without considering the labor of the human body and its work in the natural world. Jefferson's famous formulation, "Those who labour in the earth are the chosen people of God, if ever he had chosen people, whose breasts he has made his peculiar deposit for substantial and genuine virtue," appears to be a rather crude version of thinking with nature.[13] But looked at closely, his praise of farmers made them part of an intricate set of mediations between nature on the one hand and particular forms of human society on the other. "The spontaneous energies of the earth are a gift of nature," Jefferson wrote in a characteristic passage, "but they require the labor of man to direct their operation. And the question is so to husband his labor as to turn the greatest quantity of this useful action of the earth to his benefit."[14]

For Jefferson, all farming was not equal. Olives encouraged one way of life, tobacco another. Nature, in the form of climate and soil, limited but did not determine such choices. Nature affected society, but not directly. The key for Jefferson was an array of mediating factors—the size and type of landholding, the technology

[13] Jefferson, *Notes on the State of Virginia*, pp. 164–65.

[14] Jefferson to Charles Wilson Peale, April 17, 1813, in Baron, *Garden and Farm Books of Thomas Jefferson*, p. 202.

used, the crops and animals raised, the way labor was organized. Jefferson's emphasis on the human mediations that translated nature into human society gave his thinking with nature a flexibility and a sense of possibility that underlined the malleability of both nature and human society. The benefit agriculture yielded to society through these multiple mediations was not just crops and wealth, but the fundamental goods of social life itself.[15] The particular connections and results Jefferson postulated might at times be wacky, but the concentration on complicated mediations was not.

But if a stress on the numerous mediations that guide the intersection of the social and the natural is both a form of thinking with nature and a way to avoid some of the social dilemmas of thinking with nature, what is the solution to the mixed and dirty, hybrid material world that we have created? This is a world that is increasingly neither cultural nor natural but a mixture of both.

I would suggest that a beginning of a way out lies with an abandonment of fitting everything into pure categories and accepting a series of finer gradations as we take responsibility for a world that we are creating. Thinking with nature, for all its faults and dangers, warns against an absolute disentanglement of the natural and the social. And, similarly, our efforts to save nature should not lead to an attempt to disentangle it completely from the social.

The best way to give you a sense of what I mean is to close with a story. In Seattle, where I lived until last year, there are bald eagles nesting in the city, peregrine falcons amidst the skyscrapers, at least one coyote in an elevator, and mountain lions too close for many people's comfort. My students on their way to the Cascades pitied these animals; they regarded them as somehow diminished, the natural world on welfare. I have come to take comfort in them.

A moment nearly three years ago marked my own changing

---

[15] Jefferson to George Washington, August 15, 1787; Boyd, *Papers of Thomas Jefferson*, 12:38.

views on these things, a moment when I could let purity go. There was a large run of sockeye salmon into Seattle's Lake Washington that year. It was, fishery managers warned, an anomaly, a consequence of near-perfect ocean conditions and, for the moment, diminished fishing pressure in the North Pacific. Hundreds of thousands of fish ran into Elliott Bay and on to Lake Washington. For the first time in years, hundreds of small boats appeared to catch them, and tens of thousands of people came out to view them.

It seemed a triumphal return to nature in defiance of the city, but it was no such thing. The vast majority of the sockeye did not seek natal streams; they ran toward the fishponds and hatchery at the University of Washington campus. Lake Washington had never had a significant sockeye run until the turn of the century, when Seattle constructed the ship canal that linked Puget Sound, Lake Union, and Lake Washington. This was a planted run, moving through a concrete corridor with fish ladders on toward the stainless steel tanks and knives where they would end their lives. But these fish in their tens of thousands hardly seemed lesser fish for all of that.

The fish became the leading tourist attraction in Seattle during their run, and most of the people who came to see them lived in the city and its suburbs. And, at first, I thought that they were there because the return of the fish reminded them of what the region had been before the salmon declined. They were there to recollect a fuller past. But given the demographics of Seattle, this is unlikely. Most adult Seattleites didn't live there when salmon were abundant. They came to see the salmon, I think, in order to glimpse a possible future that contained Seattle and salmon. They were there to see a hybrid world that, at least for a few weeks, worked. There is a hope in that for which I would gladly surrender purity.

I am a historian; I see little evidence that people change their values or ways of thinking easily or quickly. But I do see evidence that our values and our ways of thinking contain multiple possibilities. Our values are often as contradictory as our thinking is paradoxical. And this is good news rather than bad because it creates possibilities for change without calling for the wholesale transformation of human values and ways of thinking. We can and do change without mass conversion experiences. It is easier to get a change of emphasis than a change of heart. Sometimes we need someone who can point out unconsidered implications of how we already think more than we need an oracle or a prophet. Aldo Leopold's call for a new set of values, a conservation ethic, in time, won a lot of readers for *Sand County Almanac,* but he converted very few people to a new way of thinking. Rachel Carson appealed for a new application of existing values and ignited a mass environmental movement. We don't need prophets. We don't need appeals to the Force. We need a cold assessment of the possibilities for the future, good as well as bad, that our own complicated and paradoxical values and our own messy embodiment in the natural world contain.

Representative Democracy and Democratic Citizens: Philosophical and Empirical Understandings

SIDNEY VERBA

THE TANNER LECTURES ON HUMAN VALUES

Delivered at

Brasenose College, Oxford
May 10 and 11, 1999

SIDNEY VERBA is Carl H. Pforzheimer University Professor and professor of government at Harvard University, as well as director of the Harvard University Library. He was educated at Harvard College and at Princeton University, where he received his Ph.D. In 1993 he was awarded the James Madison Award by the American Political Science Association (APSA) for a career contribution to political science. He is a member of the National Academy of Sciences, a fellow of the American Academy of Arts and Sciences, and has been both a fellow of the Center for Advanced Studies in the Behavioral Sciences and a Guggenheim Fellow. He is the author or co-author of many published works, including *Voice and Equality: Civic Voluntarism in American Democracy* (1995, with Kay L. Schlozman and Henry E. Brady), *Elites and the Idea of Equality: A Comparison of Japan, Sweden, and the United States* (1987), and *The Civic Culture: Political Attitudes and Democracy in Five Nations* (1963, with Gabriel A. Almond). *Participation in America: Political Democracy and Social Equality* (1972, with Norman Nie) won APSA's Kammerer Award for the best book on American politics, and *The Changing American Voter* (1976, with Norman Nie and John Petrocik) won the APSA award for the best book in political science.

The subject of human values is broad and daunting. When I began to consider what I might say on this topic for the Tanner Lectures, I looked at earlier lectures in this series. The lecturers were usually political philosophers or legal scholars. They analyze systems of values and beliefs and argue for one system over another. They draw on the works of other thinkers, on the writings of other philosophers, and on the opinions of judges for justification of the system they prefer.

Lurking in the background of many of these accounts, especially those that deal with my area of concern, democratic governance, is another set of values and beliefs: those held by the public. Reference is made to a "public philosophy," to "common understandings in a community," to a "public culture," to the common will, or to—the term used most often though with very varied meanings—public opinion. Michael Sandel, in his book *Democracy's Discontent,* writes of the "public philosophy," by which he means "the political theory implicit in our practice, the assumptions about citizenship and freedom that inform our public life. . . ."[1] Michael Walzer in *Spheres of Justice* writes of something similar: "sensibilities and intuitions" shared by those in a political system.[2] For theorists of democracy, like Sandel and Walzer, who ground their democratic philosophy in an interpretation of morality as practiced in particular places by particular people, the values and beliefs of the public would seem to be especially relevant. Walzer, for instance, rejects a morality based on "what rational individuals . . . under universalizing conditions" would choose, in favor of that which would be chosen by "ordinary people, with a

[1] Michael Sandel, *Democracy's Discontent: America in Search of a Public Philosophy* (Cambridge, Mass.: Harvard University Press, 1993), p. 4.

[2] Michael Walzer, *Spheres of Justice: A Defense of Pluralism and Equality* (New York: Basic Books, 1983), p. 28.

firm sense of their own identity, with their own goods in their hands, caught up in their everyday troubles. . . ."[3] Walzer certainly seems to invoke a real public with a real set of opinions.

What about those philosophers who seek to develop general, perhaps universal, principles of political morality on the basis of logic and thought experiments, rather than information about the real world of citizens? John Rawls, in *The Theory of Justice,*[4] starts in an imagined world of rational people in a contrived state of ignorance as to who they are. Even here, one has the sense that one will have sometime to face the issue of what people will actually do and actually think. Rawls assumes a citizenry capable of reason, of cooperation, and of conceptions of the good; reasoning, cooperative, and moral citizens. These attributes are discussed at a most abstract level, but they are attributes that are (or at least could be) real. Rawls moves closer to the public in *Political Liberalism,* where he asks how one can have a stable society when there exist multiple conceptions of morality that are not compatible with each other. In this book, the public is a more palpable entity. He states in the opening of the book, "We start then, by looking at the public culture itself as the shared fund of implicitly recognized basic ideas and principles."[5]

A public philosophy is, thus, not a philosopher's philosophy. It seems to be something out there; something that needs to be discovered and taken into account. But it is hard to define and hard to find. "A public philosophy is an elusive thing, for it is constantly before our eyes. It forms the often unreflective background to our political discourse and disputes."[6] In saying this, Sandel echoes comments by James Bryce a century ago about public opinion in America. Bryce noted that nowhere is public opinion more

---

[3] Ibid., p. 5.

[4] John Rawls, *The Theory of Justice* (Cambridge, Mass.: Harvard University Press, 1971).

[5] John Rawls, *Political Liberalism* (New York: Cambridge University Press, 1993).

[6] Sandel, *Democracy's Discontent,* p. 4.

important than in America. He also noted that it was "difficult to ascertain."[7]

This is one reason for the ambivalence about public opinion one finds in scholars, political actors, and the public itself. Public opinion is important; at the most fundamental level democracy rests on it. If democracy means anything, it means that in some way public values and preferences ought to have an impact on government policies; more strongly, perhaps, ought to determine what governments do. But public values and preferences are, as Bryce says, difficult to ascertain. How can public opinion guide policy when it is not clear what it is? And, even if we could ascertain it, should it be a guide? Is it not too incompetent, ill-informed, changeable, and irresponsible? You cannot follow it and, if you could, you shouldn't. Yet it is sovereign.

Empirical social scientists also address the issue of public beliefs and values and their relation to political life. There are numerous empirical studies of citizen values on social and political matters, of the ways citizens express those values. Many focus on the specific policy preferences of citizens, but there are also studies of the broader and more fundamental values they hold. These studies do not propose or justify one value system over another, but seek to describe and explain systems of values. Normative philosophers and empirical social scientists are, in some sense, in different businesses. Normative philosophers are concerned with the structure of complex normative systems, and with the justification of such systems. They pitch their arguments against alternative value systems, claiming that the alternatives are wrongly derived, or internally inconsistent, or unfortunate in their consequences—or all of these. Systematic empirical researchers usually have a different agenda. They are concerned with method and inference. They care about such matters as how one measures values or behavior in a population. They also are concerned with causal

---

[7] Quoted in James A. Stimson, *Public Opinion in America: Moods, Cycles, and Swings* (Boulder, Colo.: Westview Press, 1991), p. 8.

explanation: What causes the values that people hold? What are the consequences of those values? They pitch their arguments against alternative methods or alternative descriptions or alternative explanations.

I hasten to add that we ought not to take the distinction too far. Few normative philosophers ignore facts, and some pay a lot of attention. Few empirical researchers deny the normative foundations or implications of their work. Facts and values are not as sealed off from one another as some once tried to make them. But normative philosophers and empirical social scientists seem animated by different concerns and largely go about their businesses differently.

But for both, the issue of the public philosophy or public opinion is a problem. How then does one ascertain what the public thinks and how the public thinks? Does it even make sense to ask about such matters? Normative philosophers find public opinion elusive. No systematic social scientist who has worked on the subject would disagree.

There are several reasons for this elusiveness. Citizen values are not immediately apparent. Philosophers tell us about their normative systems. That is their business. Citizens have no such obligation. They do not spend time ruminating about their normative systems, nor do they write treatises explicating and justifying them. If one is interested in such values, one has to go out and find them.

There is a further problem in the empirical study of citizen values and preferences: the fact that they must be studied on two levels, that of the individual and that of the aggregate. The consequence of citizen values for political outcomes depends not on individual values and preferences but on the aggregate of values and preferences manifested in various ways—as votes, as public opinion, as communications to political elites, and so on. This second level of values—the values of aggregates—adds additional difficulty to the observation of citizen attitudes. Measuring the values of an individual is hard enough. Aggregating them, especially if they vary across individuals in both content and intensity, is harder still.

How then can we know about this elusive phenomenon? The answer takes us into questions of methodology, not the best subject for a public lecture on a big and important substantive issue. But at least something needs to be said about it, for public opinion is not right in front of our eyes—or, to put it bluntly, if you think it is, as many do, you are wrong. It needs to be found, and what is found depends on the method used. I do not intend to discuss methods in detail, but need to digress for some general comments. It is, in fact, not that much of a digression from my substantive theme of how ordinary citizens think about political matters since what I say about method is relevant to how citizens learn about and reason about such matters.

A CONSIDERATION OF METHOD

Let us distinguish broadly between two kinds of methods: systematic social scientific methods and everyday commonsense methods. Systematic social science is, or at least should be, interested in general knowledge about social and political reality; that is, in descriptive and causal inference about the real world. I say descriptive inference, not description, to distinguish that which we observe from the more general inferences we make on the basis of those observations. We observe some people doing things, saying things, reacting in certain ways. What we observe depends on how we observe it (are they saying things spontaneously that we overhear, are they answering our questions?). And it depends on whom we observe (how were the people we observe selected?). Thus, systematic social science depends on good measures that get at the reality in which we are interested and on a selection procedure that allows us to assume that the people we observe represent the larger population to whom we wish to generalize. If the selection is bi-ased—gets us unrepresentative people because of the way we se-lect them—we cannot generalize. The model for this is the ubiquitous social science tool used for studying the public, the sample survey.

Beyond descriptive inference, systematic social science aims at causal inference: how things go together, what causes what. We want to know not only what people say and do, but why they say and do it. Why they vote as they do; why they prefer one policy over another. And we want to know the consequences of what they say and do. Does it matter how they vote? The model for answer-ing such questions is the experiment. A perfect experiment can answer the why question, because it can take into account alterna-tive explanatory factors and isolate the ones that provide us with an explanation. The ubiquitous surveys are analyzed as if they are experiments. They are not; they don't even come close. But good analysis can get us somewhat closer to causal explanation.

Commonsense understanding of the public is less formal and self-conscious about measurement or sampling. It relies more on the vivid anecdote than on the systematic sample; on information at hand, not on information carefully selected; it often relies on in-trospection ("I am a member of this community so I know how we feel"); it may use indirect evidence about the public (what others say about it without asking how they know); it is intuitive.

Many—by no means all—philosophical works on democracy that deal with the public or a public philosophy or ethos take this approach. They are not too systematic in their sources. In many cases, a public ethos may be mentioned or invoked, the evidence for it being the intuitive understanding of the author. Philoso-phers who ground their work in actual practice—a Walzer or Sandel—often provide a rich but casually selected array of evi-dence about those practices. Writings about the public are in-voked: the writings of literary observers, social critics, earlier philosophers, journalists, and others who put their thoughts on paper. Anecdotes and interesting examples as to beliefs and behaviors abound. Reference is often made to court cases in which judges base decisions on general values or community standards. But if one looks to where the judges get their information about the public, it usually comes from their own understanding of what those standards are. A writer like Rawls, who begins from a more abstract logical analysis, also finds little in social science data. He invokes a vague common understanding of "the most reasonable conception of the person that the general facts about human nature and society seem to allow." As for a social science contribution: " . . . beyond the lessons of historical experience and . . . bits of wisdom," he tells us, "there is not much to go on" (*Political Liberalism,* p. 87).

The Problem with Unsystematic Observation

The main fault of such unsystematic observation is that it is subject to the main impediment to valid descriptive inference about the public: selection bias. In the absence of systematic observation, it is easy for philosophers or politicians or other observers of society to find that which is most congenial to their position. This is easily the case if one looks inside oneself for these values. It is also easily the case if one extrapolates from those one knows best— either personally or from their writings. And it is also easy if one interprets the values of a culture; since cultures may have many values, one can always find those that suit one's preconceptions. As Brian Barry puts it: " . . . claims to derive conclusions from the allegedly shared values of one's society are always tendentious. If they were not, it would have to be regarded as a remarkable coincidence that the shared values a political philosopher says he has detected always happen to lead to conclusions that he already supports."[8] Barry says the task of understanding the public is a futile one; that there is nothing there to understand. I think this goes too far. There is something there, but it is not easy to get at.

SURVEY RESEARCH AND THE PUBLIC

The main technique for getting at public opinion is the sample survey. Public opinion polls are ubiquitous in politics and in the press, as well as in the social sciences. Why are they used so much by social scientists? One answer might be Abraham Kaplan's law of the hammer: give a little boy a hammer, and suddenly everything around needs pounding. Give a social scientist the social survey, and suddenly every topic needs a survey. But there are better reasons. The main value of a good survey is that it is representative of an entire population. A good random sample eliminates selection bias and allows us to generalize from the units observed to the larger universe from which the units were chosen.

But about what does it let us generalize? Usually about rather superficial measures. In a systematic random sample, one cannot probe the complexity of individual value patterns. An individual's beliefs and values relevant to democracy are hard to elicit. They would be revealed only across a range of choice situations, observed over time, in varying contexts. Surveys, with their simple questions asked uniformly of a sample, run the danger of oversimplifying what is there, missing the main points, and perhaps creating rather than recording the reality we are studying. Furthermore, we care about the aggregate, not only the individual; about public philosophy or public opinion, not the values or thought processes of one person or another. The complex patterns of beliefs and values held by an individual do not add up easily to form an aggregate. You might understand individuals by writing biographies

---

[8] Brian M. Barry, *Justice as Impartiality* (Oxford: Oxford University Press, 1995), p. 5.

describing what each believes and how they got there. But it is not easy, probably impossible, to sum up a multitude of such biographies to understand a large population. To add up values across individuals requires that we reduce those values to comparable and countable items and, in so doing, we lose some of the substance of that which we count.

The problem is a general one—not only for the social scientist but for actual political choice and action situations across a large population. James C. Scott has written most interestingly about the attempt by governments to control societies by making them "legible"—that is, by standardizing things (people, towns, transactions) so that they can be counted or regulated. People and objects need to be put in categories (laws of course depend on categories), observational techniques need to be standardized, accounting schemes need to be devised. All of this smooths out the edges of a reality that is much more complex and contextually varied. Scott focuses on the pathologies this can create but realizes that some such systematization is needed in any complex society.

The problem Scott identifies in relation to the action of states is a well-known problem in the social sciences. He calls his book *Seeing Like a State.*[9] If it were a book on social science methodology, it might be called *Seeing Like a Social Scientist.* Social scientists (or at least some of us) consider the task of social science to be one of making society legible, to find order out of the chaotic business of everyday life. We, like bureaucrats, tax collectors, and planners—among other unpleasant people—like to have people neatly categorized. But, just as Scott worries about the pathologies associated with this as states use such information to impose a rigid order to society that is destructive of ordinary practices, so one might worry that systematic social science bleaches out reality in its attempt to systematize.

In democratic politics, the best example of the simplification

9 James C. Scott, *Seeing Like a State: How Certain Schemes to Improve the Human Condition Have Failed* (New Haven: Yale University Press, 1998).

of values and preferences is the vote. No one has found a substitute as yet. Millions of individuals—each unique, with a complex set of values, beliefs, and interests—can express a standardized preference simultaneously. No form of citizen control would be possible if it were not for that standardization. If all wrote long letters about what the government ought to do, they could not be translated into action. Votes capture the entire voting body and reduce it to a simple and coherent aggregate. You can vote or not vote and, if you vote, you can choose from a limited set of options. The multitudinous and varied reasons why citizens decide to vote rather than stay home and then decide for whom to vote are reduced to a couple of stylized and blunt choices.

Surveys are better than votes in terms of the information they give us about the individual. Indeed, they are used to interpret the vote—to find out why people voted as they did. But they still provide only limited insight into the public's values and beliefs.

Nevertheless, surveys are as good as it gets when one wants to typify a larger population in a valid manner. It is the technique from which I will draw my evidence about the public, flawed though the technique may be. Furthermore, good academic sample survey research—research that is not aimed at providing quick descriptions of public opinion on Kosovo or some other current issue—can go well beyond the simple report of what percent of the public favors what. Survey research can deal with variation in opinion, which is often more interesting than where the majority opinion lies. Furthermore, the answer to a single question may tell little. Such answers are sensitive to question wording. But patterns across sets of questions are more reliable and can reveal a lot about how people think. The fact that opinions change over time and vary with question wording makes many doubt the solidity and usefulness of survey results. But, properly analyzed, such change over time and variation with the stimulus presented to the respondent can give a good deal of insight into the nature of public opinion.

Furthermore, ordinary surveys can be supplemented with longer in-depth interviews or group discussions to get us closer to an understanding of citizen reasoning processes. In addition, survey researchers have, in recent years, expanded their repertoire of methods. Computer-assisted telephone interviewing allows one to explore the reasoning behind a particular answer by varying the source presented to the respondent, by varying the nature of the issue, by asking and allowing citizens to reflect on their views, by challenging views that they have previously expressed, and the like. In this manner, something approaching a dialogue with an individual is possible; more important, dialogues with samples of individuals are possible.

The studies I report will come almost entirely from the United States. The United States is a curious place with strange and sometimes frightening customs, some of which have been recently too publicly displayed. I focus on it because that is where most of the data I wish to refer to have been gathered. I am not sure of the generalizability of these data to other democracies—each of which is curious in its own way. But my reading of such works as the William Miller, Annis May Timpson, and Michael Lessnoff work on British political beliefs finds much that is consistent with what I will discuss.[10] I think there are general lessons here, but we must be cautious in generalizing.

DEMOCRATIC CITIZENS

Democratic Dilemmas

Having said something about the methods for ascertaining the public's values and preferences, let me turn to what can be learned

[10] William L. Miller, Annis May Timpson, and Michael Lessnoff, *Political Culture in Contemporary Britain: People and Politicians, Principles and Practice* (Oxford: Clarendon Press, 1996).

about the public from surveys. The substantive issue I shall consider relates to a major democratic dilemma associated with citizen participation in a democracy. It is interesting how commonly the words "democracy" and "dilemma" seem to go together. When not acting as a social scientist, I am the director of the Harvard University Library, and I sometimes look at our electronic catalogue just to see what one can learn from the catalogue records. I found over sixty records that contain the words "democracy" and "dilemma." Apparently authors like to put the terms together. Democracy seems to pose a dilemma in relation to, among other things, religion, bureaucracy, secrecy, science, socialism, nationalism, funding of the arts, school desegregation, authority, national defense, in a number of titles Germany, and—for whatever it means—the future. This is not surprising. Democracy as a system spawns dilemmas and contradictions. The very term "democratic government" is contradictory. "Democracy" refers to the people, to control from below, to procedures for giving citizens a voice over decisions. "Government" refers to policies, to authoritative decisions, to control from above, to the means for making effective policies. This is the dilemma I wish to explore from the perspective of the role of the public in democratic governance: can one have a democracy that gives the citizenry substantial and equal voice over public affairs and at the same time produces effective and just policies?

Let me spell this out. Citizen voice and participation are at the center of the democratic half of democratic government. Through participation citizens express their preferences to governing officials and induce them to respond to those preferences. They send information about themselves (who they are, what they want, what they need) and apply pressure on officials for some response. Citizens do this in many ways: by voting, working in political campaigns, writing letters, taking part in community actions, protests, and on and on. The sum of these activities represents the way in which democratic voice is expressed.

Democracy depends on such voice. It also depends upon equal voice. One of the bedrock principles of democracy is the equal consideration of the needs and preferences of all citizens, a principle embedded in the notion of one person, one vote. Note that I do not speak of equal response or equal benefit from the government. That may be much too much to ask. Even if citizens spoke with equal voice and governing officials gave each an equal hearing, equal response would not be possible. Government resources are limited; citizen preferences conflict with each other; everyone cannot get an equal response. If they cannot get an equal response, can they get a fair one? It is hard to know exactly what a fair response would be, but let us assume it to mean, among other things, that those who get somewhat less will not consider the result unjust (at least, not wildly unjust). Without an equal voice and an equal hearing, there is no chance of getting close to an equal response and very little chance of an outcome that will be considered fair and just. From this perspective equal political voice fosters beneficial outcomes. Put another way, the outcomes will be better—fairer—if everyone gets a chance to be heard. For one thing, insofar as democratic outcomes are supposed to reflect the preferences and needs of the citizenry and insofar as equal political voice fosters the communication of those preferences and needs, procedures maximizing equal voice lead to beneficial outcomes. In addition, equal political voice should foster more supportive political views among citizens. People who have a voice are more likely to accept policies of which they disapprove than are those who do not. And political voice—the chance to participate—also fosters a more enlightened citizenry. All these things, and more, suggest that a citizenry that has a real and equal voice in policy-making is a better citizenry, and where that happens there will be a better polity.

But there is another side to the story. The desirability of citizen voice and, especially, equal voice depends on some qualities of the citizenry. Why do we want to give voice to citizen preferences and needs? And why an equal voice? For some the answer lies in the belief that all people are equal before God. A more secular set of reasons expressed by such democratic thinkers as Robert Dahl and John Rawls is that people are reasoning beings, capable of understanding the world; and that they are moral beings, capable of conceptions of the good. What does this mean for the ordinary citizen, and why is it the principle on which equal citizen voice is grounded? For one thing, it means that citizens should be good (or at least adequate) moral reasoners. Their preferences and values, whatever their substance, should have some coherence and be somewhat stable. If preferences and values change from moment to moment, or if they are incoherent and self-contradictory, it is hard to know how they can be given meaningful expression. Also, citizens should be good (or at least adequate) social scientists. They should have enough information to know how to pursue their goals through politics. They should be capable of making causal inferences about how their activity might lead to desired outcomes (for instance, to be able to figure out, in the light of their preferred policy outcomes, whom to vote for or how one policy rather than another will affect their welfare). If they cannot reason about the political world, what do their expressed preferences mean?

Thus, democratic voice would seem to rest on some capacity of citizens to be moral reasoners and social scientific reasoners. It may rest on another quality of ordinary citizens: their willingness to transcend their own values and preferences. There are two components of this willingness. One is a willingness to look beyond their own narrow self-interest to consider the common good and the other their willingness to commit to (or at least accept) principles of fair democratic procedure that allow a multiplicity of viewpoints or doctrines to be expressed. Some would argue that the first is not necessary: let self-interest rule and an invisible hand will provide good social outcomes. This may work in the marketplace of commodities; I believe (though I cannot argue the case fully here) that it does not apply in the making of public policy through the political process. The second is more unambiguously tied to democracy. Rawls refers to this as a free-standing overlapping consensus on a democratic process that involves tolerating alternative doctrines. This, as he notes and as many democratic theorists have noted before, is needed to maintain a stable democracy given the inevitable plurality of competing doctrines subscribed to by citizens in a democracy.

But what if citizens are not up to the task: if they are inadequate moral reasoners or social scientists—if they don't know what they want or how to get it? What if they can't be relied upon to go beyond their own preferred value system to allow others to exist? Democratic voice becomes meaningless or undesirable. Or what if citizens are *unequally* equipped for moral reasoning or social science analysis? Some are competent, others not. And what if they are unequally committed to democratic procedures? *Equal* democratic voice might be meaningless or undesirable. These considerations have led many philosophers of democratic government to express skepticism about the public, about too much democracy, about populist democracy. The voice of the people, unchecked, coming equally from those who might be expected to be more democratically competent and supportive of democratic principles and from others who are less so, might be dangerous for democracy. And systematic social science studies have supported that position. Yet without voice and without equal voice, what happens to the equal consideration of the needs and preferences of all?

This is the democratic dilemma of my lectures. Equal citizen voice is needed for equal consideration of needs and preferences. Equal citizen voice may be disruptive of effective government and dangerous to democracy. I want to look more closely at what we know about citizen voice and public opinion to see if this is the case.

In this look at citizens, I am interested less in the substance of what citizens think—the content of their values or their policy preferences—than in how they think. I want to see how they operate as normative political philosophers; to consider, that is, the structure of their systems of political preferences and values. And I want to see how they operate as empirical social scientists; to consider, that is, how they obtain information about the political and social world, and how they deploy it to make causal inferences about how the world works.

Both views of the citizen as participant—citizen voice as a good thing and citizen voice as a bad thing—can be found in the literature and in our common understanding of politics. In the absence of closer data on what citizens do and how they reason, one might hope for the best but worry about the worst.

DEMOCRATIC CITIZENS: WHAT ARE THEY LIKE?

So let us look more closely at the data—with all due caution about the weakness of systematic data but, I hope, with respect for what it can tell us. I will proceed as follows. I want to begin with work I have been doing for a number of years on political equality, more specifically equality in political participation. This is not exactly the same thing as political voice but close to it if we think of participation as the means by which citizens exercise their political voice—by which they communicate their interests and preferences to governing elites and induce them to respond. It is empirical research based on large-scale surveys of what citizens do, work done collaboratively with Kay L. Schlozman and Henry E. Brady. I want to summarize this research briefly and then connect it, more than it has been connected, to normative issues of political equality.

Our work begins with the basic principle of equality mentioned earlier: that in a democracy citizens ought to receive equal consideration of their needs and preferences. I'd like to summarize what we found about the extent of political equality and then return to the normative principle from which we begin to look more closely at the desirability of political equality—particularly from the perspective of the capacity of the ordinary citizen to understand and reason about political matters.

ARE CITIZENS EQUAL IN POLITICS?

To begin with, as is well known—and as our studies confirm with a mind-numbing amount of data—citizen voices are not equal. Americans are as active, or substantially more active, than citizens elsewhere. But what is distinctive about political participation in America is that participation is so unequally distributed, hewing more closely to the fault lines of social class. In the United States the skew introduced by the relationship between high levels of education or income and high levels of political activity—a bias characteristic of political participation in democracies around the world—is especially pronounced.

Why is this the case? In thinking about why some people are active while others are not, my colleagues and I have found it helpful to invert the usual question and to ask instead why people do not take part in politics. Three answers immediately suggest themselves: because they can't; because they don't want to; or because nobody asked.

- "They can't" suggests a paucity of necessary resources—time to take part, money to contribute to campaigns and other political causes, and skills to use time and money effectively.
- "They don't want to" focuses attention on the absence of political engagement—lack of interest in politics or little concern with public issues, a belief that activity can make little

or no difference, little or no knowledge about the political process, or other priorities.

- "Nobody asked" implies isolation from the networks of recruitment through which citizens are mobilized to politics.

These three components—resources, engagement, and recruitment—explain the stratification in political activity. In general, the advantaged members of society are more politically motivated. Educated, affluent people are more likely to be politically interested and informed; to care about political matters. They also have more resources: not time (which turns out to be equally available—or perhaps equally unavailable—to all), but they obviously have more money. And they are better endowed with the necessary skills, which come from good education, a high-level job.

And a word on the last reason for inactivity, "Nobody asked." Some political activity is spontaneous, but a lot is recruited. We become active because someone asked us to. One might imagine that recruitment might overturn the stratification derived from resources. After all, political movements often deliberately mobilize the poor, the disadvantaged—people who would otherwise be inactive. But our research shows that, overall across the population, recruitment merely reinforces the stratification of participation. Recruiters are rational. They look for those who can participate effectively—they look where the money is—and they bring into politics people who would have been active anyway.

In recent years, the stratification in political activity deriving from resource disparities has been growing, the major reason being the relative shift in the place of time and money as the most important resource for political activity. Money has become more important, time less. The reason lies in supply and demand: time has become in shorter supply as more and more families include two earners. In addition, the professionalization of political campaigns and the increased role of television have made money more valuable to politics. Campaigns want money to buy a computer and database or television time, more than they want people who can walk the streets or stuff envelopes.

This increases the stratification of political activity for the simple and obvious reason that money is a stratified resource, time is not. The rich have money; the poor don't. All of us, rich and poor, seem to have as much—or as little—time.

From the point of view of our evaluation of political inequality, it makes a difference whether the inequality in political voice is based on a disparity in motivation or a disparity in resources. If the former is the reason—people prefer to stay home and watch television rather than turning out to vote or going to a community meeting; or they prefer a few more hours in the office rather than getting involved in a political campaign—we would be less concerned with the fact that their voice is not heard. If it is a matter of "they can't"—because of resource inadequacy—then there is a more serious problem. Our research on citizen participation shows that, though both motivation and resources play a role, the latter seem to be a much greater inhibitor of activity than the former.

Such resource disparities are, however, hard to remove. One can imagine limiting the use of money in politics. That is what campaign finance legislation in the United States attempts. It is ineffective because of the inventiveness of campaign managers. Furthermore, the U.S. Supreme Court has severely restricted the extent to which one can limit the use of money in politics, arguing that it inhibits free speech. There are many who disagree with that interpretation and who might argue that speech is freer when the ability to speak is more equal. But the Supreme Court ruling stands. In American English—I don't know about British English—there is the saying that "Money talks." It is truly appropriate for American politics, for money talks loudly and receives constitutional protection as a form of speech.

In any case, even if there were limitations on money, it would be difficult to go beyond limiting money to limit other resources. Few of us would think it appropriate to limit the use of one's cognitive skills (the ability to understand issues and see connections among them) or rhetorical skills (the ability to make a compelling case).

Michael Walzer has written approvingly of what he calls complex equality, where there are different standards of fairness in different spheres of life, where the spheres are somewhat insulated from each other, and where people may be at the top of the heap in one sphere and lower down in another. Our data on citizen participation do show some difference of standards in different spheres: the norms in politics are more egalitarian than in the economy. One person, one vote rules in politics; one person, one dollar or pound does not rule in economic matters. But the boundaries between the spheres are porous, as inequalities in the economy—in money and skills—spill over and create inequality in the political sphere.

Thus, when it comes to political activity, the three factors of motivation, resources, and recruitment work to reinforce each other and give a cumulative political advantage to those better off in other ways. The result of our analysis of political equality might be summarized in the following manner: citizen voice ought to be loud, clear, and equal: loud so officials pay attention, clear so they know what people want, and equal so that the normative idea of equal consideration of interests and preferences can be satisfied. Our data show that the public's voice is often loud, sometimes clear, but rarely equal.

Do We Want Political Equality?

That is our story in a nutshell. But let me come back to the opening normative principle and make it a question: should all voices be equal? Let's look at that from two perspectives: the substance of what is communicated to the government in terms of citizen policy preferences and citizen need (when citizens use their political voice, what do they communicate?) and in terms of the quality of decisions made by the government (what contribution does citizen voice make to the justice and effectiveness of government policy?).

On the substance of what is communicated by active citizens, the crucial point is that unequal voice makes a difference. Suppose some people are active and others not, but in terms of the characteristics that are relevant to the content and implementation of public policy—the needs and the preferences people have—the active and inactive citizens are not different. Inequality in activity would not make much difference, because the subset of citizens who are active would communicate the same messages about their needs and preferences to the government as would the inactive portion of the population. Some well-known research by Raymond Wolfinger and Steven Rosenstone shows that, if you compare voters and nonvoters in terms of their policy preferences on standard U.S. National Election Study questions (along the lines of should the government see that everyone has a good job and standard of living or stay out of such things), there is little difference between the two groups—suggesting that it does not matter much that some vote and others do not.[11]

But suppose we look at other political activities than the vote: activities like working for a candidate, writing a letter to an official, or giving a large campaign contribution. There is a vast difference between those who are active and those who are not. Those less active are groups with distinctive needs and preferences in relation to government policy. They are the more disadvantaged members of society: the poor, the less well educated, racial and ethnic minorities. It is consequential that they are less active.

Thus, equal participation would enhance the likelihood of equality in public policy. This is not to say that the expression of political voice by a group necessarily results in government response; or that government response to a group requires that the group express its needs. There are many other parts to the political

[11] Raymond E. Wolfinger and Steven J. Rosenstone, *Who Votes?* (New Haven: Yale University Press, 1980).

process. People may speak up and get nowhere. Conversely, people who do not speak up may have their views represented by proxy participants who take up their cause, by nongovernmental organizations, or by bureaucrats or legislators pursuing autonomous policy goals. Their needs and preferences can be sought out through government or foundation research. All this is true. But, on balance, groups that put their own agenda on the table and press their own case are likely to wind up better off in the policy-making and policy-implementing arena than those who do not.

But that still leaves the democratic dilemma: the competence of ordinary citizens. We want policies that are effective, that are responsive to needs in a fair and reasonable manner, and that work to preserve the democratic process. Suppose all speak up but few are competent: will we get such policies? Suppose further that citizens are self-centered, unwilling to pursue the common good, and unwilling to tolerate those with whom they disagree. Can democracy survive? Yet, if we do not have something like equality in political activity, how do we keep government policy from being skewed to the benefit of a small, more advantaged portion of the populace?

One obvious answer is representative government. It is a system, as James Madison put it, that allows the views of the people to be enlarged and refined by passing them through the consideration of a few selected and wiser citizens. But if those selected and wiser citizens—our representatives—hear only from some of the people, they will be more likely to give consideration to those from whom they hear. Views may be refined, but in the process the views of significant groups may be refined away. Thus, citizen participation remains important and citizen competence an issue.

A close look at the beliefs, values, and way of thinking of citizens is in order to see if they can perform the tasks of citizenship. How competent are they as reasoners about public matters and as moral judges about such matters? How good are citizens as social

analysts? Do they have relevant, unbiased, and accurate information or know how to get it? Can they use that information to make
valid causal inferences about the likely consequences of various actions? And do they have the moral commitments that would seem
to be relevant for an effectively functioning democracy in which
citizen voice is expressed? One would be a concern about public
matters and the public good rather than narrow self-interest. And
the other would be openness to the expression of views different
from their own.

Before systematic survey data were available, there were many
views as to the nature of the public. For some, the average citizen
was a wise and reasonable observer of politics, and public opinion
represented the sum of that wisdom. Among populist thinkers,
public opinion was far wiser and more moral than the opinion of
intellectual or economic or political elites. For others, the average
citizen was a pretty pathetic character when it came to reasoning
about public matters, and the aggregate of such opinions was even
worse. For the latter observers, political matters would be better
left to those more competent to deal with them—to the elites that
the more populistically inclined thinkers despised.[12]

The Incompetent Citizen

Perhaps the main indictment of the public—certainly the most
noticed in the social sciences—came in the important work of
Philip Converse on the nature of mass belief systems.[13] He looked
for a structure to opinions and concluded that there was not much
there. A well-structured belief system would be one in which people had a clear position on an abstract set of principles, and their

[12] Of the many statements of this principle, Walter Lippmann's is one of the clearest: Walter Lippman,, *Public Opinion* (New York: Macmillan, 1922).

[13] Philip Converse, "The Nature of Belief Systems in Mass Publics," in David
Apter, ed., *Ideology and Discontent* (New York: Free Press, 1964). pp. 206–61.

particular policy positions would derive from the more general principles. The result would be a coherent and consistent set of political positions—perhaps conservative, perhaps liberal.

Converse found that few people referred to broad ideological positions when they discussed politics. Furthermore, there was not much "constraint" in people's attitudes on issues. By constraint he meant whether the attitudes of individuals were connected to one another and whether specific policy positions could be deduced from the person's more general principles. People did not have that structure. One position did not predict another. Nor did the answer to a question asked at one time predict the answer to a question asked later; change the wording a bit and you change the response. The general view was that Americans were nonideological. Their views were neither rich, nor firm, nor coherent.

In addition, there was evidence at that time that the public was not morally competent; that they held views incompatible with a cooperative, ongoing democratic system. Citizens were narrowly focused on their own private lives and self-interest. And, as the studies of Samuel Stouffer showed, they could not be relied upon to support the basic freedoms of expression that underlie democratic rule in a pluralist society.

The result was disturbing to students of democracy. It suggested that the average citizen was not up to the job. He or she was neither cognitively competent to make the calculations needed for a reasoned voice in the policy process nor morally competent to seek goals consistent with a functioning democratic community. If this is the case, it would imply that if we seek political equality in order to get equality in the expression of citizen preferences and needs, we may lose on the quality of citizenship.

Let's see what more recent research tells us about both kinds of competence—cognitive and moral. And in doing so we can see how the reasoning of citizens resembles or differs from that of social scientists as well as normative philosophers.

The Somewhat Competent Citizen

Are citizens really as instrumentally incompetent as these early data suggested? Though much of what earlier studies said about the incompetence of citizens and the incoherence of their political positions was and remains true, there are ways in which the judgment may have been too harsh. For one thing, our research methods may overstate the absence of information among citizens or the weakness of citizen reasoning. Here is a case where survey methods and the simplification they create may do citizens a disservice by making them look more simple than they are. Surveys ask citizens about the issues that the survey researcher cares about—or thinks the public (or the people sponsoring the survey) cares about. The agenda is set by the questioner who suddenly appears at the respondent's doorstep or at the other end of the telephone line. The citizen, with no prior warning or chance to study is given a test on topics the poll-taker has chosen.

Furthermore, how competent a citizen appears in a survey may depend not only on the questions the interviewer asks, but also on the questions that the political process asks of citizens. When interviewers began to ask citizens about their voting choice and how they came to it, they found that citizens evaluated candidates on the basis of personality or party, but rarely mentioned policy positions as a reason for preferring one over the other. One reason might have been that citizens cared more about personality than policy. Another might be that there was little difference in policy between the candidates in the relatively unpolarized 1950s. When my colleagues and I followed up these studies after the more polarized election campaigns of Lyndon Johnson versus Barry Goldwater in 1964 and Richard Nixon versus George McGovern in 1972, we found that respondents spoke more about issues when they answered questions about these candidates, and that issues—the positions of the candidates and the positions of the voters—played a bigger role in their voting decisions. In other words, by offering the voters, as Goldwater put it, a choice not an echo—that is, a candidate with a clear and well-articulated set of policy positions away from the muddled median—he was posing a question to the public that allowed for issue responses.[14] (Incidentally, the elections of 1964 and 1972 show that if you offer the public a choice rather than an echo, the public will vote for the echo. But that is another story.)

Thus, it may be that these data overstate the limitations of ordinary citizens. They are not philosopher kings or even princes, but they are not as benighted as the portrait might suggest. A newer literature on citizen competence and citizen reasoning has emerged, much of it based in cognitive social psychology. It is a rich literature with many different schools that often seem, to me at least, to be saying the same thing in different words while arguing over who is right. This literature, while not rejecting the substance of the findings about the limitation of ordinary citizens, argues that they do better than one might expect. They have efficient ways of using limited information, their views are not sophisticated but they do have a structure, and, in the aggregate, they do better than their individual skills might suggest. The thrust of this literature on citizen competence is that citizens and the citizenry (individuals and the aggregate of individuals) do pretty well with what limited resources they have.

Let's begin with information. This newer literature focuses on the issue of the way in which citizens can cope in situations of limited information. Though much classic analysis in economics assumes perfect information for rational actors, much recent theorizing and much empirical work recognizes that people operate with, to use Herbert Simon's term, bounded rationality. We cannot know it all—neither the facts nor the causal relationship

[14] Norman H. Nie, Sidney Verba, and John R. Petrocik, *The Changing American Voter* (Cambridge, Mass.: Harvard University Press, 1979).

among facts. As Anthony Downs famously pointed out, information is costly. The ordinary citizen, faced with the complexity of politics, would be irrational to gather too much—in part because of the complexity of it all, more so because the individual citizen can have only a tiny voice in what the government does.

How then do citizens with little information, limited time, and limited influence on outcomes—but ultimate legitimacy—navigate the complexities of politics? Let me outline some of them. Much of the literature on citizen information has moved beyond asking what citizens know—which is painfully little—to a focus on the issue of how citizens can make meaningful, rational decisions under conditions of little information. They do so by using heuristics. These are shortcuts that allow someone to come to a reasonable conclusion with limited information. There are many types of heuristics; different authors use different categories. Anthony Downs considered ideology and party to be the heuristics most used in elections. You did not need to know more about an issue than the position on it taken by your party or by those who shared your general ideology in order to come to a decision "right" for you.

There are other similar heuristics. If there are people you trust who share your social position and your values, and if they are more attentive to some issue than you choose to be, it is a pretty reasonable approach to follow them. (We all do this in our day-to-day lives; each of us has a friend who knows about restaurants and another who can tell us what car to buy.) Or we follow some trusted government official. Members of the U.S. Congress follow the lead of specialists, if they generally share the values of the specialist. Citizens can do that as well.

Heuristics have changed the ordinary citizen from the benighted incompetent of a few decades ago to the rational user of limited information of today. However, though a shortcut may be an efficient way of getting somewhere, it is useful only if it takes you where you want to go. The information acquired through the use of a heuristic may not be valid. It may be irrelevant to the issue at hand, wrong, or biased. Citizens who take information from others often select those near at hand or those who share their views. This is the road to biased information. There is, however, evidence from an interesting study by Robert Huckfeldt that, though individuals do use the criterion of shared views in choosing information sources, they can tell who is informed and who is not and they choose information also on that basis. They are fairly good at choosing those who are in the know. They get by with the help of their friends—and can choose friends who are informed.

This is not to convert ordinary citizens into social scientists. They do place some quality control on information sources, but they also look for that which is comfortable with what they already believe. (Social scientists sometimes do also.) Perhaps the ordinary citizen differs from the systematic social scientist most in the area where I suggest there might be some weakness in the information seeking by normative philosophers—in the area of sampling and representativeness. Systematic social science depends on representativeness (that's why we like random samples and surveys). The ordinary citizen samples information, not randomly and perhaps not in terms of typicality, but in terms of the congeniality of the information to what is already there, or the vividness of an example, or the recency of acquisition of the information—none of which criteria would satisfy the canons of proper research design. The ordinary citizen always has an Aunt Edna—a person well known to students of survey research. When someone is confronted with statistics about health habits and longevity, especially when the statistics make the person uncomfortable, we hear about Aunt Edna, who drank a quart of scotch and smoked two packs every day but lived to be ninety-five. Ordinary citizens use concrete examples—a particular news story, a particular personal event—and analogize from that. Studies suggest that sample bias in information acquisition represents the biggest challenge to accurate inference on the part of the citizen.[15] In general, ordinary citizens misunderstand social reality because of statistical errors: they do not know how to make valid inferences from evidence. For instance, the notion of independent probabilities is unclear. One of my favorite examples—indeed, a statistical heroine of mine—is the woman who won the lottery in the state of New Jersey twice (each time for over a million dollars). When interviewed by the press she said she was not going to play the lottery anymore. When asked why, she said that it would not be fair—she wanted to give someone else a chance. Citizens also have logical problems making causal connections. Their reasoning often involves such statistical problems as omitted variable bias (thinking that *A* causes *B* when something else, a variable not taken into account, may cause both of them) or getting the direction of causality wrong.

In sum, citizens are not statisticians or systematic social analysts. But they do have ways of getting by.

The Reasoning Citizen

What about citizen reasoning about political choices—whom to support in an election; what policy to support; when and on what to become politically active? Recent work on the way in which citizens reason, closely related to the work on heuristics, takes what seems to me to be a more realistic view than did earlier literature. It turns the view of the public upside down. The earlier view was that citizens had little in their heads; that was why they would easily change from one position to another. The newer account of why ordinary citizens' positions on issues change over time or change with changes in question wording is not that people have

[15] Susan T. Fiske and Shelley E. Taylor, *Social Cognition* (New York: Random House, 1984), p. 253.

little in their minds, but that they have too much. John Zaller has given the clearest expression of this position in relation to survey responses. The reason responses seem to have a weak, almost random character is that people have many values or principles in their heads. Zaller calls them considerations—a broad and useful term because it encompasses what we would call values or principles but also other considerations such as narrow self-interest, social pressures, and the like. When faced with a question about public policy in a survey, people do not answer at random in order to show that they have an answer (as many theories of the survey response believe). They do answer "off the top of their heads"— that is, without much reflection—but do so by sampling from the set of considerations the question evokes. They see what kind of an issue it is, they look at the considerations it relates to, they often sample from the considerations they hold in their heads, and on that basis they come to an answer.

This description of the process accords well with several facts about the choice situation in relation to some issue of public policy. One is that almost all social issues involve a tradeoff among values. Thus, an issue position can be affected by multiple considerations. Most people have many such considerations in their minds. Some of these are inconsistent with each other, but that inconsistency is not apparent since citizens do not routinely critique their values for logical coherence. Furthermore, when faced with an issue where multiple and conflicting values may apply, individuals can choose to frame the issue as involving one set of considerations rather than another. In this way, they handle the inconsistency without reconciling the various sides.

The work of Amos Tversky and Daniel Kahneman is most prominent in this area. In a long series of experimental studies, they and others have shown that the same choice situation leads to a different decision depending on the way the choice is framed— that is, on the context in which the choice is placed. Take the same situation, change the symbolic description, and you change the response.[16] Often this is done by analogy: is intervention in Kosovo like intervening to save the Jews under Hitler or intervening in Vietnam? One of my favorite examples is an experimental prisoners' dilemma study in which the likelihood of cooperative behavior in exactly the same game was affected by whether the game was named Community or Wall Street. Call it Community and players are more likely to cooperate; call it Wall Street and they are more selfish.[17]

The point here is that citizens have many standards in their heads rather than one. Consider the self-regarding economic-type calculations assumed in most economic modeling of human behavior. Such a standard may be applied in many situations, but perhaps not in all. Experimental literature shows that the more the experimental situation "approximates a competitive . . . market" with anonymous buyers and sellers, the less other-regarding behavior will be observed. As Samuel Bowles puts it, " . . . market like situations induce self-regarding behavior, not by making people intrinsically selfish, but by invoking the self-regarding behaviors in their preference repertoires."[18] What behavior individuals choose depends on the context in which they are choosing.

The research on framing sheds light on what it means when citizens appear to have changeable and uncertain views. Changes in position from one question to another may be the result of subtle changes in the frame that the question provides or change in the context in which it has been evoked. Or it may be due to a

[16] Amos Tversky and Daniel Kahneman, "The Framing of Decisions and the Psychology of Choice," in Roben Hogarth, ed., *Question Framing and Response Consistency* (San Francisco: Jossey-Bass, 1982).

[17] Lee Ross and Andrew Ward, "The Power of Situational Effects in the Prisoners' Dilemma Game" (unpublished manuscript, 1993), cited in Cass Sunstein, "Social Norms and Social Roles," *Columbia Law Review* 96 (May 1996): 913n33.

[18] Samuel Bowles, "Endogenous Preferences: The Cultural Consequences of Markets and Other Economic Institutions," *Journal of Economic Literature* 36 (March, 1998): 75–111; quotation on p. 89.

change in the media that have primed people for one frame rather than another. This changeability is not necessarily a manifestation of the weak views of people but may be due to a change of the context in which they see the issue.

This fact does not, however, necessarily create confidence in the thoughtfulness and reasonableness of citizen views. Tversky and Kahneman find evidence for the existence of an availability heuristic—that is, issues are framed by the set of considerations that are nearest to the top of the individual's mind.[19] This may be the most recent consideration to which they have been exposed. (As an aside, one ought to note that this is not a monopoly of rank and file citizens; each of us can certainly think of high political leaders whose views depend on whom they spoke to most recently.)

This is a major way in which media coverage affects how citizens think about issues. Newspapers and TV have their major impact by "priming" people to consider one consideration rather than another more salient in relation to an issue—by giving it a particular frame. They cue citizens to place an issue in one or another category. If change of the symbol changes the position, or if the media or elites can frame issues in one way or another and elicit response from citizens, this suggests perhaps that citizens do not act autonomously; that they are manipulated by symbol spin doctors in the media and in public office.

Certainly there is evidence for such manipulation—and a large number of people spend a good deal of time and money trying to do just that. But one can put a somewhat more optimistic interpretation on citizen sensitivity to the nature and origins of the message and to context. Individuals may change their views depending on the context within which an issue or decision arises. But this is not mere reaction to irrelevant symbols. Context mat-

[19] Amos Tversky and Daniel Kaneman, "Availability: A Heuristic for Judging Frequency and Probability," *Cognitive Psychology* 5 (1973): 207–32.

ters in terms of what values are applied. The games Wall Street
and Community differ. One ought to trust and cooperate in a community; on Wall Street less trust and more defection seems appropriate. We would not have much respect for the person who acted
like a Wall Street investor in all personal relationships. And the
investor who behaved like a communitarian on Wall Street would
likely soon go broke.

Furthermore, research shows that framing is not a manipulation of passive individuals by sly framers. What frame an individual accepts depends, at least in good part, on the values or
considerations the individual already has stored. There is a running interaction between that which is stored from earlier experiences and the new input. There is evidence that individuals do
not accept just any frame. Frames are accepted if they are compatible with previously available considerations. And individuals
make judgments as to the credibility of a framer. Thus, the process of framing is not merely a matter of passive citizens and
active elite manipulators. It may go too far to consider it a democratic dialogue in which citizens interact with the media and
other elite communications, as well as with friends and others, to
consider and reconsider their positions on public matters in the
light of new arguments and changing contexts. But it may represent a quite reasonable decision process carried out by somewhat autonomous individuals. Certainly, there is evidence for
autonomous position-taking on the part of the mass public. Consider the Bill Clinton/Monica Lewinsky affair. The public clearly
responded autonomously—that is, without cues from political or
media elites. When the story first broke, all the pundits signaled
that Clinton was through since the public would not approve.
No one primed the public to make distinctions between private
and public life. Indeed, the only fully reasonable participant in
that madness seems to have been the American public.

This is consistent with several approaches to individual decision-making that stress on-line processing of political information.[20] Individuals develop overall evaluations of people or issues or groups. New information modifies that stored impression—creating an updated, running tally of favorable and unfavorable judgments on President Clinton, on Kosovo, on the Republican Party, or what have you. The point is that individuals will then know where they are—that they favor or oppose some person or policy—but they may not be sure how they got to that position. If they are asked for reasons, they are likely to create them on the spot. This presents a challenge to the observer—the journalist, or politician, or social scientist—to try to figure out what was the reasoning that went into the conclusion. But there is a structure of reasoning behind it.

This analysis also sheds light on the difference between sets of values held by philosophers and those held by ordinary citizens. The value systems of philosophers—those people whose business it is to propound such systems—are explicit, usually formal, logically consistent, and accompanied by explicit justifications. Ordinary citizens are under no obligation to explicate the logic of their positions or to justify them. Popular moral positions are not explicit and not necessarily consistent. But inconsistency can remain because there is no need to face it. The values come into play in relation to particular moments—whether this be when the individual is a respondent answering a question, a voter in a voting booth, or a citizen deciding whether to write a letter to a representative or attend a protest meeting. In that coming together, there is no need for the development of coherent justifications or a reconciliation of values. The only thing needed is the outcome—the vote, the policy position. If there is a reasoning pattern connected with it, it is often left unarticulated.

The analysis illustrates another general difference between the

[20] John M. Basili, ed., *On-Line Cognition in Person Perception* (Hillsdale, N.J.: Lawrence Erlbaum, 1989).

reasoning process of philosophers and that of citizens. The commonsense reasoning of the latter appears to be more concrete, more tied to specific exemplars. Citizens will use as examples a particular news story, a particular personal event, and analogize from that. They recognize similarity of patterns. Philosophers also use examples, but these tend to be abstractly constructed situations that illustrate a general point—how the willingness of sports fans to pay extra to see Wilt Chamberlain play demonstrates that free markets lead to just distributions or how the dilemma faced by a couple of criminals deciding whether to confess or not demonstrates the difficulty of collective action. Reasoning by analogy is not as logical as reasoning by deduction—but it is reasoning and can be reasonable reasoning at that.

In sum, citizens may appear inconsistent—the worst logical sin—but it is not an unreasonable inconsistency. They are not philosophers, but they get by. Citizens are also not social scientists; they use shortcuts and research techniques that would not pass muster in social science journals. And as social analysts, they also manage to get by.

If ordinary citizens are not moral philosophers or social scientists, what then are they? Perhaps the nearest analogy is that they are legislators, legislating for themselves. They are policymakers and must make decisions. The decisions are narrow; they can decide policy only for themselves. They decide how to vote, they decide whether and on what issues to become politically active, they decide what policies to prefer, they decide how to answer a survey question on some public issue.

Legislation involves both normative and empirical analysis. One needs to know what it is that one wants, which involves having values and goals and, one would hope, the ability to reason about such values and goals. And one needs to be able to analyze the means of achieving one's goals, which involves knowledge of relevant information and the ability to use that information to analyze the consequences of various acts. Thus, the ideal citizen should be both philosopher and social scientist. But given that no one is paying for their time, given that they have other things to do, citizens may take many shortcuts in their normative reflections and in their social science analyses. The result is not the highest level of reasoning either about values or about facts (or their combination). But it is not unreasonable.

Let's turn to some examples of the public philosophy to see how this works out.

The multiplicity of values and the absence of a need to reconcile them would lead to citizen support for fairly balanced views on issues when there is a conflict among generally accepted values. They may wind up in the middle, a position more consistent with those normative theories that seek to balance or reconcile various views than with those theories that take a clearer position on one side or the other. Consider the following democratic dilemmas.

I began by saying that the terms "democratic" and "government" contain a built-in tension—between democracy, which implies power from the bottom up, and government, which implies power from the top down. It parallels the tension between the legislator as delegate and the legislator as trustee and many other democratic dilemmas involving the need for a citizen voice and the need for effective government that cannot respond to every citizen demand. Citizens—if one reads the results of polls—agree with both positions. They do not want leaders who do nothing but follow the polls or leaders who ignore them. They want both leadership and responsiveness.

Similarly, in relation to their own competence as citizens they are relatively balanced. The average citizen is not a populist— at least that is what survey studies show. Most members of the American public seem to be quite modest about their own capabilities. They believe that most citizens don't know what is best for them, that they don't understand issues and arguments, and that they are too uninformed to make sensible choices in public matters. Nonetheless, more support the view that "every citizen

must have an equal right to decide what is best for the country"
than accept the proposition that those of character and intelligence ought to have more voice.[21] They are not sure they know
what's best, but they do not think anyone else has the right to decide that for them. I find that a somewhat contradictory but actually quite reasonable position.

THE COMPETENT CITIZEN AND THE COMPETENT PUBLIC

Individual citizens may be better citizens than one might expect.
However, democratic choices depend, not on the views of any individual citizen, but on the aggregate of citizens. As with the issue
of the competence of the individual citizen to function well within
a democratic system, there are conflicting views of the capacity of
the aggregate of citizens to do so. Various arguments can be and
have been educed as to the analytical and/or moral incompetence
of citizens in the aggregate:

1. The aggregate is immoral. The argument here is that peo-
    ple in the aggregate may behave in ways that they would
    find unacceptable if they were acting as individuals—either
    because their responsibility (to themselves or to others) for
    acting can be submerged in a group or because group pres-
    sures push them to act this way. Mobs, "mass publics," can
    be undemocratic or unjust in ways that individuals would
    not be.
2. The aggregate can distort the positions of the individuals
    who make it up. Pluralistic ignorance and spirals of si-
    lence exist when individual members of a group mistake
    the views of their fellow citizens but, because of weak

[21] Herbert McClosky and John Zaller, *The American Ethos: Public Attitudes toward
Capitalism and Democracy* (Cambridge, Mass.: Harvard University Press, 1984), chap. 3;
quotation on p. 79.

communications or fear of rejection, act in ways that distort what would be the sum of their individual positions.
3. There may be no stable summary of the position of a group
   due to Arrow problems of aggregation. It may be that a collective view is an oxymoron.

There may be a good deal of validity to each of these reservations about the mass public. But let me focus on the opposite argument: that the public is superior to the individual. Benjamin
Page and Robert Shapiro in their book *The Rational Public* argue
that individual instability of opinion need not be incompatible
with a relatively stable set of reasonable preferences among the
public as a whole. "Even though individuals may hold only weak
and poorly informed opinions, subject to measurement error and
random change due to new information, there can still exist a stable, meaningful public opinion based on the underlying central
tendencies of individuals' opinions. And sample surveys eliciting
the expressed opinions of many individuals at a given moment
may quite accurately reveal what collective public opinion looks
like."[22]

How does this happen? As they put it, "Individuals exposed to
random bits of information may err or be misled about an issue
and may form policy preferences not well suited to their needs and
valuers; but the public as a whole, so long as the errors are randomly distributed, will make use of all the available information
and choose the appropriate policies."[23] The well-known argument
comes from Condorcet's jury theorem and was made 200 years
ago. The argument is that given modest amounts of information,
imperfect individual judgments are more likely to lead to correct
aggregate judgments the larger the group of judges. Thus, the
jury does better at coming to the truth than would any individual

[22] Benjamin I. Page and Robert Y. Shapiro, *The Rational Public: Fifty Years of Trends
in Americans' Policy Preferences* (Chicago: University of Chicago Press, 1992), pp. 25–26.

[23] Ibid., p. 26.

member, and public opinion may be sounder than the opinion of individuals.

But the condition for a Condorcet outcome is that the errors of the several individuals are random. If the individual voters are exposed to a systematic bias in what they hear in one direction or another, the aggregate may not come to the right decision more frequently. It is one of those areas where there is much reasoning, but little empirical work. Larry Bartels has attempted to study this empirically using election studies. His results are not conclusive. "How likely is it that the effects of voter ignorance would persist even in the aggregated choice of a mass electorate? The simple answer is that no one knows."[24]

One of the more interesting approaches to the relationship between the attitudes of individuals and the aggregate of those attitudes is found in the work of James Stimson. Using some innovative ways of summing up the positions of individuals across a range of issues, he traces the movement across time of the average position of the American public in broad policy orientation— essentially its average position on a left to right dimension of government policy that might be thought of as running from the unfettered free market to the full-fledged welfare state. Though many individuals have unclear and inconsistent positions on these issues, the movement of the position of the citizenry has an interesting regularity. In general the public moves away from extremes. When government policy is off to the left, the public begins to move right; as policy moves right consistent with public opinion, the public moves back to the left. Thus, the public favored a diminution of social services before the Ronald Reagan administration, but when Reagan started to implement those policies it moved back. And this pattern has been repeated—more recently in relation to the Republican Party's movement to the right and its alliance with the religious right in the 1994 election.

---

[24] Larry M. Bartels, "Uninformed Voted: Information Effects in Presidential Elections," *American Journal of Political Science* 40 (1996): 200.

The public wants change, but when it sees change going too far, it backs off. Stimson likens the effect to that of a thermostat. When things get too cool, it raises the temperature until it gets too hot, and then it lowers it. Such moderation can look like inconsistency, and to some extent it is. And it can be maddening, I assume, to politicians who think they have won the support of the public for a new direction to policy only to find the public turning against them as soon as they try to move in the new direction. But the position seems not unreasonable. In this sense, the civic aggregate may indeed be better than the civic individual.

THE PRIVATE AND THE PUBLIC CITIZEN

Let us consider the other set of reasons why one might oppose equal citizen voice: that citizens are morally incompetent and hold values incompatible with an ongoing democratic polity. It is hard to delineate what values are needed for democratic functioning. Let me focus on two that seem basic and have the advantage of having been studied empirically. These are having some consideration for the public good and having tolerance for opposing and unpopular views.

Let us begin with the issue of the consideration of the common good. The ordinary citizen is commonly believed to be a narrow, somewhat selfish, parochial person, concerned only with his or her narrow world and seeing the broader society as a projection of his or her inner needs. If that is the case, who will think of the common good? I realize that this is an issue only for those who believe that citizens can and ought to think beyond their narrow self-interest. From a more economistic point of view, narrow self-interest is what we would expect and, probably, what we would want. I cannot get into that debate, so let me state that I think it good if people think about the common good. In any case, let's see if they do. And for this I can return to my own research on citizen activism.

The interest in this subject for myself and my collaborators actually came from a different direction: from our concern with the paradox of participation. This is a puzzle derived from the conclusion of rational actor theory that it is irrational for the individual citizen to participate in politics unless there is some selective benefit. To participate for some collective outcome (something in the public good) makes no sense from this perspective since the individual, through, say, a vote, cannot have much effect on a policy outcome and can benefit from it even if inactive. Thus, the individual ought to take a free ride. The argument is well known, and I won't elaborate it here. And the paradox is that, despite the seemingly impeccable logic, millions in fact participate.

Our attempt to understand the paradox led us to a better understanding of the ordinary citizen as private and as public person. We did something rarely done: we asked individuals why they were active. More specifically, we asked them what gratifications they obtained from their activity.[25] It is, of course, tricky to ask the kind of question I am referring to: to ask people to tell you why they did something or what they got out of some action. Citizens may give what they assume to be the socially correct answer. One way we obtained what I think are compelling answers to the question of why people participate is by asking them to name the issue that animated their activity. Why did they take the time and effort to do what they did? For some activities such as voting the reasons for acting may be many and somewhat uncertain. But we were asking about specific acts: thus the motivation may be easier to recognize and the purpose ought to be clearer to the actor. Most of us know what it is we want when we write a letter to a representative or when we take part in a protest or go to a community meeting.

We found their answers compelling. Sometimes, they describe

---

[25] The data from these questions and the full analysis of the material discussed here can be found in Sidney Verba, Kay L. Schlozman, and Henry E. Brady, *Voice and Equality* (Cambridge, Mass.: Harvard University Press, 1995), chap. 4.

the issues on which they are active as involving narrow selective benefits, which would seem to fit the expectations of rational actor theory. But narrow issues were relatively rare. The issues or problems they say animated their activity are ones they describe as affecting many people, the community, or the nation, not just themselves. Indeed, they are usually issues easily labeled collective. And when we ask for descriptions of these issues, they fit that categorization. We believe that these are sincere descriptions of their motivation.

In general, we found that some of the reasons why people are active fit the narrow, material, self-interested, selective benefit categories that social choice theory might lead us to expect: to get a job, a contract for one's firm, or a particular government benefit. Some activity is animated by such concerns, but not much. More is animated by other concerns. Some are active for what can be called social reasons: they enjoy working with others, or they want to please a friend or someone else with whom they want to be in good repute. More still get gratification from doing what they consider to be right—they are active because it is their civic duty, or because, as they say, they think of themselves as the kind of person who cares about social matters. From a rational actor perspective, such motivations can be—and have been—considered self-interested gratifications. But that makes self-interest a rather broad and not very useful rubric. And, even if we subsume social and psychic gratifications under the rubric of self-interested benefits, it does seem to make a difference whether someone who is active is so for a material benefit or to satisfy a feeling of good citizenship. The latter feels a lot more like civic virtue. Lastly, many of the answers as to why people participate explicitly invoke a public purpose: to make the community or nation better, to influence public policy. And such public purposes clearly do not fit rational actor calculations.

In sum, the people we studied act more often as civically minded citizens than as narrowly selfish individuals. Aristotle may not be right that humans are by nature political animals, but the economists are not right either that they are rational calculators of narrow, individual self-interest. In sum, if by civic virtue we mean "the disposition to further public over private good in deliberation,"[26] citizens appear to manifest it—indeed, they proclaim their commitment to it.

This is all consistent with another body of literature that shows that citizens evaluate policies and candidates as public issues, not in terms of the specific effects on them. In research on attitudes toward unemployment policy, Kay L. Schlozman and I found that individuals (in deciding what policies to support or what candidates to choose) were guided more by the national situation in terms of unemployment than by their own experience.[27] Similar findings exist about attitudes toward racial matters, schooling, American involvement in war, medical care, and other issues. General commitments (self-identification as liberal or conservative, party affiliation, general attitudes on matters of race, etc.) are more likely than the impact of the issues on a person's narrower self-interest to predict the specific policy preferences of an individual or a voting decision.[28]

A comment on rational actor theory and the understanding of ordinary citizens: Surely, if there is a candidate for a theory of citizen involvement in public life that would universally explain citizen behavior, it is rational actor theory. It is, in one form or another, appearing as an explanation of behavior in many fields outside of economics, from whence it came, and certainly in political science.

---

[26] Quoted in Richard Dagger, *Civic Virtues: Rights, Citizenship, and Republican Liberalism* (New York: Oxford University Press, 1997), p. 14

[27] Kay L. Schlozman and Sidney Verba, *Injury to Insult* (Cambridge, Mass.: Harvard University Press, 1979).

[28] See, for example, Richard R. Lau, Thad A. Brown, and David O. Sears, "Self-Interests and Civilians' Attitudes towards the War in Vietnam," *Public Opinion Quarterly* 42 (1978): 464–83; David O. Sears, C. P. Hensles, and L. K. Speer, "Whites' Opposition to Busing: Self-Interest or Symbolic Racism," *American Political Science Review* 73 (1979): 369–84; and David O. Sears, Richard R. Lau, Tom R. Tyler, and Harris M. Allen, Jr., "Self-Interest vs. Symbolic Politics in Policy Attitudes and Presidential Voting," *American Political Science Review* 74 (1980): 670–84.

As I indicated, the concern that my colleagues and I had for the motivations behind citizen activity derives from the difficulty that rational actor theory has with citizen participation: the fact that many people who ought to be free riders are in fact active. Our analysis of the motives that individuals have for such activity suggests that, if we take their statements to be true—which I argue we can more or less—they show that citizens are active for many reasons. Some but not many of the reasons fit a rational actor, narrow, self-interested cost-benefit calculation model. Some might fit if the scope of benefits is extended to include the psychic benefits of being a good citizen, though if that is done the theory loses discriminatory power. And some motivations—such as the desire to influence public policy, which is quite common—do not fit the theory at all.

But earlier in my lectures, I mentioned our analysis of the strategies used by those people who act as political recruiters—the people who make telephone calls or in other ways contact citizens to get them to give money or time to a campaign or a political cause. I said that they act as rational recruiters. We find we can model their strategies quite well using cost-benefit calculations. We show, for instance, that they deploy information in a rational manner to find those people who are most likely to say yes to a request and, having said yes, have the capacity to make contributions to the campaign or the cause. They quite rationally follow the advice of Willie Sutton, the famous American bank robber, who, when asked why he robbed banks, replied: "That's where the money is." In addition, they use personal connections in a rationally calculating manner.

How do these parts go together—our inability to model the activity of citizens in general in rational actor terms and our ability to model the activity of political recruiters when they seek activists? The answer sheds light on the circumstances under which rational actor theory works and is useful for understanding citizen political behavior. We could not model the reasons why individuals become recruiters—why they decide to spend their time on the telephone calling others to support some political cause. They have many and varied motives. Some do so out of narrow self-interest—they are hired to do that work. Others do it for social reasons—perhaps their friends are working in the same campaign. Others do it out of commitment to the cause. As with political activity in general, there are many reasons for becoming a recruiter.

But once people have decided to be active as recruiters, they pursue their recruitment activities in a carefully calculated and efficient manner. They look for people who have the money to contribute, have past records of contribution, are known to be supporters of the cause—all characteristics that make them useful targets of requests.

The reason, we believe, that cost-benefit calculations work in the recruitment case is that there is a well-defined task (to mobilize support) and such calculations can be made. It is similar to a market decision where one wants to get the most for the least cost.

In general, we found that rational actor approaches to citizen activity fit some contexts and not others. They are sometimes quite useful, but not always.[29] We have made that point at several conferences in the United States, and the reaction has been interesting. The conclusion has been attacked. The grenades have been thrown from both directions—and, in a way, for the same reason. Rational actor fundamentalists have objected to the idea that the theory is *sometimes* useful; they would prefer to think it is *always* useful. The rational actor rejectionists—of whom there are many, though they are not as well organized—have also objected to the notion that the theory is *sometimes* useful. They would prefer to think it is *rarely or never* useful. So be it.

[29] For a fuller discussion of the uses of rational actor theory for the study of political participation, see Sidney Verba, Kay L. Schlozman, and Henry E. Brady, "Rational Action and Political Activity" (unpublished manuscript).

FREE SPEECH AND TOLERANCE

There is another basic value that underlies democracy and that we might hope would be shared by ordinary citizens: tolerance of the views of others. Here is an issue that has been studied a good deal by social scientists and that is closely related to normative issues. The issue is that of stability in a society with multiple, incompatible doctrines. John Rawls assumes that in any pluralistic society, there will inevitably be a number of comprehensive doctrines that will conflict with each other. How then can they live side by side? His assumption as to the nature of the doctrines held by a democratic population and his description of the solution fit the clear and comprehensive principles often found in political philosophy: differing comprehensive and internally consistent conceptions of the good exist side by side. This would cause instability in a society committed to peaceful and noncoercive means of political decision-making—that is, in a democratic society. Stability is maintained and the strain of multiple incompatible doctrines is moderated by a free-standing overlapping consensus on a democratic process that involves tolerating alternative doctrines. The conception of a fair democratic procedure is free standing in that it is not derived from any of the competing conceptions of the good.

This is an area in which there is a fairly long tradition of empirical research on what citizens actually believe about the variety of doctrines to be found in a democratic society (not cited by Rawls), and about whether they are committed to some overarching conception of a democratic process that would lead them to tolerate doctrines incompatible with the ones in which they believe.[30] What does the empirical literature tell us about the issue? The

---

[30] See, among others, Samuel A. Stouffer, *Communism, Conformity, and Civil Liberties: A Cross-section of the Nation Speaks Its Mind* (Garden City, N.Y.: Doubleday, 1955); John L. Sullivan, James Piereson, and George E. Marcus, *Political Tolerance and American Democracy* (Chicago: University of Chicago Press, 1982); Paul M. Sniderman et al., "Principled Tolerance and the American Mass Public," *British Journal of Political Science* 19 (1989): 19–44. For a discussion of the relation of Rawls's work to empirical material on free speech, see George Klosko, "Rawls's Political Philosophy and American Democracy," *American Political Science Review* 87 (1993): 348–60.

matter is a subject of debate; there are various studies done with somewhat differing assumptions and different methods, so I cannot give a definitive reply. But the studies are illuminating about the issue.

To begin with, it appears that political philosophers such as Rawls—as one might expect—take doctrines of the good more seriously than do ordinary citizens. It may be that comprehensive competing doctrines of the good exist, but most citizens do not hold such a doctrine. Competing doctrines may not be that hard edged, so there can be overlapping conceptions of the good. Such conceptions need not be mutually exclusive among individuals or groups of individuals. If people have different conceptions of what is right in relation to the family and the economy and religion and the polity, they may disagree with their fellows on some things but agree on others. This overlapping applies to social groups as well. African Americans in the United States are quite at odds with many of the religious right when it comes to matters of economic policy—but not that far away when it comes to such issues as abortion and homosexuality. Such overlapping consensus—perhaps better called by an older name in political science, cross-cutting cleavages—can hold a system together.

What about evidence of a free-standing commitment to tolerance of competing conceptions of the good? Much of the earlier literature suggested that this was not something on which to count as a support for democracy. The studies of Samuel Stouffer and others found that most citizens did subscribe to what seemed to be a free-standing commitment to the general principles expressed in the Bill of Rights. The hitch was that these citizens did not seem to deduce from those principles a more specific commitment to tolerate unpopular groups. Almost all supported a general right to free speech, but many opposed allowing someone to speak in their community if that person espoused communism or atheism.[31]

There are several possible interpretations of this phenomenon:

---

[31]   Stouffer, *Communism, Conformity, and Civil Liberties.*

citizens may merely be giving lip service to support for the Bill of Rights (a positive symbol), or may be inconsistent in their positions (an illustration of inadequate logic), or may be placing one value (free speech) against another (the desire to protect democracy or religion from attack). But whatever the interpretation, there did not seem to be much comfort for those who would base democratic stability on a free-standing commitment to a more open society.

The work of John Sullivan and his associates modified Stouffer's design and carried the research forward. He and his associates argued that Stouffer's examples of groups to which people might deny free speech rights were mostly groups that would be anathema to conservatives—socialists, Communists, atheists. If one expands, and lets the individual choose his or her enemy (that is, respondents are asked to name groups they really dislike and then asked whether they would accord them free speech opportunities), then intolerance is found to be even more endemic. Similar research in Britain comes to a similar conclusion. What Sullivan's research seems to show is that people report commitment to some free-standing principles of free speech and tolerance and may indeed have such commitments—but when it comes right down to it, their opposition to people espousing doctrines they dislike swamps their commitment. Again this can be seen not as intolerance, but rather as a greater concern about social stability. The least-liked groups in the United States include the Ku Klux Klan and the American Nazi Party; in Britain, the National Front and Sinn Fein.

The studies did suggest several mechanisms by which this general expression of principle coupled with specific rejection of free speech did not create instability or a loss of such freedoms. The mechanisms include the fact that those citizens least committed to freedom of speech for specific groups were also the least educated and the least active citizens. Their views may be more threatening to democratic freedoms, but they are not likely to act on them. The argument was that intolerance among the mass public did not harm democracy—except perhaps in times of mass political arousal—because it was irrelevant. The apathy and ignorance of the intolerant mass neutralized its potentially deleterious effects. Elites—more active and more tolerant than the mass—saved democracy. Stouffer found community leaders to be much more supportive of democratic free speech than was the average citizen. And the impressive massive survey work of Miller, Timpson, and Lessnoff in Britain confirms this.[32] Similarly, John L. Sullivan et al. found legislators in the U.S.A., the U.K., and several other countries to be much more supportive of civil liberties for unpopular groups.[33]

One more body of research is relevant to this topic. Paul Sniderman and his associates, using some sophisticated analytical techniques, found what strikes me as good evidence for a free-standing commitment to tolerance. People who are tolerant of one group are tolerant of others regardless of the closeness of the group to the individual's own preferred position. Thus, tolerance is free standing and does not depend (certainly not fully) on one's views of the substance of the doctrine one is tolerating or not. Put another way, among citizens who are generally tolerant, they are more supportive of the free speech of groups they oppose than intolerant citizens are tolerant of the free speech of groups of which they approve. A generally tolerant racial liberal is more tolerant of free speech for a racial bigot than an intolerant racial bigot is for other racial bigots.

Sniderman and his associates call such general tolerance across groups and doctrines principled tolerance. But it is interesting

---

[32] Miller, Timpson, and Lessnoff, *Political Culture in Contemporary Britain.*

[33] John L. Sullivan et al., "Why Politicians Are More Tolerant: Selective Recruitment and Socialization among Elites in Britain, Israel, New Zealand, and the United States," *British Journal of Political Science* 55 (November 1993): 51.

what they mean by this. It is not that these principled tolerators have explained that they hold to such a position because it derives from some general view of society or a general theory of democracy. They have given no such justification, and Sniderman et al. suggest they would not be able to do so if asked. Rather their analysis suggests that principled tolerance means general tolerance; tolerance that transcends one's support for or opposition to the views tolerated. It is, thus, a good example of a Rawlsian free-standing commitment to a political principle of justice.

What still seems to be missing is a principled commitment arrived at by reasoning from the nature of a pluralistic democratic system. Rather than coming to their general tolerant position by reasoning from a more abstract set of principles, Sniderman and associates present evidence (based on how one instance of support for free speech relates to others) that these tolerant citizens reason by analogy. They focus on some vivid example of tolerance—on an example of free speech for some group—and then support tolerance for other groups because they see the situation as similar. It is an example of framing. A particular situation—tolerance for some group—is categorized as an example of free speech. If tolerance of another group is seen to fit the category, the individual favors free speech again. Principled consistency is not a matter of a logically connected structure of argument, but of a connected set of recognizable objects.

But this still leaves out reasoning. Is there really none? The new standard view of citizens derived from the cognitive social psychological literature is that citizens reason their way to conclusions through a commonsense, results-oriented process. They recognize specific patterns in specific cases; they put together a variety of considerations and come to a conclusion. It is a form of logic and reasoning. It differs, however, from the reasoning of philosophers in that citizens do not tell you how they got there. They may reason, but do not give you their reasons.

The difference is not trivial. Reasons and their public statement are crucial if democratic decision-making is to involve deliberation and is to be more than a clash of preferences or wills or interests. We are supposed to be able to reason together—to argue and persuade. It is too bad if citizens come to decisions that are reasonable, that are consistent with their set of stored considerations, but they cannot tell you why.

But again, maybe we do not hear citizens reason because they have not had the chance. We ask specific questions and get their responses, but do not ask them why they said what they said. However, experimental studies where one modifies the wording of questions and the presentation of issues do seem to show us a reasoning process. We change the frame and the respondent changes the response. This, as I have suggested, is not necessarily weakness of belief, but what we expect from democratic discourse—desiccated though the examples may be. In a sense, changing the frame of the questions is saying to someone, as we say in discussion: you are saying yes, but have you thought about the following consideration? Oh yes, you respond, now that you mention that, I think the opposite.

But in these experiments, the individuals do not explicate. Maybe they can't, but maybe they can if we ask them, and maybe they can if we ask them and they have some time to think about it. They are faced with important issues that they have not confronted, and need some time to reflect.

What if we give people time to think and ask them to explain themselves? There is a tradition of this kind of research, the tradition of depth interviews. They make it difficult for us to generalize because the numbers are too small. But if they are selected more or less at random—not interviews of our professional colleagues or our students—they give us a good hint at the reasoning processes that would be found in a larger sample of the population. This is the tradition of the work of Robert Lane and Jennifer Hochschild, of the discussion groups of William Gamson and Roberta Segal.[34] Let me illustrate what can be found by looking behind some of the answers to questions about civil liberties.

Herbert McCloskey conducted pilot interviews in order to design the forced choice questions for his large study of attitudes toward free speech. Dennis Chong unearthed this trove of conversational material on free speech, in which people were asked about their views and were allowed to reason about the issues.[35] Issues of free speech almost always involve conflicting considerations. Free speech is desirable for lots of reasons, but the problem arises, of course, when it is speech for people who will say bad things: things that offend others, that hurt others (sometimes children), that lead to social unrest. Ambivalence about free speech ought to be expected from most people who are reflective. And this is what is found in the discussions with interviewers. People change their minds. They say they favor free speech, but they are afraid that people will be convinced by Nazis or by Communists. As one woman says, she believes in free speech but opposes letting groups of this sort open a bookstore. As she puts it, ". . . that's trampling on their rights a bit, but maybe to protect other people, I would say no [to allowing them to open a bookstore]." Another moves the other way, opposing free speech rights for various radical groups. But when the interviewer asks in general about people "who stand up and advocate the forcible overthrow of our government," she replies, ". . . that would be in a sense what the Nazis and communists were trying to do. They do have the right, they

---

[34] Robert E. Lane, *Political Ideology: Why the American Common Man Believes What He Does* (New York: Free Press of Glencoe, 1962); Jennifer L. Hochschild, *Facing Up to the American Dream: Race, Class, and the Soul of the Nation,* Princeton Studies in American Politics (Princeton: Princeton University Press, 1995); William A. Gamson, *Talking Politics* (New York: Cambridge University Press, 1992); and Roberta S. Sigel, *Ambition and Accommodation: How Women View Gender Relations* (Chicago: University of Chicago Press, 1996).

[35] See Dennis Chong, "How People Think, Reason, and Feel about Rights and Liberties," *American Journal of Political Science* 37 (1993): 867–99.

do have the right. I know they do. . . . That's what freedom is all about. Freedom of speech. Yeah. I'm all just doing a topsy turvy here. I know they have the right and our government isn't perfect and they might, you know, bring out a lot of things that would change for the better, but I would not want to go to the extreme of turning all of a sudden communist. . . . "

One further example illustrates how people are likely to come out if they reflect on such matters. James Kuklinski carried out an interesting experiment.[36] He asked about free speech rights for members of the Ku Klux Klan and tried to get answers that were more or less reflective. Some respondents were told to answer with whatever they first thought; others to reflect on the consequences of the position they espoused. He found a not insignificant difference. Interestingly, it was not that the more reflective respondents were more favorable to free speech opportunities for the KKK; they were less so. More reflection did not raise the importance of the free speech perspective in the balance of values, but apparently led them to think of the social harm coming from speech whose content they found hateful. Reflection did not lead to more tolerance, but to less. There is a point to be made here. I am not sure whether these results would always hold up. But they contradict the assumption we sometimes make that people, if they only reflected, would become enlightened and more committed to free speech. They may indeed come to a different position on reflection—but maybe it will not be the one we imagine.

In sum, the reasoning found in these interviews is not elegant; the individual has not thought much about it and is deciding on the spot. But one cannot expect most people to have spent much time mulling over such issues, and the considerations are reasonable.

---

[36] James Kuklinski et al., "The Cognitive and Affective Bases of Political Tolerance Judgments," *American Journal of Political Science* 35 (1991): 1–27.

THE EDUCATED CITIZEN AND PARTICIPATION

One last point about the relationship between equal participation and quality participation: Though I have suggested that the ordinary citizen is not as benighted as one might imagine, this does not mean that all citizens are equally competent. Some are more so than others, the biggest predictor of such competence being education. It is no wonder that almost all students of citizenship have hoped for a more educated citizenry, and some, of course, have argued for special participatory rights for the better educated—whether that be achieved through extra votes for university graduates or through literacy tests. In fact, one need not have policies that favor the educated as participants, because they participate more than others anyway.

This fact illustrates the dilemma of unequal participation. Let's explore this a bit further. The best predictor of political activity is education. In our research on participation, my colleagues and I tried to answer the question: why is education so potent a predictor of political activity? Was it that it made people more informed? Made them feel more efficacious? Made it easier for them to see connections between their values and preferences and governmental action? Was it that it inculcated the values of citizenship—that one ought to be a participant? Did it increase the store of resources that people had—skills that made one an effective participant or income useful in making political contributions? Did it put the individuals into networks so that they were surrounded by others who were active and by others who could help them act effectively? The answer was—to use the forced choice language of tests and surveys—all of the above. Education fosters activity though its effect on information, skills, values, resources, networks, and more. No wonder it is so potent. Furthermore, the potency grows after education ends.

The educated citizen is not only more active; he or she is a better citizen. The educated citizen is more informed, has a more coherent or consistent set of political values, and can make better connections between means and ends. Educated citizens have other virtues: they are in general more supportive of the rules of democracy, more tolerant of unpopular voices, more committed to cummunal rather than individualistic goals. Some simple data from our studies will make this clear. Compare individuals with no college education with college graduates. The latter are more active in any of the activities we measure, and by a long shot. They are, for instance, four times as likely to have contacted a government official (a good way to express political voice) than is someone with only a high school education. They get twice as many information items right. When they contact, they are four times as likely to deal with an issue that has broad relevance, rather than some issue limited to themselves and their family; they have, thus, more civic concern. And in other ways they are exemplary. They are five times as likely to support the right of someone who opposes religion to speak in the community. And on and on. They are better citizens.

I don't want to overstate this case. There is the possibility that we give educated citizens more benefit of the doubt when it comes to civic virtue than they deserve. And this may be because they speak our language. Some early research on the civic-mindedness of citizens found that better-educated citizens were more likely to have a long time horizon and to think of the public good when contemplating social and economic issues. Less well educated citizens and newer immigrants had a shorter time horizon and thought of policies from the point of view of their immediate impact on themselves.[37] I think there is some truth to this, but many years of looking at what respondents say about public issues have also made it clear that those who are more articulate have little difficulty in expressing their own self-interest in broad social terms. In our research on unemployment we found that less well educated

[37] James Q. Wilson and Edward C. Banfield, "Public-Regardingness as a Value Premise in Voting Behavior," *American Political Science Review* 58 (1964): 876–87.

people need a job and ask for a job. More educated respondents need a job and discuss the problem of unemployment—while also asking for a job. Neither I nor my colleagues who have sent in research proposals to the National Science Foundation ever argued that the research funding would allow us to do what we like better to do (research) than what we might otherwise have to do (teach) or that the funding would increase the prestige of our research institute, etc. But it may be (just may be) that some of us have such things in mind—as well as having a sincere commitment to the substance of the research and its value to scholarship and the understanding of society.

It is to the good that the educated are more active. That education fosters activity means it fosters better democratic participation. But the educated do not differ from the rest of the citizenry only in their greater competence and commitment to democracy. They are also wealthier, more likely to be male, more likely to come from the dominant race and ethnic groups. They are less likely to support spending on programs to aid the poor. More important, perhaps, they are less likely to face the deprivations faced by those with less education. On a large number of measures of need (the need to put off medical treatment, the need for better housing, etc.) they differ substantially from those who did not attend college. In sum, educated activists are more civically competent, which makes for a more enlightened input into the democratic policy process; they are wealthier and more advantaged, which means they have policy preferences and needs different from those of the population as a whole, and that makes for a more biased input into the policy process. Insofar as the participation of the educated is driven by the democratic values of tolerance or by the civic beliefs they acquire in school, this creates a better citizenry. Insofar as their activity is driven by the components of their social class position (their income, the networks of connections that come with various jobs), this creates the more biased polity.

We may want an educated citizenry, but we wind up with a wealthy one.[38]

CONCLUSION

Where does this all take us in relation to citizens as social scientists and moral philosophers? Individual citizens fall far short of the reasoning of either group. But they have ways of making not unreasonable choices about what to support and what to do. In sum, the individual citizen is not a philosopher; he or she could not articulate a coherent social philosophy, nor give full justifications for the positions held or the political choices made. But the individual citizen is—as the political scientist V. O. Key made clear—not a fool.

Is the ordinary citizen a rational actor, calculating from a self-interested perspective the costs and benefits of his or her own actions and the actions of others? The answer may depend on how narrowly or broadly one defines self-interest and what one considers to be costs and to be benefits. But using any definition not so broad as to make the question vacuous, the answer would seem to me to be: sometimes. It depends on the venue. Citizens do think about the collectivity when it comes to public issues. They think about their narrow interests as well. And they balance the two. It

---

[38] My colleagues and I, in our studies of political activity, tried to disentangle the effects of education and income on civic activity and, in turn, on the consequences of that activity for the kinds of messages sent to the government. We linked three components of a model: what social characteristic is connected to the activity (allowing us to distinguish the effect of education from the effect of income); what was the nature of the political activity (distinguishing activities that involve giving time from those that involve giving money); and what were the preferences or values that were given greater voice in the participatory process. We found that time-based activity derived directly from education while money-based activity came from income and only indirectly from education through its effect on income. In turn, the income-driven, money-based activity led to a greater voice for the affluent and policies that favored the wealthy; the education-driven, time-based activity led to a greater voice for the informed and for those who were more tolerant.

could not be otherwise. Rabbi Hillel wrote: "If I am not for my-self, who will be for me? If I am only for myself, what am I?" The average person agrees.

Is the ordinary citizen the free and equal person that Rawls assumes, with a capacity for a conception of justice and of the good? Again the answer may depend on exactly what such conceptions entail. But if one looks at what we know about individual citizens—and looks at both the representative but sketchy information we get from surveys and the more rounded picture we get from depth studies—the answer would seem to be pretty much yes.

Does this mean that representative government with its ability to refine the preferences of the people can or should be replaced by more direct citizen control—through referendums, or polls, or other direct democratic means? I hope no one takes that to be the implication of my remarks. There is a long distance between the subtle complexities of policy-making and the preferences of ordinary citizens as revealed by surveys and others means. The public itself, so it would seem, does not favor that much unfiltered citizen voice. But I do suggest that the collectivity of citizens can add useful input to the political process, input that will make the government more democratically responsive. I am not sure that the input ought to be labeled wisdom, but it is not foolishness. Wisdom may, in any case, be in somewhat short supply throughout the political process—among ordinary citizens, and among our leaders as well. But that is another topic.

THE TANNER LECTURERS

1998–99

OXFORD Bernard Williams, Cambridge University

MICHIGAN Joel Feinberg, University of Arizona
"Voluntary Euthanasia and the Inalienable Right to Life"

STANFORD Joel Feinberg, University of Arizona
"Voluntary Euthanasia and the Inalienable Right to Life"

1977–78

OXFORD John Rawls, Harvard University

MICHIGAN Sir Karl Popper, University of London
"Three Worlds"

STANFORD Thomas Nagel, Princeton University

1978–79

OXFORD Thomas Nagel, Princeton University
"The Limits of Objectivity"

CAMBRIDGE C. C. O'Brien, London

MICHIGAN Edward O. Wilson, Harvard University
"Comparative Social Theory"

STANFORD Amartya Sen, Oxford University
"Equality of What?"

UTAH Lord Ashby, Cambridge University
"The Search for an Environmental Ethic"

UTAH STATE R. M. Hare, Oxford University
"Moral Conflicts"

1979–80

OXFORD Jonathan Bennett, University of British Columbia
"Morality and Consequences"

CAMBRIDGE Raymond Aron, Collège de France
"Arms Control and Peace Research"

HARVARD George Stigler, University of Chicago
"Economics or Ethics?"

MICHIGAN   Robert Coles, Harvard University
                "Children as Moral Observers"

STANFORD   Michel Foucault, Collège de France
                "Omnes et Singulatim: Towards a Criticism of 'Political Reason'"

UTAH   Wallace Stegner, Los Altos Hills, California
                *"The Twilight of Self-Reliance: Frontier Values and
                    Contemporary America"*

1980–81

OXFORD   Saul Bellow, University of Chicago
                "A Writer from Chicago"

CAMBRIDGE   John Passmore, Australian National University
                "The Representative Arts as a Source of Truth"

HARVARD   Brian M. Barry, University of Chicago
                *"Do Countries Have Moral Obligations? The Case of
                    World Poverty"*

MICHIGAN   John Rawls, Harvard University
                "The Basic Liberties and Their Priority"

STANFORD   Charles Fried, Harvard University
                "Is Liberty Possible?"

UTAH   Joan Robinson, Cambridge University
                "The Arms Race"

HEBREW
UNIV.   Solomon H. Snyder, Johns Hopkins University
                "Drugs and the Brain and Society"

1981–82

OXFORD   Freeman Dyson, Princeton University
                "Bombs and Poetry"

CAMBRIDGE   Kingman Brewster, President Emeritus, Yale University
                "The Voluntary Society"

HARVARD   Murray Gell-Mann, California Institute of Technology
                "The Head and the Heart in Policy Studies"

MICHIGAN   Thomas C. Schelling, Harvard University
                "Ethics, Law, and the Exercise of Self-Command"

STANFORD   Alan A. Stone, Harvard University
                "Psychiatry and Morality"

UTAH   R. C. Lewontin, Harvard University
                "Biological Determinism"

AUSTRALIAN
NATL. UNIV. Leszek Kolakowski, Oxford University
    "The Death of Utopia Reconsidered"

1982–83

OXFORD Kenneth J. Arrow, Stanford University
   "The Welfare-Relevant Boundaries of the Individual"

CAMBRIDGE H. C. Robbins Landon, University College, Cardiff
    "Haydn and Eighteenth-Century Patronage in Austria and
     Hungary"

HARVARD Bernard Williams, Cambridge University
   "Morality and Social Justice"

STANFORD David Gauthier, University of Pittsburgh
   "The Incompleat Egoist"

UTAH Carlos Fuentes, Princeton University
   "A Writer from Mexico"

JAWAHARLAL
NEHRU UNIV. Ilya Prigogine, Université Libre de Bruxelles
    "Only an Illusion"

1983–84

OXFORD Donald D. Brown, Johns Hopkins University
   "The Impact of Modern Genetics"

CAMBRIDGE Stephen J. Gould, Harvard University
   "Evolutionary Hopes and Realities"

MICHIGAN Herbert A. Simon, Carnegie-Mellon University
   "Scientific Literacy as a Goal in a High-Technology Society"

STANFORD Leonard B. Meyer, University of Pennsylvania
   "Music and Ideology in the Nineteenth Century"

UTAH Helmut Schmidt, former Chancellor, West Germany
   "The Future of the Atlantic Alliance"

HELSINKI Georg Henrik von Wright, Helsinki
   "Of Human Freedom"

1984–85

OXFORD Barrington Moore, Jr., Harvard University
   "Authority and Inequality under Capitalism and Socialism"

CAMBRIDGE Amartya Sen, Oxford University
   "The Standard of Living"

HARVARD Quentin Skinner, Cambridge University
"*The Paradoxes of Political Liberty*"

Kenneth J. Arrow, Stanford University
"*The Unknown Other*"

MICHIGAN Nadine Gordimer, South Africa
"*The Essential Gesture: Writers and Responsibility*"

STANFORD Michael Slote, University of Maryland
"*Moderation, Rationality, and Virtue*"

1985–86

OXFORD Thomas M. Scanlon, Jr., Harvard Univesity
"*The Significance of Choice*"

CAMBRIDGE Aldo Van Eyck, The Netherlands
"*Architecture and Human Values*"

HARVARD Michael Walzer, Institute for Advanced Study
"*Interpretation and Social Criticism*"

MICHIGAN Clifford Geertz, Institute for Advanced Study
"*The Uses of Diversity*"

STANFORD Stanley Cavell, Harvard University
"*The Uncanniness of the Ordinary*"

UTAH Arnold S. Relman, Editor, *New England Journal of Medicine*
"*Medicine as a Profession and a Business*"

1986–87

OXFORD Jon Elster, Oslo University and the University of Chicago
"*Taming Chance: Randomization in Individual and Social Decisions*"

CAMBRIDGE Roger Bulger, University of Texas Health Sciences Center, Houston
"*On Hippocrates, Thomas Jefferson, and Max Weber: The Bureaucratic, Technologic Imperatives and the Future of the Healing Tradition in a Voluntary Society*"

HARVARD Jürgen Habermas, University of Frankfurt
"*Law and Morality*"

MICHIGAN Daniel C. Dennett, Tufts University
"*The Moral First Aid Manual*"

STANFORD Gisela Striker, Columbia University
"*Greek Ethics and Moral Theory*"

UTAH   Laurence H. Tribe, Harvard University
              "On Reading the Constitution"

1987–88

OXFORD   F. Van Zyl Slabbert, University of the Witwatersrand,
                  South Africa
              "The Dynamics of Reform and Revolt in Current South Africa"

CAMBRIDGE   Louis Blom-Cooper, Q.C., London
              "The Penalty of Imprisonment"

HARVARD   Robert A. Dahl, Yale University
              "The Pseudodemocratization of the American Presidency"

MICHIGAN   Albert O. Hirschman, Institute for Advanced Study
              *"Two Hundred Years of Reactionary Rhetoric: The Case of the
                  Perverse Effect"*

STANFORD   Ronald Dworkin, New York University and University
                  College, Oxford
              "Foundations of Liberal Equality"

UTAH   Joseph Brodsky, Russian poet, Mount Holyoke College
              "A Place as Good as Any"

CALIFORNIA   Wm. Theodore de Bary, Columbia University
              "The Trouble with Confucianism"

BUENOS AIRES Barry Stroud, University of California, Berkeley
              "The Study of Human Nature and the Subjectivity of Value"

MADRID   Javier Muguerza, Universidad Nacional de Educatión a
                  Distancia, Madrid
              "The Alternative of Dissent"

WARSAW   Anthony Quinton, British Library, London
              "The Varieties of Value"

1988–89

OXFORD   Michael Walzer, Institute for Advanced Study
              "Nation and Universe"

CAMBRIDGE   Albert Hourani, Emeritus Fellow, St. Antony's College,
                  and Magdalen College, Oxford
              "Islam in European Thought"

MICHIGAN   Toni Morrison, State University of New York at Albany
              *"Unspeakable Things Unspoken: The Afro-American Presence
                  in American Literature"*

STANFORD   Stephen Jay Gould, Harvard University
"Unpredictability in the History of Life"
"The Quest for Human Nature: Fortuitous Side, Consequences, and Contingent History"

UTAH   Judith Shklar, Harvard University
"Amerian Citizenship: The Quest for Inclusion"

CALIFORNIA   S. N. Eisenstadt, The Hebrew University of Jerusalem
"Cultural Tradition, Historical Experience, and Social Change: The Limits of Convergence"

YALE   J. G. A. Pocock, Johns Hopkins University
"Edward Gibbon in History: Aspects of the Text in The History of the Decline and Fall of the Roman Empire"

CHINESE
UNIVERSITY OF
HONG KONG   Fei Xiaotong, Peking University
"Plurality and Unity in the Configuration of the Chinese People"

1989–90

OXFORD   Bernard Lewis, Princeton University
"Europe and Islam"

CAMBRIDGE   Umberto Eco, University of Bologna
"Interpretation and Overinterpretation: World, History, Texts"

HARVARD   Ernest Gellner, Kings College, Cambridge
"The Civil and the Sacred"

MICHIGAN   Carol Gilligan, Harvard University
"Joining the Resistance: Psychology, Politics, Girls, and Women"

UTAH   Octavio Paz, Mexico City
"Poetry and Modernity"

YALE   Edward N. Luttwak, Center for Strategic and International Studies
"Strategy: A New Era?"

PRINCETON   Irving Howe, writer and critic
"The Self and the State"

1990–91

OXFORD   David Montgomery, Yale University
"Citizenship and Justice in the Lives and Thoughts of Nineteenth-Century American Workers"

CAMBRIDGE Gro Harlem Brundtland, Prime Minister of Norway
"Environmental Challenges of the 1990s: Our Responsibility toward Future Generations"

HARVARD William Gass, Washington University
"Eye and Idea"

MICHIGAN Richard Rorty, University of Virginia
"Feminism and Pragmatism"

STANFORD G. A. Cohen, All Souls College, Oxford
"Incentives, Inequality, and Community"

János Kornai, University of Budapest and Harvard University
"Market Socialism Revisited"

UTAH Marcel Ophuls, international film maker
"Resistance and Collaboration in Peacetime"

YALE Robertson Davies, novelist
"Reading and Writing"

PRINCETON Annette C. Baier, Pittsburgh University
"Trust"

LENINGRAD János Kornai, University of Budapest and Harvard University
"Transition from Marxism to a Free Economy"

1991–92

OXFORD R. Z. Sagdeev, University of Maryland
"Science and Revolutions"

CALIFORNIA
LOS ANGELES Václav Havel, former President, Republic of Czechoslovakia
(Untitled lecture)

BERKELEY Helmut Kohl, Chancellor of Germany
(Untitled lecture)

CAMBRIDGE David Baltimore, former President of Rockefeller University
"On Doing Science in the Modern World"

MICHIGAN Christopher Hill, seventeenth-century historian, Oxford
"The Bible in Seventeenth-Century English Politics"

STANFORD Charles Taylor, Professor of Philosophy and Political Science, McGill University
"Modernity and the Rise of the Public Sphere"

UTAH   Jared Diamond, University of California, Los Angeles
"The Broadest Pattern of Human History"

PRINCETON   Robert Nozick, Professor of Philosophy, Harvard
University
"Decisions of Principle, Principles of Decision"

1992–93

MICHIGAN   Amos Oz, Israel
*"The Israeli-Palestinian Conflict: Tragedy, Comedy, and
Cognitive Block—A Storyteller's Point of View"*

CAMBRIDGE   Christine M. Korsgaard, Harvard University
"The Sources of Normativity"

UTAH   Evelyn Fox Keller, Massachusetts Institute of Technology
"Rethinking the Meaning of Genetic Determinism"

YALE   Fritz Stern, Columbia University
"Mendacity Enforced: Europe, 1914–1989"
"Freedom and Its Discontents: Postunification Germany"

PRINCETON   Stanley Hoffmann, Harvard University
"The Nation, Nationalism, and After: The Case of France"

STANFORD   Colin Renfrew, Cambridge University
"The Archaeology of Identity"

1993–94

MICHIGAN   William Julius Wilson, University of Chicago
"The New Urban Poverty and the Problem of Race"

OXFORD   Lord Slynn of Hadley, London
"Law and Culture—A European Setting"

HARVARD   Lawrence Stone, Princeton University
"Family Values in a Historical Perspective"

CAMBRIDGE   Peter Brown, Princeton University
"Aspects of the Christianisation of the Roman World"

UTAH   A. E. Dick Howard, University of Virginia
"Toward the Open Society in Central and Eastern Europe"

Jeffrey Sachs, Harvard University
"Shock Therapy in Poland: Perspectives of Five Years"

Adam Zagajewski, Paris
*"A Bus Full of Prophets: Adventures of the Eastern-European
Intelligentsia"*

PRINCETON	Alasdair MacIntyre, Duke University *"Truthfulness, Lies, and Moral Philosophers: What Can We Learn from Mill and Kant?"*
CALIFORNIA	Oscar Arias, Costa Rica *"Poverty: The New International Enemy"*
STANFORD	Thomas Hill, University of North Carolina at Chapel Hill *"Basic Respect and Cultural Diversity"* *"Must Respect Be Earned?"*
UC SAN DIEGO	K. Anthony Appiah, Harvard University *"Race, Culture, Identity: Misunderstood Connections"*

1994–95

YALE	Richard Posner, United States Court of Appeals *"Euthanasia and Health Care: Two Essays on the Policy Dilemmas of Aging and Old Age"*
MICHIGAN	Daniel Kahneman, University of California, Berkeley *"Cognitive Psychology of Consequences and Moral Intuition"*
HARVARD	Cass R. Sunstein, University of Chicago *"Political Conflict and Legal Agreement"*
CAMBRIDGE	Roger Penrose, Oxford Mathematics Institute *"Space-time and Cosmology"*
PRINCETON	Antonin Scalia, United States Supreme Court *"Common-Law Courts in a Civil-Law System: The Role of the United States Federal Courts in Interpreting the Constitution and Laws"*
UC SANTA CRUZ	Nancy Wexler, Columbia University *"Genetic Prediction and Precaution Confront Human Social Values"*
OXFORD	Janet Suzman, South Africa *"Who Needs Parables?"*
STANFORD	Amy Gutmann, Princeton University *"Responding to Racial Injustice"*
UTAH	Edward Said, Columbia University *"On Lost Causes"*

1995–96

PRINCETON   Harold Bloom, Yale University
            I. *"Shakespeare and the Value of Personality,"* and
                II. *"Shakespeare and the Value of Love"*

OXFORD   Simon Schama, Columbia University
            *"Rembrandt and Rubens: Humanism, History, and the
                Peculiarity of Painting"*

CAMBRIDGE   Gunther Schuller, Newton Center, Massachusetts
            I. *"Jazz: A Historical Perspective,"* II. *"Duke Ellington,"* and
                III. *"Charles Mingus"*

UC
RIVERSIDE   Mairead Corrigan Maguire, Belfast, Northern Ireland
            *"Peacemaking from the Grassroots in a World of Ethnic
                Conflict"*

HARVARD   Onora O'Neill, Newham College, Cambridge
            "Kant on Reason and Religion"

STANFORD   Nancy Fraser, New School for Social Research
            *"Social Justice in the Age of Identity Politics: Redistribution,
                Recognition, and Participation"*

UTAH   Cornell West, Harvard University
            "A Genealogy of the Public Intellectual"

YALE   Peter Brown, Princeton University
            *"The End of the Ancient Other World: Death and Afterlife
                between Late Antiquity and the Early Middle Ages"*

1996–97

TORONTO   Peter Gay, Emeritus, Yale University
            "The Living Enlightenment"

MICHIGAN   Thomas M. Scanlon, Harvard University
            "The Status of Well-Being"

HARVARD   Stuart Hampshire, Emeritus, Stanford University
            "Justice Is Conflict: The Soul and the City"

CAMBRIDGE   Dorothy L. Cheney, University of Pennsylvania
            "Why Animals Don't Have Language"

PRINCETON   Robert M. Solow, Massachusetts Institute of Technology
            "Welfare and Work"

CALIFORNIA Marian Wright Edelman, Children's Defense Fund
            "Standing for Children"

YALE   Liam Hudson, Balas Copartnership
            "The Life of the Mind"

STANFORD	Barbara Herman, University of California, Los Angeles *"Moral Literacy"*
OXFORD	Francis Fukuyama, George Mason University *"Social Capital"*
UTAH	Elaine Pagels, Princeton University *"The Origin of Satan in Christian Traditions"*

1997–98

UTAH	Jonathan D. Spence, Yale University *"Ideas of Power: China's Empire in the Eighteenth Century and Today"*
PRINCETON	J. M. Coetzee, University of Cape Town *"The Lives of Animals"*
MICHIGAN	Antonio R. Damasio, University of Iowa *"Exploring the Minded Brain"*
CHARLES UNIVERSITY	Timothy Garton Ash, Oxford University *"The Direction of European History"*
HARVARD	M. F. Burnyeat, Oxford University *"Culture and Society in Plato's* Republic"
CAMBRIDGE	Stephen Toulmin, University of Southern California *"The Idol of Stability"*
UC IRVINE	David Kessler, Yale University *"Tobacco Wars: Risks and Rewards of a Major Challenge"*
YALE	Elaine Scarry, Harvard University *"On Beauty and Being Just"*
STANFORD	Arthur Kleinman, Harvard University *"Experience and Its Moral Modes: Culture, Human Conditions, and Disorder"*

1998–99

MICHIGAN	Walter Burkert, University of Zurich *"Revealing Nature Amidst Multiple Cultures: A Discourse with Ancient Greeks"*
UTAH	Geoffrey Hartman, Yale University *"Text and Spirit"*
YALE	Steven Pinker, Massachusetts Institute of Technology *"The Blank Slate, the Noble Savage, and the Ghost in the Machine"*

STANFORD	Randall Kennedy, Harvard University *"Who Can Say 'Nigger'? . . . and Other Related Questions"*
UC DAVIS	Richard White, Stanford University *"The Problem with Purity"*
OXFORD	Sidney Verba, Harvard University *"Representative Democracy and Democratic Citizens: Philosophical and Empirical Understandings"*
PRINCETON	Judith Jarvis Thomson, Massachusetts Institute of Technology *"Goodness and Advice"*
HARVARD	Lani Guinier, Harvard University *"Rethinking Powers"*